NO DAMAGE

An adventure in courage, survival and the pursuit of dreams

Kathryn Hodgson

Copyright © 2014 Kathryn Hodgson

All rights reserved.

ISBN-13: 978-1507693421

ISBN-10: 1507693427

For Sp,

My Man of the Sea

Acknowledgements

Thank you to my family, friends and colleagues for refusing to give up on me when the going got tough. I am forever grateful that you all surrounded me with love, acceptance and encouragement when I needed it most.

Particular thanks to my mother for being a wonderful friend, to my father for picking me up and dusting me down when I stumbled and to the Hester and Paddington for making me laugh when I thought all was lost.

Thank you also to my dear friend Erin for proof reading and editing No Damage without complaint.

Finally I would like to thank Nicholas, for teaching me how to love again and for holding my hand throughout the highs and lows of life. I adore you.

1

Kathryn stared through her reflection in the window, her amber grey eyes flickering and searching for answers in the dark night beyond. The moon had already lit up her stark, country garden and she realised it was getting late. 'Where is he?' she whispered to herself as she plunged her hands deep into the kitchen sink and thick soap suds covered her arms. The warm water began to calm her neurotic mind but, as the scent of cinnamon candles drifted past her, she remembered it was almost Christmas and panic clenched her chest. In ten weeks' time she was getting married; her fairytale ending and everything she had dreamed of was just weeks away yet Kathryn had never felt more alone. The clock above the sink ticked loudly as she waited for her fiancé to return. Yet again he was absent from their perfectly planned life together.

Minutes that lasted a lifetime passed and then Kathryn visibly relaxed, her shoulders dropping at last, when she heard the familiar sound of heavy footsteps and a key turning the lock within the front door. She knew it was her fiancé Graham, how could she not? His familiar footsteps and routines had been ingrained in her for the past seven years of their life together. As he entered their home with a flurry of wind and ice billowing behind him, her heart skipped a beat and she turned, beaming with love and relief, to welcome Graham into her arms. Her husband-to-be was finally at home where he belonged. She could at last share the seating plan and other final wedding preparations with the man she adored.

In her excitement, Kathryn reached towards Graham with her soapy arms dripping pools of water onto the tiled kitchen floor and stopped mid-stride as Graham stepped firmly back and away from her embrace. Graham stood in the kitchen, his head bowed and his broad mountaineer's shoulders hunched defensively. His hands shook continuously and his heart pounded in his chest as slowly he forced himself to look up at the woman he was about to marry, at her face of freckles and the beaming smile that told him of her innocence and unwavering love.

Can I really do this? It will destroy her, she has absolutely no idea. Oh God, how can I find the words to say...?

His thoughts were interrupted by Kathryn's light touch on his arm as she stepped closer again.

'Sweetheart what is the matter? Are you okay my love? Where have you been? You are so late again and I was worried. We have our wedding guest list and stationery to finish tonight and my parents have been waiting for you in the lounge so we can begin.'

Kathryn was chattering excitedly and Graham's head began to swim with the endless noise of her voice and what he was about to do. He reached for his shoes and backed out of the kitchen towards the front door. Clutching his bag and favourite shoes in his hand, he looked one last time towards Kathryn and the home they shared. Unblinking, he spoke.

'Kathryn I am leaving you. I am a shell of the man I used to be. I just, really just can't take this anymore.'

Without further word Graham strode out of their house and into the dark, cold night. As he started the still-warm engine of his car he opened the window to catch his breath and clutched the steering wheel tightly, disbelieving of what he had done. He had at last set himself free but he had also turned Kathryn's life upside down without warning or discussion and had walked away from everything he knew she wanted. Now what would she do? What would happen to their home, their dogs and their wedding? Graham had no more idea of how Kathryn would cope than of where he would stay for the weeks and months to come. He was brought back to his senses as he heard Kathryn sobbing in their home and her parents shouting in disbelief as they tried to open the front door to reach him. With a sharp screech of the brakes he reversed onto the slippery road and disappeared into the cloudless night, never to be seen by Kathryn or her family again.

Every time I read those paragraphs I find myself questioning if that *really* happened to me. Was I really unceremoniously dumped by my fiancé during the festive season of 2008 on an icy cold night as I did the washing up? Did my fiancé really check out of our life together that swiftly, never to be seen again by me? And was I honestly that clueless as to what was coming my way? Yes. Yes I was that naïve, yes that was me being ditched and yes it all happened in much the way I describe it above whilst doing the washing up. On the brink of turning thirty, that notorious milestone in a woman's life, I was left at the almost-altar. I had a runaway groom to my name. I do not recall asking for *that* to be a part of my life plan when I imagined leaving my twenties behind and entering the decade of supposed domestic bliss, a successful career, perfectly styled hair and an unwavering inner certainty about who I am.

I assured myself after the event, as I sobbed into my glass of champagne on New Year's Eve, that life would not and could not get any worse. All I had to do was maintain some form of dignity, pretend not to be deliriously angry and heartbroken every time I spoke, muster a strong sense of humour and swiftly cancel our wedding whilst hoping nobody would notice a thing. Surely it would be that easy.

How wrong was I? Not that it requires an answer but, I was very, ridiculously wrong. That one night was just the beginning of my life spiralling utterly out of control throughout my early thirties. It was less a time of perfect hairstyles and domestic bliss, more a time of emotional chaos, cancelling not one but two of my own weddings, rat infestations, a jam obsession and one day finding myself detained in a South African prison. But first let us go back to that Christmas.

2

'You want to return this dress? Oooh it is really pretty,' the elderly shop assistant cooed as she fingered the silky dress gently and smiled.

I am rigid with fear, a fake smile spread across my face as I wait for the assistant to somehow know I have been left by my fiancé just yesterday. Old people are like that, they seem to know everything without you even speaking about it.

'Yes, I really am sure and yes it is, er, very pretty.'

'Are you sure now young lady? Hang on! Weren't you in here just the other day buying it?' She chewed on the arm of her embellished purple glasses as she decided.

'So, tell me. Go on! Why do you want to return it then darling?' The shop assistant dropped her hands theatrically onto the checkout desk, her big eyes enquiring with honesty through layers of powdery make-up and a fug of rose perfume.

'Because yesterday my groom left me and he's not coming back.

Because in ten weeks' time I am supposed to be getting married, this is my hen do outfit and my hen do also happens to fall on my thirtieth birthday. Now isn't that just delightful?! There isn't much point in me wearing this dress now is there? No groom. No wedding. Kind of makes the hen do a little pointless don't you think? Now, I would be delighted if you would hurry the sod up and refund me before I die of shame and embarrassment. And guess what? Next I have to return my wedding underwear and I have no idea how I'll explain that one. Oh and then I am going home to a nice cup of tea and to inform one hundred and twenty dear friends and family members that my fiancé left me. I really must hurry for I simply cannot wait for that humiliation!'

I clapped my hands together in mock delight, with a fake excited squeal and a slightly hysterical look in my eyes.

Or alternatively, being English, I actually just explained to the dear lady that the dress didn't fit anymore. Yes you heard me correctly; the dress that was a perfect fit two days ago no longer fitted me. It doesn't matter that I remember this assistant witnessed it fit like a glove; I prayed internally that she was too old and adorable to remember such trivialities and would refund me before I broke down in tears. It was painful enough putting my mother through this as she stood by my side with a broken look in her eyes and an umbrella on her arm. She is all of 5ft tall and such a gentle soul. I can't begin to imagine how hard it must have been on her to witness her youngest daughter having to do this. Thankfully the assistant bought my story, after a little more chewing on her glasses, and refunded me without question.

Okay, it's the underwear boutique. Breathe Kathryn, breathe.

The mannequins trussed up in their fancy pants glared at me from the window like guards, ready to strike my shamed and humiliated form down at any moment with their bald heads and plastic eyes. I paced back and forth outside, prowling like a leopard about to make its kill as I plotted how on earth I was going to convince them to give me a refund for underwear. No one gives refunds for underwear unless the item being returned is an unopened multi-pack of cheap rolled up cotton knickers, which clearly my bridal underwear was not. It is one of the unwritten laws of nature that underwear cannot be returned, much like digestive biscuits are the best biscuit to dunk. It is irrefutable. I am partially aware of being watched by a couple at the café next door as I prowl some more, bobbing my head like a bird of prey between the mannequins as I identify my prey: the shop assistant. I say shop assistant, but she couldn't have been further from the lovely powdery old lady. This one was more akin to a haughty lady of the manor. The boutique was far too exotic to have shop assistants.

I look like a bag of crap. I really don't belong in there. No. Come on, you can do this.

The old fashioned bell rang loudly as I entered and it announced my arrival. Haughty lady was lounging against the counter, svelte and dressed to kill (me in all likelihood). No doubt she wore perfect underwear to match her perfect outfit and perfect figure. She glanced upwards, she glanced downwards, she identified that I clearly hadn't gone near a mirror this morning when I dressed myself and then she spoke.

'Oh, well, look at you. Hmm. Welcome. How may I help you darling? Special occasion?' She arched her back as she slowly and gracefully eased herself off the counter edge.

'Er, I'd like to return these please and, um, have a refund. Yes, a refund. Thank you.' I shoved my bag of underwear at her face with a wild look in my eyes and fiddled with my fleece that I then realised was absolutely covered in dog hair. I was less a bird of prey, more a furry rabbit caught in the headlights. Excellent. Well done me.

'Oh. Oh, I see. Ooooh these are divine.' Haughty lifted the bridal underwear high out of the bag with a flourish and began inspecting it closely.

'One assumes you would like to exchange them for something more, um, you?' She waved the underwear in my face and smirked as she admired my dog hair fleece.

'No thank you. Just a refund please,' I trilled in a high-pitched tone, followed by a nervous laugh.

I was well aware that this shop contained nothing 'me', what with it being a boutique of ridiculous expense. My daily life didn't require me to wear a garter to work – perhaps that is why Graham left. By the look of me that day I would have been more at home with a five pack of cotton pants from the nearest supermarket and an old grey bra with holes in it and underwire poking out of the side.

'We don't do refunds darling. Why on earth would you need a refund?' she snorted as her eyes widened in surprise.

Oh God help me. I didn't know what to say. I was cornered, surrounded by bras and bald mannequins and suddenly I couldn't breathe. I couldn't find the words to explain as I scanned my brain for a reason and answer to her question.

They don't fit? No, she'll give me a different size. I don't like the style? No, there are a million fancy pants in here to swap them for. Come on Kathryn, there is every size, shape and colour a bride could possibly desire. Think woman, THINK!

'Because I love this perfume! Wow! I mean it is just divine darling and I simply must have it. Yes, I must and I knew that the other day and thought to myself I really do love this perfume. Yes and I will exchange this wonderful underwear for this even more wonderful bottle of perfume.' I had grabbed the first bottle of perfume I could find and waved it in her face triumphantly. Ha Haughty, now look who is in charge.

Say what? Did I really do that? Well yes, I did. Somehow and I have no idea how, she bought my story. She bought it hook line and sinker and I left with the most expensive bottle of perfume I have seen in my entire life. I marched out of the shop, shoulders back, head held high like a lion and promptly collapsed at the nearest café for a very large coffee. It took me two years to use up that perfume. Two stupid, smelly years. The quality perfume just wouldn't evaporate overnight like my groom.

'Kathryn. Debbie. You are well?' Ah, the short, clipped yet friendly tone of my solicitor. I had returned home from the underwear hell. Debbie was the solicitor that had seen Graham and me through the purchase of our home, a flood, criminal builders and more. It had been an interesting few years and Debbie had been strong, efficient and an all round superhero. She was definitely someone I wanted on my team again and I explained what had happened.

'Right. Okay. What a shame. You sound remarkably well. Well done. I will of course represent you. Speak in the New Year. Goodbye.' With that Debbie was gone.

Well yes, I was faking being 'remarkably well' that day and had it down to an art form. I had just done battle with a shop assistant, a lady of the manor and came out triumphant. I was high on caffeine, adrenaline, shock and it was Christmas Eve, which meant Debbie's practice closed very shortly for a week. I still had cancellations to complete on email, guests to inform and all before the world shut down to celebrate Christmas. I decided at that point that faking it was the new me and would continue indefinitely. It worked, it got the job done. Otherwise I suspect I would have just keeled over and died from a broken heart and lack of food.

I rested my head on the sofa, relieved to have hired Debbie before Graham, and then turned my laptop on. There was one lone email and it was from Graham. Just a day after his departure, he had sent me an Excel spreadsheet of every item in our home, complete with original prices, each item's current value, the purchaser (conveniently listed as G or K) and who it should therefore belong to after our separation. The spreadsheet was colour coded and contained everything, absolutely everything we had ever owned. I curled up and cried.

There are no words to explain how painful that moment was. I was exhausted and the man I had thought cared for me was already tearing us apart piece by piece with colours, lists and money. I was nothing more than a spreadsheet to him now. A problem to be calculated, solved and ultimately discarded.

So followed more coffee, more emails, and more tears as I contacted every wedding supplier we had hired in order to cancel our arrangements, to beg for refunds or at least avoid full charges. It hadn't escaped my attention that we were a week beyond the last cancellation dates and were due to pay the full balance. I refused the help of my parents that day as I wanted to spare them the agony and humiliation. After explaining in every cancellation email what had actually happened I felt numb enough to contact the guests. Between emails and texts I told them all. I told my family and best friends, Graham's friends and relatives and our colleagues. It was hard enough writing it down, let alone doing it dispassionately and without judgement. I wrote my shame out, knowing that with each click of the send button everyone would know. I had become *that* person, the girl that everyone would talk about in the weeks to come. Forever labelled:

LEFT AT THE ALMOST-ALTAR

I looked up towards Mum and Dad sitting by the fire and realised it was already dark outside. Mum and Dad had aged overnight and looked so very tired, huddled over a bottle of wine and cup of tea. Paddington was snuffling gently and testing his puppy teeth on the carpet at their feet, whilst Hester was still upstairs hiding and searching for Graham. I hit send on the final email; at least the first day of being single was done and I had notified everyone. In a week's time I had to show my face at the office and I was dreading it. But first I needed to tackle the festive season and somehow welcome in the New Year.

3

Christmas passed relatively uneventfully given all that had occurred the day before. The world had shut down and so all I could do was eat, drink and surround myself with family. All of which I did in abundance. By the time New Year's Eve arrived I was home alone and crying quietly into my glass of cheap supermarket champagne as the clocks chimed midnight. It was a horrible end to the year and my only hope was that the coming year couldn't and wouldn't be any worse.

My first day back at work came all too quickly. Whilst my colleagues had been incredibly supportive by sending texts and emails to offer their words of encouragement and understanding I was still terrified. I didn't know how I would find the strength to hold it together as I faced fifty or so different people that knew me well and would want to be there for me. I arrived extremely early, expecting and hoping for an empty office, and was surprised to see my friend and colleague Alex waiting for me. He scooped me up in a big bear hug and I held back my tears as I listened to his words of comfort; nodding and acknowledging that life could turn on a dime but that it would go on. He had made my day easy by giving me permission to be sad and quiet and other colleagues were equally as supportive and caring as those early days went by. It is only now when I look back at this period of time that I wonder how Graham got the support he needed given he was no doubt painted by many as the bad person for how he treated me. Did he find space and comfort from others in order to grieve for our broken dreams, for the loss of joint friends that felt they could no longer be in his life? I still don't know the answers to those questions but I do know those first few weeks were an extremely painful rollercoaster for us both and we were at each other's throats via our solicitors. There was a constant stream of emails as Graham and I battled through our initial negotiations and it was all muddled up with stress, swear words and an outraged anger I had never felt before. It was not pretty, we were cruel to each other (as many people are when they separate) and my strongest memory is of the horror of trying to juggle this with my work and home life every day. How had it come to this when we had loved each other for so many years? My family all lived miles away and my parents had returned to Cornwall by the time I went back to work. I was standing on my own two feet and dodging bullets that seemed to be fired at my face every single day.

The morning journey to work was the hardest part. When I woke up I often forgot what had happened and it took a moment to register. When it did I felt like giving up. I had never felt this low and if I could have opted out of life easily and painlessly at that time I was very tempted to do so. I drove the country lanes to work every morning and played the Foo Fighters at full blast. I sang lines such as 'A little bit of resolve is what I need' at the top of my voice whilst the tears streamed down my face and I wondered if the pain would ever end. I stared longingly at the hedges I drove past and on many occasions I felt like turning the car into those hedges and watching my light go out. I was desperate and felt deeply alone. The only thing that kept me going was the knowledge that without me my two dogs would have no one. I would not let them down and if that meant fighting every day until my situation improved then resolve was exactly what I would need and I would dig deep to find it. That resolve, courage and sheer doggedness kept me from falling to the side of the road and waving a flag shouting 'I quit' at the top of my voice as I crawled into my favourite month of the year; February.

This is normally my favourite month for four very important reasons:

1. It is my birthday
2. It is Valentine's Day
3. It is Pancake Day
4. And finally....Easter is on the horizon

Perhaps I should explain this more clearly. I love those days because they all involve the excuse to eat more cake, chocolate and other sweet treats - mostly in celebration but usually in commiseration on Valentine's Day. Still, chocolate is chocolate and I will eat it whether I am miserable or not.

That year though, it was not a month I was looking forward to. Yes it was my birthday and my thirtieth birthday at that but it was also the time of my hen do and my first Valentine's Day without Graham. Both of which were only six weeks after our separation. I was in the depths of despair and a cruel fight to try and keep my home for my dogs and me. I had toyed with cancelling my hen do but in an act of defiance I had decided to go ahead with it and turn it into a birthday celebration as best as I could. There was no way a runaway groom was going to ruin the milestone that was my thirtieth birthday. I had more self-respect than that. Nerves and adrenaline had flooded through me though when I typed an email invitation to my girlfriends. I just didn't know if this was appropriate. What would Graham's family think? Could I hold it together for a weekend in London? Would my family cope and would people even want to be there? I was astounded at the response from my friends and family alike. Without hesitation they all pulled together and insisted they would be there for me and with me. My mum hadn't been well since Graham left and was undergoing various tests to explain the pain she was in. It meant everything that she was well enough to be there for my birthday.

'I just look wrong, please help me. I don't know what to do, what to wear. My make-up looks awful. I can't do this. I can't do this Melody.'

I stood shaking in the dim light of our hotel room in central London, imploring my beautiful friend Melody to help me as tears pooled in my eyes. We were due to meet my girlfriends and family for drinks in the hotel room next door to toast my birthday and I just couldn't do it. I couldn't begin to imagine how I was going to hold it together and fake happiness when inside I felt so hollow and downright embarrassed to be me. I was frightened like a child that they would see my broken heart and my shame.

'Come here darling, let's start again and try this instead.' Melody pulled me towards her gently.

Melody is an angel and has spent fifteen years being my friend, helping me and sorting me out from our teenage years onwards. We have shared shopping trips, cups of tea, laughter, tears, broken hearts, happy moments and nights on the town with our fairy wings or fancy dress granny outfits and more. I have lost count of the number of times she has turned up at my house ready for a night out and swapped outfits because I loved her clothing more than mine. Not once did she say no, not once. I was the ugly duckling in her beautiful and talented shadow and she did everything to change that for me in our youth. As I held out my make-up brush shakily in that hotel room, I hoped she would work her magic on me just one more time. I hoped that our time-worn ritual would help me through.

'Okay. Come on sweetheart, you look beautiful, let's go.' Melody took my hand and led me firmly next door with a smile in her eyes and love in her heart. She had transformed me, painted on a mask that I was proud to wear and happy to hide behind. I looked pretty good for me.

There were shiny metallic balloons everywhere emblazoned with '30 today', champagne corks were popped, streamers flew and birthday cards and presents were handed to me with the loving smiles of my dear wonderful friends. The room trilled with the voices of ladies giggling and chatting and each held me tightly in their warmth. My beautiful Mum and sister looked proud and happy as they mixed with my friends and welcomed them all to the party. I just stood there taking it all in feeling incredibly loved and supported. Mum's eyes sparkled and her smile lit up the room as she gave her speech for me. I took a deep breath as she began, wondering if I could keep smiling and not let my tears fall. I didn't want to let my wall down and falter for a moment after everything my friends had done in order to be here. I wanted them to have a wonderful time.

I wish I could recall all of the words my Mum spoke that evening but I can't. No matter how hard I try I can't find the exact words or her tone of voice but I know it was a speech filled with love. I know she thanked everyone for being there and I know she told them all how proud she was of me for having the courage to carry on in spite of recent events. I know her beautiful smile faltered and her voice wobbled as she held her champagne glass high in congratulations and her eyes, the colour of oceans, filled with tears. As I raised my glass I realised I had been silently letting my tears fall all along and it just didn't matter. I was surrounded by love and laughter as we raised our glasses and it was fantastic. The weekend was incredible and filled with good food and laughter from there on in. We giggled on red tour buses, stared at Big Ben and admired the dusting of snow in central London. We wrapped our hands around mugs of hot chocolate and spent time just being girls.

Next up was Valentine's Day. How was I going to deal with that day of love and rejection? I circled the thought and stared at it from every angle with a furrowed brow and feelings of determination on my post-London high. I paced the office kitchen one day and considered my options:

a) Go home after work and cry as per usual with my Bears as companions until I fall into an exhausted sleep. Ignore Valentine's Day

b) Go home after work and cry as per usual with my dogs as companions. Acknowledge Valentine's Day. Cry some more.

c) Go to the nearest supermarket, purchase myself a 'Valentine's Romantic Meal for Two with pink cava and single red rose'.

Then go home, skip the crying and eat like a pig whilst getting incredibly drunk on a work night.

I plumped for option C. I was not going to be defeated by a day of love and fluff, a day I had always secretly longed to be a part of, no matter how miserable I felt. That was not going to happen. I was instead going to treat myself like a princess, eat like a pig and consume the entire bottle of cava. I marched into town after work and selected my luxury meal for two, proudly held the slightly tired-looking rose and clutched the bottle of cava tightly. Yes checkout lady, I thought to myself, this is all for me and you have no idea. I bought my Bears a little treat of some chicken and headed home. I should point out that by 'Bears' I am referring to Hester and Paddington and not stuffed toys that I feed chicken to. Those two dogs have and always will be known as the Bears because they are enormous with bear-sized paws and personalities to match.

By 7pm I was so tipsy I had burned the scallops and chorizo. They were bouncy and practically leapt off my plate and into Paddington's ever ready and hungry mouth. By 9pm I felt sick from eating the entire luxury meal including both desserts and I tried to focus on a film by the fire and failed. By 9.30pm I had given up on the film, had polished off the cava and was merrily singing songs to myself about lost love as Paddington howled along with me and we jumped around my bedroom. By 10pm I had passed out on my bed surrounded by dogs. Happy Valentine's Day. I may die alone but I do believe I did that day proud. Until I woke up the next day with a raging hangover and realised I had to go to work.

If only that had been the end of February and it hadn't held any other surprises. Those two acts of courage and defiance had been more than enough for one month; I was exhausted at the prospect of the fight to come with Graham. What came next made our separation feel like a walk in the park by comparison. Who knew that was even possible.

4

It was just eight weeks after my separation from Graham and I was at home, sitting by the log fire, when I heard the telephone ring. I had been waiting for this moment all day and my heart raced as I heard my father's familiar deep voice. Try as I might, I couldn't decipher from his tone what had happened and then it hit me as he talked me through the results of Mum's test. I listened as he numbly told me that Mum had been diagnosed with cancer. That she would undergo surgery and six rounds of chemotherapy to fight her illness and they didn't know if it would be successful. Cancer. My mother, who did everything in moderation, had never spent a moment unwell and had always been our tower of strength. Cancer. In my preoccupation with my own problems it hadn't occurred to me it could be that serious. I had been worried but never thought it would be cancer. Surely this couldn't happen to us? Cancer. My knees buckled and I sobbed into the telephone guiltily and loudly. I didn't want my Dad to hear me cry, he needed me to be strong and to be there for him, but I couldn't keep my shock and tears to myself. Like a child I wanted my Dad to tell me it would all be okay but he couldn't give me that. We just didn't know. I don't know what we said or how long the silence lasted as the news sunk in but I rang off and stared. I stared at the floor, stared out of the window, and stared hopelessly wishing time would erase the diagnosis. Finally I slumped on the sofa.

I was already exhausted and couldn't have imagined this turn of events was on its way. It was at that moment I took a deep breath and made the decision not to talk about Graham to my family or to anyone else from now onwards. My problems would be my own, I would cope alone, and I would be there for my family when they needed me most. I would fake it, put a smile on my face and be strong. I didn't know how or what to do for Mum but I knew that I would give everything possible to make her well again. The telephone rang endlessly that evening as my brother and sister called and we cried our way through the terrible news and tried to find some words of comfort and hope for each other; tried to find a way to fill the miles that separated us all.

For the second time I faced a return to work with bad news and I let my closest colleagues and boss know of the diagnosis. I said it quickly, as if ripping a painful plaster off a wound, and just kept smiling and saying 'I'm fine' in the hope that I wouldn't be rumbled as secretly falling apart on the inside. I made the effort to stand tall at work, dress in my favourite high heels, plaster a smile across my face and convince myself I was not only coping but was in fact absolutely fine.

No surprise that shortly after my attempt at faking it I began to experience anxiety attacks and then nose bleeds on an almost daily basis. I refused to take the happy drugs my doctor prescribed and just carried on listening to the Foo Fighters every day, putting a smile on my face and reeling through my anxiety whilst holding on to the Bears and my home tightly. With hindsight, it is a blessing my family didn't live close by as I could not have kept up that charade if they had seen me in person. It is that much easier to lie on the telephone as no one can see the pain that is reflected in your eyes and so I faked my way through every day. I walked through the front door each night, kicked my heels off and bolted the door twice as if to secure not my home but me from the outside world. Only then did I drop my shoulders, fall to my knees and genuinely smile as my team of Airedales licked my tears away and gave me a reason to keep on fighting. Their utter playfulness and tails that wagged furiously were all that I needed to know life would come good in the end.

I would be okay and, on the up side, I had lost a tremendous amount of weight from the lack of eating properly coupled with my flying pulse rate and stress. For the first time in years I was thin and my squidgy thighs did not meet at the top. There was a definite gap and, as shallow as that is, I really enjoyed knowing that. There was indeed one silver lining to the turmoil that had become my life; being able to wear skinny jeans.

5

I feel like a criminal. I feel like I have a sign around my neck pulling me down that says I no longer belong in this club, I shouldn't be allowed inside.

It was the weekend after cancer and I gazed at the steamed up door and 'Welcome' sign that stood against the backdrop of the Shropshire Hills inviting me into the beautiful bridal boutique. I breathed deeply and walked away from the frosty morning air biting my cheeks. The bell tinkled delicately to announce my arrival, as I pressed the icy cold door knob into my palm and entered. I was enveloped in sights and sounds that were familiar and comforting to me. As a bride-to-be it was impossible not to fall in love with this boutique and I fell backwards into the memories of my mind.

It had been my favourite place to be as I planned our wedding. The first thing that strikes you is the warm yet quiet chatter of women as they excitedly discuss wedding plans and begin their search for the perfect dress. The rooms are filled with mothers and daughters, sisters and best friends. All nestled amongst a sea of exquisite dresses; fabrics of every kind, the colours of ice cream, milk, candy, pale coffee, pistachio and adorned with jewels that sparkle in the spotlights. Feathers and ribbons, pearls and diamanté line every display cabinet and highlight the curve of silk satin, chiffon and velvet. There is the soft noise of hangers touching the rails as dresses are excitedly pulled out for further inspection by brides eager to feel like a princess on their special day. The list is endless and it is a sweetshop for grown-up girls. I can still feel the magic of being one of those brides and finding my dress many months before. I can still remember welling up when Mum said she would like to buy my wedding dress as a gift. We were in the large, beautifully furnished changing room and sharing such a special time together as mother and daughter. I stood in The Dress; I felt beautiful as the silk satin hugged my curves and the intricate diamanté pattern trailed down my back and away with the gently rounded train. Reflected back at me was a woman I didn't recognise as me. Mum and I giggled throughout the day, trying on dresses and tiaras, and I am so thankful we had that time together. I had spent the previous months with a serious back injury and it was wonderful yet frightening to be able to stand upright and try on dresses for most of a day without the support of my walking stick. I explored every imaginable style, fabric and colour. It was a moment I had waited for since I was a little girl.

I was brought up on a diet of romantic Disney films and fairytale endings and had two girlish dreams as a child; to wear a dress as beautiful as that of a princess and to have a library in my home. I had adored Belle's dress in Beauty and the Beast, the pale yellow fabric and layers of material that swished and swayed as she danced, and I had adored books since I was able to read. By the end of that day with my mum both dreams had come true. I had found my dress, which was thankfully not primrose yellow or enormous like a meringue, and at home that year my Dad had lovingly converted our spare bedroom into a study/mini-library. It was filled with books I had cherished from my childhood onwards; books filled with memories, photograph bookmarks and notes that meant everything to me. Each one held a story personal to my life and I spent hours thumbing through them. Had there ever been a house fire I would have been very busy saving my dogs and my books.

The bell tinkled delicately to announce my arrival, as I pressed the icy cold door knob into my palm and entered. I was enveloped in sights and sounds that were familiar to me. But that familiarity didn't bring me comfort on that day as I tried to melt into the background. I stepped backwards into the mother-of-the-bride outfits that lined the first room within the boutique. I was surrounded by every ridiculously bright colour you can imagine and I realised it was quite difficult to conceal myself here. I was a drab pea hen surrounded by peacocks in bright plumage, fluff and feathers. In fact I was the only person there that wasn't smiling and giggling, the only person there that didn't have a mother, a sister or best friend by her side. I told myself I would do this alone and so be it, I did.

I looked at my reflection and realised that yet again I was wearing my old dog walking fleece and yes it was generously covered in hairs and had been teamed with a ragged pair of jeans. That was perhaps not the best choice of clothing. Evidently I hadn't learnt from the nightmare of returning my wedding underwear just weeks previously.

I took steps gingerly towards the room of wedding dresses. This is the room I had adored and my memories of happy times, promises and laughter visited me. I scanned wildly for the assistant that I had spoken to on the telephone when I explained I would no longer be getting married. She had helped me choose my dress with my mum and was gentle and kind every time we had spoken. I knew she would make this easy because she had already made the arrangements for me to take home the bridesmaid dresses that day and sell my dress. Sell my dress – three simple words to write but painful to actually admit.

'Can I help you?' Instead of being greeted by my nice assistant I was greeted by an impossibly small, glossy twenty or so year old girl with very shiny hair.

Where do they find these perfect people and why do they always work in bridal shops?! She was greeted by me; a pale-faced ex-bride covered in dog hair. I feared the deck was stacked in her favour and my eyes widened as I tapped the counter in front of me and mumbled a half response.

'Er, my name is Kathryn. Hello' I dipped my head.

Please don't ask me what I know is your standard next line.

'And when is your wedding? Are you here for a fitting? How exciting!' She beamed at me with the genuine innocence of someone that had no idea why the lady covered in dog hair wasn't as excited.

'Friday 13th March and I am here to collect my bridesmaid dresses and make some arrangements' I squirmed at my half-truth.

It was so hushed in there and I was painfully aware that every bride, mother, sister and friend trying on dresses could hear me. Nice assistant was nowhere to be seen when I needed her most. I was tempted to back into the mother-of-the-bride outfits again and hope for the best that I could hide amongst them until everyone else had left. As that was really not an option other than for the clinically insane I just waited quietly whilst glossy lady found my details. I smiled internally at how ridiculous our wedding date had been anyway. Friday 13th March. Not only was it a Friday 13th and therefore inevitably bad luck, it was also the Ides of March that year.

Beware the Ides of March

From Shakespeare's *Julius Caesar*, 1601. It was the soothsayer's message to Julius Caesar, warning of his impending death. I wish a soothsayer had warned me of my impending doom a little more gently than sneaking up on me shouting 'Surprise! Plot change! Wedding is off'.

There she is! Quick grab her! And for the love of God what is her name? No, put your arms down Kathryn. Far too desperate.

Nice assistant had appeared and I stifled a woop of relief in my throat. She was busy with brides and their dresses and squeals of joy. I tried to catch her eye repeatedly but realised I looked slightly odd as I bobbed my head like an owl and appeared much like a stalker. Perhaps glossy lady would have to help me after all and I would just have to admit my shame and be done with it. You'd think by now I would be used to it but no. It was still raw and I fought back tears at the prospect of admitting in a bridal shop I was that person – you know, the one with the runaway groom.

Come on nameless nice assistant. Rescue me from glossy lady and make just one day easier for me. Please.

I jumped as the telephone rang and glossy lady was distracted for a moment. Now was my chance and I coughed loudly in an attempt to gain nice assistant's attention. She smiled and finally she joined me at the counter, her name badge reminding me that she was called Louise. I didn't need to say a word and Louise was intuitive and calm as always. She quietly retrieved my details after asking after me and offering her condolences. My world swam and I swallowed hard as she brought my dresses out for inspection. I had forgotten not only the beauty of those dresses but the promise they held of a future which had rapidly shifted and changed into something I didn't understand.

'Here you go sweetheart. The bridesmaid dresses are ready for you to take home and we will sell your dress for you. I am so sorry.' Louise passed me the bridesmaid dresses and went on to explain that it was difficult to sell my dress as they already had a display version on sale but that they would try all year.

I couldn't even begin to imagine what a year from then would look like with so much uncertainty and change. There was little I could do to reassure myself it would be okay and, with bridesmaid dresses clutched tightly to my chest, I thanked Louise for her kindness and stumbled out of the boutique. The frosty air was cold in my lungs, the Shropshire Hills were golden in the late afternoon light and I walked briskly to my car with adrenaline surging through me. I fought back tears as I passed new arrivals to the boutique and then finally I was in my car and safe. I started the engine, took a deep breath and began the drive home. As the sun dipped lower and disappeared behind the hills, music blared out of the car stereo and a sense of achievement and determination pushed through me. I had survived and another hurdle had been overcome.

6

The weeks passed by and the cherry tree in my garden was soon in bud. The daffodils were swaying their heavy yellow heads in the morning sunshine and spring was stretching her limbs for another year. Sap was rising within the trees and hope began to rise within me when I walked the woodland paths near my home. I swung my apple wood stick lazily with each step, supporting my recovering back, whilst the polished brass end pushed the old autumn leaves aside as they decayed in damp soil. Birds sang their day in the trees around me and dappled sunshine brought a smile across my cheeks. It was my time in the woods with spring and the Bears as my companions and I found such precious moments of peace with nature by my side.

Hester and Paddington roared across the path in front of me and brought me to a well-practised halt on one such day. I had lost count of the number of times they did this; waving their tails from side to side, auburn ears rising and falling rhythmically as they skidded and chased the nearest moment of happiness. I couldn't help but smile at their eternal optimism as I walked on slowly. They were totally out of control, of course. I didn't have the strength to rein them in and they didn't listen to me anyway. They knew plenty of commands and would do anything for cheese. However, they were also ill-mannered , stubborn, defiant and utterly brilliant. They were having fun, the woodlands were peaceful, they made me laugh until my belly ached and I enjoyed being able to give them the freedom to run. I came to know the local dog walkers in the woodland throughout that year, as they helped me find one Bear or the other that had roamed a little too free and disappeared into the nearest field of sheep, a garden, an old badger set, into a pond or down a bridleway. My nerves were fried already and the extra dose of fear from those occasions was merely a drop in the ocean. I was however terrified that the Bears would either cause damage or be hurt themselves. I knew I was pushing my luck letting them run free.

The Bears must have thought it was hilarious when they ran circles around a field of sheep on one occasion that spring whilst I frantically waved my stick at them; shouting like a crazy person in bright pink wellies with no idea of how to control her dogs. I had hobbled around the field after them as fast as possible, hair flying in the wind, as I lurched from side to side in a bizarre comedy walk. Waving my stick like a signal man and swearing like a trooper. I am sure Hester actually stopped at one point and smiled at me, head cocked to the side, as if to say 'do you realise how stupid you look?' Paddington, in his infinite laziness, gave up running after about five minutes and came back for some cheese. Cheese inventor I salute you for giving me control of one dog.

Hester however was a demon when she ran free, fast as lightning and utterly disobedient. She had flown past me whilst she herded up the sheep and, every time I got close, she leapt out of arm's reach just at the last moment and with a big grin on her face. I admired her spirit but I was fast approaching a mini meltdown after thirty minutes of that. I was reduced to childish tears of frustration as I knelt on the grass amongst the pretty daisies.

'Cheeeeese,' I shouted repeatedly in a high-pitched tone. I clutched Paddington, my stick and my bag of sweaty cheese chunks. Tears rolled down my cheeks and onto my pink wellingtons.

'Cheese, Hester! Look, cheeeeeeeeese!'

It was such a mournful cry and I must have looked pathetic. I was a grown woman in pink wellington boots; sobbing and shouting about dairy products in the middle of a field of sheep. Desperation finally set in and I threw cheese chunks at Hester whilst she raced past, hoping the scent of cheese would distract her. The cheese bounced off her face and curly beard. She gave me a quizzical look and skipped on in the sunshine and long grass. I sobbed quietly.

I was all out of tricks and I had no idea what to do next to resolve this situation. The poor sheep had run a marathon in circles, Hester was having a jolly old time chasing them and Paddington was merrily eating his way through the bag of cheese he had now torn open. I sat there and, quite frankly, gave up. I stared down at the daisies, looked up at the sunshine and wondered how it had come to this. Then I started to laugh and couldn't stop. I snorted and guffawed at how ridiculous we looked as I clutched my side and laughed so loudly that I could barely breathe. I felt a presence beside me followed by Hester pushing her big wet nose in my face as she wagged her tail profusely and licked my cheek for all it was worth. Cheese may not have worked but the sound of laughter had brought her running to me and we fell about in a tumble of auburn fur and sweaty cheese chunks. I couldn't bring myself to be cross; which clearly explained the general lack of obedience in this team.

But what the hell, at least she was back. Figuring out what to do next could wait until another day. We ambled back to the car and I breathed a deep sigh of relief as I clicked the doggy seatbelts in place. With that click I knew my lunatic dogs were safe and we could at last head for home.

As I walked the aisles of the local pet store I placed my hands on my hips and furrowed my brow. I was surrounded by every style, colour, shape and design of lead imaginable. It was inevitable after the adventure with the sheep that I realised my need to keep Hester and Paddington on the lead at the woodland. But which lead should I choose? I wanted to give them the maximum amount of freedom possible whilst also keeping them under some form of control as we walked. I had already tried chest and face harnesses in the weeks after the sheep and they were not very successful at preventing them from pulling. Hester had quickly cottoned on to how to remove a face harness and run free. Paddington couldn't have cared less that the chest harness tightened when he pulled; he just pulled harder and seemed to enjoy the challenge. I trailed my hands along the silver clips of the leads on display and listened to them jangling together. As I moved along the aisle I caught sight of two sturdy looking, long retractable leads. I eyed them suspiciously and began to smile at the realisation. They would be perfect for giving the Bears freedom yet with the click of a button I could stop them mid-walk and retract them back to short lead length. Or so I thought. I practically skipped out of the shop with my purchases in hand, excited to give them a try.

- Click and hold down button next to handle. Lead stops reeling out. Dog stops walking
- Release button and walk towards dog to retract excess lead
- Click and hold down button again to walk at new lead length
- Release to allow the lead to reel out again and give dog more freedom

Easy. I looked down at my two dogs clipped onto their new leads and held a lead in each hand as we walked purposefully into the two woodlands. I shifted my thumbs off the buttons and listened as the leads reeled out whilst the dogs followed their noses along the wide path. This was brilliant! They had the freedom to walk and so far I hadn't been entangled. We carried on like this, enjoying the woodland scents and sounds around us, and I practised retracting the excess lead whenever the Bears paused for a moment. We had a few minor entanglements around branches and tree trunks as they wandered further together but it was easily solved by walking around the trees after them. I couldn't believe I had waited this long to purchase such wonderful leads. How had I lived without them in my life? I walked tall, proud even, as if I alone had solved the problems of the modern dog world.

Pass me my prize now please, for I am great

I pointed at the sky to emphasise my point about this. They say pride always comes before a fall.

A rabbit streaked across the woodland path in front of us and within seconds the flaw of my plan became very evident. The Bears leapt from the ground and sprinted after the rabbit ahead of us as it darted back and forth across the path. Leaves flew from the mark where they had stood a moment ago, the leads let out a high-pitched whirr as they spooled and my mouth fell open. My world slowed down as I realised in horror what was about to occur...

1.0 second: The Bears are running and they are running fast...

...There is only one way to stop them. Press the lead buttons...

...At that speed the sudden halt could choke them or damage their necks...

...Don't press the buttons...

...Oh my, they are gaining speed. Press the buttons?

1.5 seconds: If I let go of the leads I am unlikely to see my Bears again...

(Recalls sheep adventure and shudders)

...If I press the lead buttons I will damage my back from the sudden halt...

...Wow, they really are fast. Look at them go!

1.9 seconds: The lead only has a certain amount of length...

2.0 seconds: THE LEAD ONLY HAS A CERTAIN AMOUNT OF LENGTH. It will end.

2.1 seconds: Do something. Quick!

Whoomph.

2.2 seconds: Too late...

And with that thought I ate dirt; a lot of dirt. The Bears dragged me along the woodland path, stomach bouncing along the bumps and pink wellingtons flying. My face was buried in a curious mix of leaves, soil and stones. We bumped along the path as I prayed I wouldn't be dragged across any dog mess and tried to breathe through soil-filled nostrils. I held tightly onto the leads – a little late now but I was not giving in. Suddenly we stopped. Perhaps the Bears had become bored of dragging the extra weight or the rabbit had disappeared down the nearest hole. Either way I leapt to my feet before anyone could see what had just happened and tried to act nonchalantly. Never mind the fact I was covered in woodland detritus and was missing one wellington. I was not going to be caught face down in the woods. I shakily retrieved my wellington and two dogs and with a tear-streaked face we hobbled quietly back to the car. I swore never to use those leads again as I looked at my reflection in the car window. I had leaves in my hair, soil in my ear and what looked to be the remains of some creature smeared down the front of my jacket.

7

In the midst of my trial and error as a single dog and home owner that spring, Mum had undergone her surgery and first round of chemotherapy. It is true what they say; it isn't the cancer that makes you feel ill. It is the treatment. I had listened on the telephone as Dad explained the surgery procedures and the chemotherapy that had a 50% chance of success. It was a severe type of therapy that would essentially poison my mother from the inside out in a bid to save her life. In the coming months we would become familiar with the medical terms surrounding cancer and the probabilities of success that changed constantly with blood counts and more. We would become familiar with the highs and lows and try to just live in each moment. In spite of my best efforts though, my heart always fell when I realised that if the treatment had a 50% chance of success it also had a 50% chance of failure. Then what would we do? I knew there was only one other type of chemotherapy that could be tried. I couldn't allow myself to think like that out loud but at night time my thoughts ran free as I stared at the stars and prayed every night for Mum to recover.

I was desperate to visit my parents in Cornwall but I knew I first needed to finalise my separation from Graham and allow my parents time to adjust to living with cancer before they received visitors. They needed time to shutter the windows, close the doors and find a way to cope with each tomorrow when so much was unknown. They adored each other, always had done, and it was their time to talk and be together. Their time to understand what they had to do next, how cancer would rampage noisily through their lives every single day without respite and figure out a way to find moments of peace among it all.

As spring wore on and the cherry blossom came into bloom it

signified the final steps of my separation. Graham would soon be visiting the house to remove his furniture and the items listed within that multicoloured spreadsheet that he wanted to keep or be paid money for. It had been a painful process acknowledging the end of the life we had shared together for many years and I had watched as joint friendships fell away. People inevitably didn't know what to say or do for either of us once the initial shock had passed and slowly those close bonds began to fray and disappear without argument. We had both lost an extended family and friends we cared about. I was lonely and mostly alone as we had fought bitterly for possessions. It was ugly, it was cruel and we were as guilty as one another for only seeing it from our own angry perspectives. I didn't share details with the friends I still had by my side, as I knew I wouldn't be able to keep going if I walked into their supportive arms. As with every separation, money became important because we both had to make a fresh start. Every penny was counted and we both thought we were in the right and fought over items small and large. I was indignant when Graham suggested if I wanted to keep the furniture I should pay him half the value of those items 'as new' when they had been brand new seven years ago and were now worthless if he forced them to be sold second hand. I was outraged when he threatened to cease paying his half of the mortgage and force a sale of the house if I didn't agree to all of his demands. He could leave me homeless, in serious trouble with the bank and unable to afford anywhere else to live. I was terrified at the prospect of then having to give up my dogs and deeply hurt that someone who had loved me could act that way. It took everything I had not to give in to anger and burn his childhood possessions and cherished items that he had left behind. I dreamed of burning his scout uniform on the wood burning stove and cackling as his collection of vintage t-shirts went up in acrid smoke. I didn't want to be that person though and just pushed his clothing further under my bed, whilst pretending the multicoloured scout woggle didn't exist.

I scrawled my signature across the legal papers in my solicitor's office. That room had been witness to Graham and I purchasing our home together years previously, young and in love, and had seen us through our home then flooding. The walls crowded around me on the day a final flourish of my left hand across the papers confirmed it was done. My life with Graham and our dreams of a future together were over. I was free to begin again. I owned my own home, my Bears were safe and whilst the future felt shaky at least I had a future. I was one of the lucky ones. I walked out of the solicitor's office, leant against the heavy stone wall and closed my eyes. Relief, loss and tension all mingled in as my knees ached below me. It was done. All that remained was to hold steady whilst Graham moved his belongings out. Then I could begin to forget; begin to carve a new chapter of my life, walk onwards and think of hope.

Graham and I had barely spoken since separating and our business had been conducted through solicitors, emails and the power of the Internet. Neither of us could have coped with seeing and talking to one another. What would we have said after such a swift and unexpected departure anyway? In the one conversation we had shared on the telephone early on, Graham offered no explanation and hadn't wanted to discuss a future together. It was clear from his words that there was never to be a fight for us. Once the gloves were off, the phrases 'amicable separation' and 'let's talk about this' just didn't exist. I spent months hiding behind supermarket shelves, dashing through town and ducking low for fear of bumping into Graham or his family. I knew I would have fallen apart in the face of their questions and concern. I couldn't risk the humiliation when I was busy trying to keep some form of backbone and hold it together. By the time it came to moving

Graham's belongings out I was still standing strong for the finale. We swiftly agreed on email that it would be best for the Bears and me to be absent whilst he packed up and cleared out.

I slid my hand across the smooth oak bed frame that Graham's father had made for us when we first moved in. Memories came rushing back of us furnishing the house together, choosing colours and patterns and creating our home. We had shared so many precious moments through those years and it had been reduced to this. I committed to memory every curve and texture of the different furnishings as I walked each room. The sunshine followed me across the hallway and down the stairs to the front door. It was eerily quiet as the Bears were staying at the kennel overnight. I glanced to my right and couldn't help but suppress a mixture of laughter and guilt. In the Bears' final flourish, one of them had eaten through the leg of Graham's dining room table. I hadn't planned it yet I still felt guilty. The Bears had never chewed furniture that voraciously before but for some unknown reason had chosen yesterday to really leave their mark. I knew Graham would think I had done it on purpose and there was nothing I could say. It was moving day and all I could do was close the door firmly behind me, get in the car and drive to work. My high heels hit the accelerator hard; I glanced in the rear-view mirror and wondered how my home would feel that evening.

It was empty, dusty and somehow lacking in warmth. For a split second my home felt like a ghost town as I glanced at the marked walls where pictures had hung. Bare bulbs glared down from the ceilings where once ornate shades had given the rooms warmth. I noticed the absence of small stupid items such as knives and cutlery, more so than the lack of big furniture and that some rooms were empty. The lounge carpet bore the old weight of tables and chairs that were now gone and had left dusty circular dents deep within the pile and in the echo of the room. I slept in a strange new bed that evening. The cool iron bedstead was unfamiliar to my feet as I fidgeted across the sheets in the night. Paddington had a difficult time adjusting to the new bed height and headbutted the mattress as he tried to leap up to cosy with me. With a helping hand I lifted him up and Hester looked at us disdainfully from 'her' side of the bed. It was our first night in an empty, dusty house and from now on this was to be our bed. I had after all bought a king-size bed and it seemed a shame to keep it just for myself.

I began to furnish my home as life rolled on towards summer. I picked pretty new furnishings, new beds for the Bears and tried to figure out how to mow the lawn with a bad back. In those weeks I became a demon at hanging pictures, using a spirit level, organising furniture deliveries, rewiring plugs, drilling holes and mastering the boring art of D.I.Y. I discovered that mowing the lawn is absolutely impossible with a bad back, lawn strimmers should not be used whilst wearing flip-flops and growing fruit was the way forward. It became the year of making jam. I may not have been able to heal my heart overnight, find the cure for cancer or make the past go away entirely but I could make jam; a lot of jam. I was going to be a domestic and D.I.Y goddess (in my pink wellingtons of course). Meanwhile, the Bears were having a field day of trashing the house and garden during Paddington's teenage months. I came home from work to a variety of chewed items on various days including skirting board, pipe work boxing, staircase spindles, dog beds, the front of the television and some expensive new speaker cables. Hester had taken to digging her way into the sofas and clawing at the window frames whenever a dog passed us by. She was on edge since Graham had left, I was on edge because that's who I was then and Paddington was consuming the house. This was not very 'domestic goddess' and I suspect it was a reflection of the madness inside my head. I did however find the good grace to laugh and just accept my team with their foibles. I loved us with all my heart.

There was the time I looked out of the kitchen window though and realised that my once beautiful lawn surrounding the cherry blossom tree had been turned into what resembled a badger set. There was not a scrap of lawn remaining. There was merely dry cracked earth pocked by enormous holes and skid marks from the Bears careening around the tree. I looked to my left and saw Paddington was busy chewing his way through the fence panel to reach the chickens next door. He was determined, I'd give him that. I promptly shook my head and poured myself another glass of wine. Even domestic goddesses needed assistance and I flicked through the local parish newsletter for someone to help me repair the damage. I was looking for a Handy Man but perhaps a dog psychologist would be more appropriate.

As fate would have it Dave the Handy Man was just what I needed and within a matter of weeks he had taken us under his wing. He nearly choked on his cup of tea the first time he saw my badger set lawn and looked deep into my eyes with a shake of his portly head. He enquired kindly as to what had happened. I sipped my tea, raised an eyebrow and smiled my standard line 'the groom ran off'. Dave toiled in the sun and created a pretty picket fence across the patio in my garden. At last my lawn could recover and I could keep the dogs off the grass in boggy winter months. He taught me how to fix and insulate outdoor pipes for the coming winters, he helped me lift heavy manholes when my drains became blocked and we shared many cups of tea as the summer progressed that year. His strength and male company helped me feel less alone and his lawn mowing skills were second to none. I gave him my first jar of strawberry jam that summer and a jar of every flavour I produced as the year wore on. I hope he liked jam.

I also hesitantly contacted a dog psychologist. She was cheery, covered in dog hair like me and spent quality time with us. She quite simply told me to relax, stop worrying and recognise that some dogs just didn't like others. In time Hester would be fine and just needed space and peace to recover. The dog lady made sense as she stuck another plaster on our wounds and I wondered if she was really referring to Hester's recovery or mine.

8

As summer began to show herself, Mum was ready for visitors. It was time to combat my fear of motorway driving and get down to Cornwall with the Bears. I had successfully avoided all forms of motorway driving since passing my test six years before and the thought of five hours on a motorway, with two enormous hounds, left me in a cold sweat. I wasn't sure how my back would handle sitting still for five hours in a car, how the Bears would handle sitting still for five hours and how I would navigate them through service stations for breaks along the way. In fact I wasn't quite sure how I would navigate at all, given I didn't have a clue where I was going and had never driven on a dual carriageway let alone a motorway. I was nervous and decided upon arming myself with a vast quantity of cheese cubes. I rammed the glove box of my car with bags of Red Leicester and Cheddar as if there was going to be a mouse convention in my car. I strapped the dogs in their seatbelts behind me, placed some more cheese beside me and hoped for the best. If they misbehaved I could reach the cheese and throw it at them.

I was deaf within the hour. I knew that Paddington was obsessed with sheep and that Hester was neurotic. I didn't however realise they would spend their time barking and howling along the country roads of every single county as we passed sheep, dogs, people and cars. People actually turned their heads and pointed at my demonic crazy dogs as we drove through peaceful historic town centres. My head slumped onto the steering wheel and I began to throw cheese at my dogs as the traffic lights turned red. Lord knows what we looked like. By the time we reached the last set of traffic lights before the motorway the back windows were covered in dog spit, there was cheese everywhere and still the dogs barked on. Paddington, in his excited flailing at life, discovered the electric window button. In my rear-view mirror I saw him half fall out of the window as he eyed the nearest field of sheep with a wild look in his eyes. I promptly let out a squeal, hit the window button by my side and watched as Paddington regained his balance and fell back into his seat with a loud thud and legs in the air. I began to eat the cheese myself and wept quietly in my mind. We had another four hours to go.

We descended onto the motorway and I was tempted to close my eyes as I would have done on a rollercoaster ride. I quickly realised that wasn't going to help me and hoped for the best as I joined the slow lane and hid behind an enormous lorry. The cars in the other lanes whizzed past me and I closed my right eye in an attempt to ignore their existence. After an hour of one-eyed driving in the slow lane I became bored of 50mph and the back of lorries. The dogs had settled down into a quiet sleep and I realised there were two other lanes. Foot down, shoulders hunched ready for disaster, I attempted the fast lanes and survived. I was doing it; I was actually driving on a motorway and was not yet dead. Hours slipped by as I sang our way past county boundaries and cities. The dogs slept on. When they eventually awoke for a service station break all went smoothly and I fuelled up on caffeine and chocolate. The Bears sank deep into their cosy dog beds and settled down as the evening wore on and the miles passed by.

The stars came out to greet us as I left the motorway, turned off my music and revelled in the silence of the Cornish roads. I pulled over on a familiar lay-by and admired the view of the moon rising overhead. I had travelled this road countless times as a child on the way to Cornwall with my family for our holidays. Now I was an adult bringing my own little fur family to Cornwall. I breathed deeply as my old anxiety began to rise as I realised that within the hour I would be seeing Mum and Dad for the first time since Mum's diagnosis. What would I say? How would I stop them from seeing my fear and pain? They needed me to be strong, cheerful and positive. I had been practising that attitude for months but that was on my own. How was I going to pull it off in person when I just wanted to be their child? I wanted to feel their arms wrapped around me and be assured it would all be okay. As I looked at the moon that night I realised the parental comfort of childhood was long gone. I was an adult and now it was my turn to be the carer. It was my duty to stand tall and tell them it would all be okay. A sudden gust of wind whipped my hair and brought me back to the night as I closed the car door quietly. I drove onwards towards the star-filled horizon, weary and chewing my lip in quiet anticipation. I passed childhood memories as moorland and then seaside towns passed us by, their golden lights sending out warmth into the cool summer night. I recalled long journeys on those very roads, strapped into the back seat of our old family car. My hand was always clutched tightly around a bag of sugary sweets as I constantly chattered and asked if we were nearly there yet. I had cherished my times in that family car; they signified the start of adventures in Cornwall and holidays by the sea. I had spent a lifetime exploring the sandy beaches and every flavour of Cornish pasty and ice-cream you could imagine. My Dad and I had spent hours walking the shoreline looking for shells, rock pooling and building sand castles whilst we walked our scruffy mutt Toffee. My love affair with food, all things sandy and the oceans started early.

I pulled up and over the last hill before Padstow and admired the view of the estuary; the River Camel curling away from her banks, along the coastline and out into the open ocean. The moon reflected on the water and beaches that I knew surrounded the estuary on either side. Lights nestled in the sand dunes that hid seaside villages and tiny boats bobbed up and down on gentle waves. The night was peaceful. The Bears woke quickly from their slumber as they smelt the sea air and knew we were nearly there. They knew when they were close to their second home. Five minutes passed and we were snaking down the twisting road into Padstow. I felt my old excitement building as we descended towards home. I turned towards Hester and told her where we were.

'Hester, we're going to see Granddad. Granddad!'

She had known the word Granddad since she was a puppy and leapt to her feet, pawing at the window and whining in anticipation. Her back legs twitched as she sniffed the air. Paddington, picking up on the excitement, began his deep, low howl as he held his head high and proud out of the back window. We were a virtual choir descending the hill, waking the neighbours, and I laughed until my belly ached. For a moment I forgot everything there was to be anxious about and just lived. Lived and smiled and laughed as I pulled the car into the garage towards Dad.

Dad looked tired in his eyes and I held him close. At last we were a family again and I could do something to help them; starting with providing two enormous Bears that were bouncing up and down all over Dad and refusing to give up. They went berserk with their greeting. Hester wriggled between Dad's legs for bottom rubs, stamping her front legs in excitement, and her paws pattered on the cold stone floor. Dad bent down with a weary but genuine smile and let Hester nuzzle and thoroughly cover him in licks and wet nose pokes. Paddington barged in with his big wagging flag of a tail and gumdrop nose and pushed Dad over. He never did know his own strength and batted his giant paws at Dad, begging for attention. Those two dogs were the absolute masters at making people smile and covering them with love and affection. That night they did me proud and broke any tension there could have been.

Nothing had changed at home and cancer hadn't yet curled her icy fingers around the house. Every corner was filled with familiar sights and sounds as we walked upstairs to the kitchen of this unusual, upside-down house. Family photographs sat atop wooden shelves and Mum and Dad's beach treasures and trinkets sat beautifully, immaculate, alongside paintings of seabirds and ocean views. My shoulders dropped with each pace up the stairs as Dad pulled the cork on a bottle of red wine. Mum was sleeping soundly and I would see her in the morning. As we leant in companionable silence on the balcony, we looked towards one another and registered how much had changed in the months since Christmas. Life had turned upside down and back to front for us all but we had survived this far. We raised our glasses in mutual celebration, commiseration and sheer exhaustion.

She was always so beautiful, so perfectly calm and gracious even as cancer ran through her body and spirit. How did she manage to always be so serene? I watched Mum walk across the kitchen to make her morning cup of tea as the steam from the kettle curled around her. But for the brightly coloured scarf on her head and the slightly slower pace you would never have known Mum was unwell. She was her usual smiling, perfectly coordinated and loving self when we embraced that morning and I held back tears. Mum had always taken exceptional pride in her appearance; enjoyed her femininity and clothes to the point of them being an art form. She was neither vane nor plastic but a natural beauty, carefully enhanced with fabrics and colours and her stunning blue-green eyes. Her smile lit up the room and her cheeks were lightly dusted with freckles. People adored and confided in Mum time after time as she walked through life with her calm and gentle manner. She was everyone's counsellor and support and would do anything for her beloved children. Her wicked sense of humour brought out a hint of a Liverpudlian accent when she really laughed and joked. Mum stirred her tea and the tinkling of the teaspoon brought me back to now. Tea and 30g of Bran Flakes for breakfast were time-honoured traditions in our family. I don't think Mum had eaten a different breakfast in the past thirty years. She was a creature of habit, of moderation and never one for excess. But what good had it done her now? For all those efforts cancer had come to Mum in the end.

Crimson red with black and white paisley swirls, pale lilac with tiny white and magenta flowers, rich purple with black and white paisley, bright sunshine yellow, turquoise of Mediterranean oceans and the softest knitted caps of baby pink and blue. There was every colour of head scarf you could imagine in the wicker drawers of Mum's bedroom. Even in illness she had found a way to bring colour and fashion into play, a way to make it easier to bear the horror of losing her hair. We sat on Mum's bed overlooking the garden. Steps led down from the French window in front of us towards a patio covered in pots brimming with flowers and a garden full of birds, fluttering to and from the bird table. They twittered over fallen seeds and bread and darted between clematis and rambling roses that hung thickly from the trellising and balcony upstairs. The bedroom was sun-filled, light and airy and was the perfect place to rest and recover. Mum showed me each scarf with care and we discussed outfits and combinations, matching jewellery and more. It was a familiar and comforting routine of mother and daughter sat side by side, sharing a love of clothes and colour as we had done for as long as I can remember. We were two best friends weaving in and out of conversation, pauses and gestures. We barely needed words to express our understanding.

I knew the time had come to see Mum without her head scarf and Mum was nervous and steeling herself, preparing for my reaction and hers, as she looked at her dressing table mirror. There was fear and sadness in her eyes as she slowly lifted her delicate hands to her face. For a woman to lose her hair brings a sense of losing her femininity, her identity and sense of beauty. I knew Mum felt unattractive, a shadow of her former self and no longer a woman as she lifted the scarf away and turned to me with tears in her eyes. She looked so frightened of what I might say, of what she saw in the mirror but all I could think was how her courage and vulnerability made her even more beautiful. I knew she hated her reflection right now. Soft baby hairs cradled her face and I held my mother as she cried in my arms and let out her fears and grief. I couldn't have loved her more at that moment. If only she could see her beauty came from within, not from the hair she was now lacking. I stroked her head and felt the soft down upon her olive skin as I reassured her that she was still the same person, we still loved her and it would be okay. As her tears subsided Mum explained she also had a wig but she wasn't really sure about it. She tried on the blonde cropped wig designed to imitate her old hairstyle and we laughed. It looked nice but it wasn't Mum and we agreed it also looked a little bit like shredded wheat. I tried on some head scarves and the short wig and we were in stitches. I looked like a man with very blonde hair and very black eyebrows.

The tension dissolved in our laughter and we were inseparable for the rest of the day as we talked about the past few months of our lives. Mum was in her cycle of chemotherapy that gave her a brief respite from sickness and exhaustion and we made the most of every moment together. We bitched and moaned and laughed about my separation over numerous cups of tea and moments in the garden shade. Together we found a way to just shake our heads at the entire fiasco. We talked about men and relationships, the dogs, life post-separation, friendships and dreams for the future. Mum gently encouraged me to return to my passions for art, piano and singing. One day.

Dad meanwhile had taken on the role of superhero at home since the moment of Mum's diagnosis and we heard him hurrying around upstairs across the hard kitchen floor. He lived for Mum every second of every day, he always had done, and worked his anxieties and fear out through cleaning and cooking. Chemotherapy had killed off Mum's immune system rapidly and Dad filled the house with every type of disinfectant, antibacterial hand gel and more in a bid to protect his wife from harm. He tended to her every need with wholesome foods and his loving heart. He was a true hero whizzing the vacuum cleaner across already clean carpets in the lounge and hallway and we heard him talking to the Bears. As Mum rested that evening after our first day of chatter I joined his ranks and we talked amongst a cloud of laundry and boiling pots of meals for the freezer. My cleaning ability had never been up to Dad's standards but I poured my love into cooking and laundry. The smell of flowery detergents had always reminded me of my childhood, of Mum. I piled dirty sheets and bedding onto Paddington in the utility room and watched as he squirmed and wriggled his way out, clacking his teeth excitedly whilst Hester leapt on top to tussle.

Dad and I walked the golden sands of the beach near home every day that week, feet sinking into the soft sands at low tide as we watched the dogs careening through sand dunes and long tussock grasses. We talked of cancer and I began to understand more of the harsh realities of chemotherapy, how it killed from the inside out in a bid to save lives. Dad told me that Mum was no longer allowed to sit out in the sunlight for chemotherapy brought on light sensitivity that could further damage her already painful skin. I learnt that chemotherapy robs its patients of their sense of taste, stole their eyelashes, eyebrows and the expressions they held. I realised that the pain inside manifests itself through agonising stomach pains and digestive problems, sickness and nausea that brings people to their knees time and again, exhausted and eventually bedridden when certain days of treatment cycles drag on. It is utterly brutal for both patient and carer, for my mum and dad as they held tightly onto each other in those early days and lived from one moment to the next. Their lives had already become a constant round of exhausting journeys to hospital for treatment followed by weeks of sickness, rest and simply not knowing if it would work. I couldn't begin to comprehend their anxiety and their strength, when they had no respite and no answers. Yet not once did Mum complain. Not once. In the months that followed I never heard Mum talk of her fears, of being in the excruciating pain she endured. She just showed quiet acceptance as she lay in bed with her books and watched the garden birds day after day. We showered Mum with magazine subscriptions, novels, anything we could find to at least vary her days a little. Mum just smiled and held our hands in genuine thanks and appreciation. She was incredible, an inspiration to us all as she fought her battle with grace and patience.

There was also laughter. As we sat together in the lounge one evening after dinner we found an upside to the hormonal treatment Mum was given after her surgery. Bigger boobs.

'Seriously Mum, they're massive. Look at them!' I whispered quietly as Dad washed up in the kitchen, unaware of our hushed tones.

'You think so? I wasn't sure but I did think my bras were a bit tight lately.' Mum had a wicked smile spreading across her cheeks.

'They're huge! Bigger than mine now for sure and that's saying something,' I giggled.

'I don't know...' Mum chuckled as she peered down at her chest and I checked Dad wasn't looking.

'Let's go, follow me. Quick'

I gestured quickly and helped Mum up. We scurried off to the cloakroom and locked ourselves in before Dad could see what we were doing.

We were two women, mother and daughter, side by side in the cloakroom with top halves entirely naked and staring at our reflections in the mirror. We had our hands on our hips as we admired ourselves unashamedly.

'Yeah I do think yours are bigger Mum. Those are some hormones you're taking.'

We turned sideways, first to the left and then to the right. Shoulders back and down, we pushed our chests out comically.

'And your nipples are nicer than mine. God, mine are like big hairy dinner plates.' I frowned at my reflection.

'Some chemotherapy would soon sort those hairs out love.' Mum patted me gently on the shoulder as she spoke.

Mum tried to suppress her laughter with a quiet snort but failed miserably. At that we couldn't stop laughing and leant on each other and the sink, half naked, as we tried to laugh quietly knowing Dad was next door. It was no good, we laughed long and loud and tears fell as Dad's voice came to the door.

'You alright in there love?' Dad asked in a confused tone.

'Um, yeah, *we're* fine. Thanks Dad. Any chance of a cup of tea?'

I smiled to myself at the memory of that evening as I prepared to drive the miles back from Cornwall to Shropshire. That week in Cornwall had been a blessing in disguise. It had been painful and sad but we had laughed and built precious new memories. The roles had changed but we were still a family, we were still my family. I wanted nothing more than to stay by Mum and Dad's side but knew I couldn't. It was a wrench of the worst kind when we hugged goodbye and I wondered if the next time I saw them Mum would be recovering or fading away. I saw the fear and tears reflected in Dad's eyes as Mum cried openly in my embrace. I held my tears and sorrow in until I rounded the corner and then I let them fall all the long miles home.

9

I knew we were home because of the overwhelming smell of dog. I reminded myself that I really must do something about that or I would most probably die alone surrounded by dogs. At that point in my life I felt I actually would die alone anyway. I had emotional baggage, two enormous ill-mannered dogs, a home that smelled of dogs and, as one colleague kindly phrased it after my post-holiday return to work;

'No one will ever put up with you and your dogs. Not a chance.'

Simple yet effective. Admittedly I was at the time discussing my 'baggage' in the office kitchen and yes he had always been ridiculously blunt but I classed him as a friend. He proceeded to explain that I had been lucky to have found one person that would tolerate me and my dogs. His coffee breath lurched at me whilst he wittered on, gesticulating and raising his chin high for maximum effect.

'Kat you've just got to accept there is no way it will happen twice. No one will ever put up with you and your dogs again. Fact.'

So apparently I was destined to be single forever; the hairy dog woman of Shropshire. That arrogant and misguided colleague had confirmed my greatest fears about myself and my future and his opinions remained with me and festered in the depths of my insecurities. I didn't want a relationship at that time but a part of me wanted to believe I was at least lovable in theory. Really is that so much to ask? No it isn't but from the moment he spoke I began to feel shame and loneliness more completely than before. I was ashamed that I had been left by my fiancé and I truly believed I deserved it. Despite all of my courage and strength and repeated 'I am fine' moments, there was a part of me that believed it was all my fault and my colleague was right, nobody would ever want me again. I was good for nothing, washed up, on the shelf, damaged goods, slowly gathering dust and tears as shoppers passed me by in search of brighter goods. The kind of goods that had shiny new packaging, perky bottoms and definitely no issues, craziness or giant woolly dogs.

Thankfully I found a distraction that summer from my ridiculous insecurities in my friend Amber and in singing. Amber and I had been colleagues for many years yet had never really known each other. From afar I had always admired her calm, hippy walk and serenity as she glided through the open plan office with long glossy hair and a genteel smile upon her face. She was utterly unaware that the men all adored her and had named her 'Miss June July August' in their imaginary work hotties calendar. Fate had brought Amber and I together that summer in joint misery to be honest. We were both reeling from painful separations and, as they say, opposites attract. I would skip by Amber with my fake smile and 'I am fine' response whenever she asked me how I was and I had a wild look in my eyes from too much caffeine. Amber on the other hand would pass by me slowly, melancholic in her separation whenever I asked her how she was. She allowed herself to feel her grief honestly whilst I tried to push mine away as if it were a persistent and annoying fly. We fascinated each other with our polar opposite approach to 'Survival of the Ex' and one day, over a confessional cup of green tea, I admitted that actually I wasn't fine. Life was a bag of crap. I was doing my best to just keep going but it was all so hard. With that moment of honesty our friendship began and Amber burst out laughing. It was a good start.

We shared our first woodland walk with the Bears shortly after that cup of tea. I was terrified she would reject us, would dislike the unruly woofs and not understand why they stayed on the lead. I put my pink wellingtons on shakily as we got out of the car and looked towards her with fear and self-judgement in my eyes. Amber just smiled her peaceful smile and looked at me with genuine care and understanding. We walked for hours and admired the trees surrounding our blossoming friendship. We talked of failed love affairs, relationships, sex, personal growth, neuroses, wine, fake friends, sex yet again, cake, spiritualism, adventures, adrenaline and who we were. It was crazy good for both of us, just what we needed and I was delighted to find her wellington boots were as brightly coloured as mine. But not pink. Amber had informed me early on she did NOT wear pink. Ever. Much like I do NOT share dessert. Ever. Important life rules established early on as we marched on whilst being dragged by the Bears snuffling delightedly at the soil. A summer of pizza and wine nights followed that walk, as did endless cups of tea as we helped each other heal. We also endured a work do where I utterly humiliated myself and flashed my senior manager. Most importantly we coined the phrase 'performing monkey'.

Everybody has a performing monkey; some just don't know it yet.

The monkey is that part deep inside that shouts 'I am fine' when actually we are not fine at all. We need someone to listen but are too scared and proud to let them in. It is easier to just keep smiling and pretend. It is a monkey with the maniacal grin, a jaunty fez hat tilted on its fuzzy head and wild eyes darting from side to side. It is a monkey that bangs its cymbals loudly and constantly in a bid to convince the world all is good with its grin and noise; marching onwards like a clockwork toy. It is fake, a fraudster and keeps us all from making genuine connections, from being the real deal.

The performing monkey was strong in me. And yes I am aware how ridiculous that sounds but it is true. My monkey was rabid, on drugs and really going for it. High on caffeine, sugar, wine and anything else legal it could get its hands on. It clashed the cymbals louder and louder, I was becoming more isolated and more ridiculous as time went by until I met Amber. She outright refused to do business with my inner-monkey and forced me to take my barriers down one step at a time. Amber stood there with her mental arms crossed and repeatedly told me to get real and drop the monkey. Drop it every time it dared to show up and kick it in the nuts.

I found it incredibly difficult to kick my monkey in the nuts no matter how big a swing I took at it's dangly parts. That monkey was on fire and refused to go down at times despite our best efforts. But Amber persisted, I kicked harder and improved my aim and slowly I began to open up and be real. By no means did I suddenly become perfectly vulnerable and talk it all through but at least I was able to occasionally be genuinely me. Which, at that point in time, mostly consisted of tears, anxiety and admitting my fears of dying alone surrounded by dogs.

That monkey though, it came back for a sequel one evening at a work summer BBQ. As a thank you for our work (what work? I had been busy drinking tea with Amber in the kitchen all summer) our senior management organised a BBQ one Friday afternoon. We gathered to eat enormous amounts of pork products, wilted salad and chat about all things work-related. It went smoothly and professionally until I went home to walk the dogs, changed my clothing and returned to the pub to meet my colleagues. I don't get out much, I was feeling quite pleased with myself for surviving thus far and in the mood for a good night out. On went the skinny jeans and high heels and off I trotted to the pub in high spirits.

By the time of my arrival at 6pm my colleagues were already tipsy and I had some catching up to do. It seemed a good idea to consume four enormous glasses of wine in the space of thirty minutes. I downed the lot and ordered two more glasses. It was a beautiful summer evening in the beer garden and we sat by the river, watching rowers pass by. It was all very relaxed and entirely appropriate until my performing monkey showed up. By 7pm I was wobbling around on my high heels and flirting with everything male that walked past me. I slurred at friends and had deep discussions about how awful the year had been. I puffed my chest our proudly and admired my pretty shoes. By 8pm my friends and I were deep in discussion with our senior manager about sex and relationships. God only knows how that happened and what we admitted to. I have long buried any memory of that one and pray it never resurfaces.

By 8.30pm I was talking about boobs and decided to show two

colleagues (whom I didn't actually know) my boob. Not just a sneaky peak but a proper 'here is my boob' moment. They looked at me with wide eyes as I whipped my boob out of its cosy bra in a flourish, much like a magician produces a white rabbit from a top hat. Tada! Here it is; my boob. Have you seen one of those before? A man nearby simply closed his eyes and walked away shaking his head. The colleagues just stood there and stared a lot. As if it hadn't actually happened, except it had. And if that were not enough humiliation I then decided to show my senior manager my boob. Excellent. The manager I barely spoke to in the office for fear of his seniority was going to see my boob. I teetered over, swished my hair out of the way and, with another magician-like flourish, whipped out my mammary once more. He had not asked to see my boob, I just showed him. It seemed a great idea at the time. He was utterly speechless and choked on his pint of Shropshire Lad. This is why I should not be allowed out. Ever.

By 9pm I was herded into a taxi and sent home. I wonder if I showed the taxi driver my boob as well. I have no recollection of getting home. It wasn't until Monday morning I realised what had happened when I bumped into the first colleague I flashed. He raised an eyebrow and smiled as he passed me by. Slowly it dawned on me and I spluttered into my green tea and emailed Amber for the full low-down. The entire office knew by the 11am coffee break. I hid at my desk that day, Amber brought me tea, and I spent the rest of the week being a new kind of *that person*: the one that flashed her boob at not just one colleague but two AND a senior manager.

Fantastic. I was the office gossip for the second time that year. I kicked my monkey hard in the nuts and wept silently onto my keyboard.

Paddington had continued to busy himself with chewing the fence during my work humiliation and was well into his third attempt to enlarge the hole in order to reach the chickens next door. He had also taken to chewing sticks and, despite my best attempts to remove them from him, I knew that one day he would eat a stick on the sly and injure himself. I walked sleepily into the lounge one morning before work, bleary eyed with wild bed hair, and found Paddington fast asleep on the sofa. He didn't open his eyes as I stroked him and when he turned towards me I realised his head had swollen so much that one eye was no longer visible. Never mind Elephant Man, I had Elephant Airedale and he was clearly in a lot of pain. Half of his face had turned into a furry balloon.

I rushed Paddington to the vet. They knew us well from various puppy ailments ranging from random lameness through to dog psychology follow-ups and a refusal to eat food. Yes we were high-maintenance. Poor Elephant Airedale was rushed into surgery and they opened up his entire head to see what was in there. I would like to think they found a brain but that is debatable with Paddington's silly nature and his known ability to get lost in the corner of rooms and stand there morose and confused as he whines for me to help. It seemed that Paddington had chewed a stick and a splinter had worked its way into his gums and up into his head. They did find his brain, drained half a pint of fluid and then stitched him back together.

My poor Bear lurched out of the recovery room doors and bounded towards me in his post-surgery drug haze. In his enthusiasm and confusion he ran into the row of waiting room chairs with his plastic lampshade collar and hit the deck, legs splayed like a fawn as he skidded to a halt. He looked appalling. I used to work as a veterinary assistant and had seen some sights in my time but this one took the biscuit. Paddington appeared to have tagliatelle coming out of his head where his brain should be and a bruised, bloodied eye. Thick stitches zigzagged across his head and down his face to where the tagliatelle came to rest. I couldn't have loved him more or also felt more like vomiting. He wobbled to a sitting position and buried his grizzly face in my lap as he swished his tail on the tiled floor. As much as I felt a little queasy looking at him (sorry Paddington) I couldn't help but admire his resilience. I smothered him with love and care over the next week as he recovered at home. It turned out the tagliatelle was in fact a wound drain and needed to be cleaned a number of times each day. It did exactly what it said in the description; drained the wound and did so a LOT. The main challenge was stopping Paddington from spraying blood throughout the house all week whilst he bounced around oblivious to his pasta appendage and lampshade collar.

The house looked like a murder scene, Hester was completely freaked out by his pasta head and Paddington made the most of being boss whilst Hester hid in the corner and shook. My magnificent Mr Bear ripped his collar off every single morning as he raced into the garden after the pigeons and left the collar crumpled against the back door like an overused accordion. He ate his food with gusto, he ate Hester's food with gusto (again, still hiding in the corner) and scared the crap out of the postman with his Frankenstein face as he leapt up at the lounge window and barked. Blood sprayed up the glass theatrically every time. The postman looked horrified every time and Hester continued to hide. I drank red wine, invested in large quantities of bleach and window cleaning solution and vowed never to eat tagliatelle again.

10

Before I knew it Paddington was back to his usual self and normal service had resumed. Hester was back to being boss and it was time to turn some attention towards myself. I looked in the bedroom mirror at my reflection and cocked my head to one side. I took a deep breath and tried to muster some courage as I zipped up my favourite boots and pushed my shoulders down. I had longed to sing for years and I knew I had a reasonable voice but fear had always stopped me. After much deliberation and browsing of choir websites, I had contacted my local choir of choice. They all looked so happy on the website, like one big family and they did wine tasting frequently. Sold to the lady with woolly dogs. Singing, wine and new friends were surely the ideal combination. I reminded myself of this as I stepped into my car and drove to the musical director's house for an introduction and voice test. I was fearful of failure but the time had come. I could no longer hide myself away from the world. There was life in the old dog yet and I needed to put myself out there and just get on with it. My mobile phone brought me back to reality as Amber messaged me good luck. She was always there cheering me on.

There were purple soft furnishings, lilac walls and candles of every shape and size, all wrapped up in soft music and I was surrounded by a feeling of warmth and home. The musical director and his fiancé, Franz and Emily passed me a hot mug of tea and I sank into the soft sofa quietly. I was shaking in my favourite boots and hoped I could bluff my way through, pass the voice test and run before they noticed my fear. We talked of life, of our love of music and then a need to tell my story washed over me. I couldn't help but admit that my fiancé had left me just before our wedding, my mother was seriously ill and I was *that* person. For crying out loud, they hadn't even asked me but it all came pouring out as I gulped my tea and blinked back vulnerability and tears. It was the start of many times in the months and years to come during which I felt compelled to admit my circumstances. As time went by I narrowed it down to what I termed my Circumstance Sentence; my standard explanation of what had happened followed by a hearty Santa laugh and smile to brush it all away. With that laugh I was effectively preventing anyone from offering compassion, understanding or even trying to get beyond the surface. A closed book as it were. But for now it was a waffling long diatribe and I welcomed a listening ear as I admitted my shame and drank more tea. Safe and warm in the room of lilac, Franz and Emily offered gentle expressions of comfort and stories of their welcoming choir.

The keys of the piano lurched at me and grimaced angrily, or so I thought. I attempted to repeat scales of varying tone and screeched the high notes out with tension and a belly full of tea. I was expecting Franz's ears to bleed, Emily to snigger in the next room at my efforts and my voice to crack. Thankfully none of that happened, my voice sounded okay after years of not being heard and I was admitted to the choir with Franz and Emily's kind smiles. I would be joining sixty other voices and finding my way through scores of music, familiar and new, and introducing myself to strangers the following week - to a lot of strangers that all knew each other. Stranger Danger came to mind and I drove home laughing, excited and nervous. A new beginning was on the horizon.

What do you wear to a choir rehearsal? I appreciate that fashion isn't the first consideration for a choir practice but it is when you are attending your first rehearsal and everyone will be looking at you. Sixty sets of eyes on the new girl at school and fashion suddenly matters. When I was actually at school it didn't go so well in the fashion department and I was mindful of having no friends again. I was chubby, very chubby, had a wild and enormous monobrow and three (yes three) corkscrew perms one atop the other. I looked like a cross between Oscar the Grouch from Sesame Street and Tina Turner in her 80s heyday. And to top it off our school uniform was a thick woollen kilt and a grey felt hat or a straw boater in the summer. I understand why I had no friends, really I do. In a bid to avoid a repeat of that period of my life I opted for my favourite boots yet again. Never mind a stiff drink, I had faux leather. They were not exactly a fashion statement but I definitely had no hint of Sesame Street character or 80s pop icon about me as I dressed.

'Good evening everyone. Please take your seats for the announcements.' Franz gestured to the sea of faces and we took our seats.

I was placed between the tiniest, quietest mini person I had ever seen and a scrumptious buxom English rose whom I expected to produce homemade farm goods at any moment and lamb some sheep whilst she was at it. They were two welcoming and happy faces that became much-loved friends in the months to come. For now they had at least passed the test of not being Stranger Danger and I breathed a sigh of relief whilst scribbling down their names. All was going well right up until the moment Franz 'announced' me and instead of waving quietly in response I leapt to my feet and beamed a big loud hello to everyone and waved vigorously - new girl at school and desperate to be liked. At least I didn't have a perm that time. The hour was a blur of trying to keep up with the choir as they sang songs they clearly all knew by heart and had practised for months. I fumbled with my standard issue red plastic file of songs and flicked pages in a bid to identify which song we were actually singing. I belted out the notes I knew and mouthed the rest, hoping nobody would notice. The high point was half way through the rehearsal when we took a break from singing. Little did I know that choir break time included tea and baked goods. Cake is my heroin and I practically ran to the queue. It was so much better than school and the free carton of milk. High on cake sugar, the rest of the evening went smoothly with more mouthing of songs and introductions to people. Two years down the line and I'm afraid I still didn't know half of their names but that night I tried to scribble some of the more memorable ones in my file.

I had never encountered such a diverse and welcoming group of people before and, despite feeling like a fish out of water, I left that evening hopeful and eager for more. Franz and Emily had created something special in their choir and I imagined everyone that joined had a similar story of heartache to mine. People of every age and background had come together to create something better, something to hold onto when life hit rough seas.

I didn't miss a single rehearsal that summer and relished my weekly outing to sing beautiful songs and eat cake with my sixty new friends. Okay, I didn't know them all, but it felt like we were all friends, all part of one gloriously supportive team that worked hard and had fun with music through life's twists and turns. They became my support group, my strength and a distraction to pull me away from the anxiety and fear that followed me daily like a lost and pitiful hound. Their talent left me speechless and humbled and they showed what true commitment and passion could create.

Around the same time as choir, I discovered a new minor obsession of mine. Jam. My garden had produced an enormous quantity of glossy soft fruit that summer and it hung heavily in the sunshine. I hadn't made jam since I was knee high to my Dad and we had made redcurrant jelly. Armed with nostalgia I stepped into the garden and was determined to recreate that lost happiness. Raspberries, loganberries, redcurrants and blackberries filled colanders draining in the sink and strawberries bobbed in their rolling boils upon my hob. I couldn't get enough of making jam and people from work kindly donated the extra fruit from their gardens. Greengages, Mirabelle and Victoria plums were conjured up into jewel-coloured delights such as plum, ginger and brandy jam, greengage and vanilla and deep dark damson. It was sugar heaven, though I admit I had no idea quite what to do with the enormous amount of jam I had produced. In my enthusiasm it hadn't occurred to me that it would need to be eaten.

11

Cancer. It is just a word. Five tiny letters lined up next to each other in the shadow of a big curly C. Yet that one word has the ability to strike fear into the hearts of people of all ages when it is brought into their lives. We hear the word cancer and we may as well hear the word death, for all the attention we pay to how treatable it actually is. With a diagnosis of cancer we falter, we let hope walk away in an instant and grasp onto loved ones' hands for support. No matter how positive the prognosis, we initially close our minds in fear and assume the worst and understandably so. Cancer terrifies us because it changes lives in an instant. It is a cruel disease and the treatment can be long, painful and humiliating. You cannot walk through cancer and remain unaffected, unchanged. It exposes vulnerability and fears, shines a spotlight on our own often ignored mortality and asks unconditional love and support of families, nurses and doctors for months. Years even. It is a modern day nightmare yet it also brings moments of true love, courage and self-sacrifice. In the hands of cancer there are precious gems of heartfelt laughter and survival to be found. For as the world moves ever forwards, people are cured of their cancer every single day and live on to enjoy the next chapter of life. Families are changed but by no means diminished. Beautiful in their warmth and courage, the cancer survivor smiles all the more deeply for having been granted a moment more in which to love this life.

As I marched through summer and autumn with my jam-making

and singing, cancer continued to be a part of daily life for my Mum and Dad. I don't think I can ever truly understand the impact that summer of cancer had upon my parents, for I was not there on a daily basis and I don't know how it feels to have cancer or be the devoted husband of such a person. Mum and Dad had a lifetime together before I appeared in this world and I only ever saw what they allowed me to as their youngest daughter. I have no doubt that, in their absolute love of their three children, they protected me and my siblings from the worst of the illness and, even in their darkest moments, they held on tightly to each other and ensured their family was safe. The unconditional and unshakeable love of parents continued on. But I *can* tell you that I learnt all about how cancer brings families closer and makes you appreciate every single moment that you share together. It literally forces you to live from one day to the next and holds you in a strange suspended animation where there is no future. There is only the present moment with an absolute *uncertainty* of tomorrow. It is terrifying and leaves you feeling utterly defenceless, sick to your stomach, yet it also makes you fiercely determined to fight and live on. Grateful and thankful and deliriously happy when you hear the slightest piece of good news. A telephone call from Dad confirming a good blood count that summer indicated a step towards recovery. I felt like we had won an Oscar, felt like we were cheating death and could go on. There was hope quietly walking back through the open door. It was an emotional and mental rollercoaster of highs and lows and that was merely how it affected me. How did Mum feel on a day-to-day basis? I don't truly know. I only know she held it together incredibly well and I never once heard her complain in my presence. She bore the weeks of horrendously painful chemotherapy and its vicious side effects with quiet grace and a steady supply of love from us all. There were weeks when Mum couldn't move from her bed, couldn't taste the food she ate and didn't sleep yet she didn't give up. She was an inspiration to me every single day; the reason I got up each morning and told myself 'onwards'.

Dad didn't leave Mum's side and spent every waking moment caring for her. In those months he became the cleaner, carer, chauffeur, chef, nurse, interpreter of medical reports and devotee to disinfectant and tea tree oil. Yet he also continued to be a loving husband, father, grandfather and friend. He ran the show, he kept the family informed and fought with every fibre in his being to support his wife and never once did he put himself first. He would have taken on Mum's cancer himself if he could have done so to ease her pain. I watched him as I visited Cornwall throughout the summer and autumn months, a car full of jam and Airedales, and it broke my heart wide open to see his love and devotion. I longed to take away his pain but all I could do was stand by Dad's side and join in as another pair of hands to disinfect the world around us and hold hope close. He was incredible in his strength and endurance and we shared many bottles of red wine of an evening when Mum slept. We sat and passed the time like any other family and remembered our shared past. We laughed at childhood memories of visits to the zoo and of our weekly trips to feed the ducks together. It was a release and distraction for us both.

As Mum and Dad leant upon one another they adapted to their new, slower pace of life and pulled themselves through each day. Months went by and the chemotherapy dictated what could and could not be done in its three-weekly cycle. Week One was essentially a good week and offered Mum the opportunity to venture outside before chemotherapy killed from the inside out and called her back to her bedroom. It was followed by the dark times of Week Two; which passed like an endless hell of side effects every single month. A slight improvement occurred during Week

Three, just enough to be able to get out of bed again for another round of poisonous chemotherapy. I don't know how people survive it; how Mum coped with such relentless treatment for six months straight and kept stepping up to the mark after every fall.

It was during Week One that Mum and I could go out into the world and enjoy a glimmer of the old times we shared, shopping together and chatting away the days arm in arm. The first time we went to town I was apprehensive and felt responsible for Mum's welfare. She had been issued with a disabled badge due to her limited mobility, another chemotherapy side effect, and it allowed us to park close to the shops. It was a new experience for us to be allowed to park right outside our favourite little shops and I quickly realised how valuable these badges are. We could speed shop! People often misjudge, including me, and assume that if someone has a disabled badge and can walk, they are not disabled. I am thankful that badge opened my mind and made me see that they can be needed by all sorts of people with disabilities both visible and invisible. That little badge provides a vital lifeline for those that are otherwise cut off from the outside world due to no fault of their own. Nonetheless I was nervous as we stepped out of the car. Mum looked far too well to be classed as disabled, she always was gorgeous, and I was concerned that other people would judge us. How ridiculous that I even cared what others thought but I admit I did. I wondered how people would react to Mum in her head scarf with her daughter by her side. Would they assume the worst? Would they stare? Would they even notice? I knew I would want to tell anyone that looked at us that my Mum was recovering. That she would be well again and would not die. I wanted a guarantee where there was none to be found.

I took Mum's arm to walk slowly out onto the cobbled streets and felt overwhelmingly protective. Everyone moved so quickly and whizzed past us with children coated in sticky ice-cream and with dogs at their heels. Shoulders bumped past me, oversized handbags that I feared would knock Mum over went swinging past and it was all too much. I was concerned someone would sneeze on Mum and finish off her already bruised and battered immune system. It was supposed to be fun but I soon realised the average high street doesn't have time for those that need to move more slowly, need to be given leeway and understanding. It wasn't long before we found a quiet café away from the noise and bustle of a summer's day and quietly drank our cups of tea. I could see over the swirling steam rising from my mug that Mum was trying her best to be strong but she was clearly tired and wanted to go home. We beat a hasty retreat and put the disabled badge to better use in Week One in the future; with trips to quiet National Trust tea rooms alongside ocean views and rugged Cornish coastline. There would be no speed shopping but we simply enjoyed sitting aside one another at home, watching the garden birds and admiring the bees dipping from one flower to the next in pots of all shapes and sizes.

Yes cancer changes your world and it certainly makes it smaller and slower but, as I said, it also brings precious gems. And those moments in Week One were ours.

12

I arrived at the woodland just as the sun was heading towards the hills. It was autumn and the leaves were beautiful shades of gold and deep red. The canopy of the trees looked to be on fire and nature was beginning to draw her year to a close. I breathed in the scent of damp earth and touched my hand to my trusty walking stick. The end had been worn away by a year of walking; a year of ups and downs but also of adventures and fitness. It had been a long year and I had needed the apple wood support of my stick during my daily walks but perhaps I didn't need to carry my prop anymore? I trusted I could support myself and placed the stick gently back in the car boot. I turned my face skywards at the clouds skittering overhead and glanced at my watch. We were late starting our evening walk today and I knew the light was on the way out. I didn't want to be caught walking around the hill and woods in the dark; I had always been scared of the dark and shivered at the thought of it. As I pulled my coat firmly around my shoulders, I clicked red leads onto Hester and Paddington's collars and we began to walk up into the woods. There was not a sound to be heard other than leaves crunched down by paws and the gentle hooting of owls. I checked my pocket and touched my head torch and mobile phone lightly. They were always there, just in case. I smiled down at the Bears and laughed to myself. I had become overprotective with them this year; forever trying to keep them from harm but I couldn't help myself. They each wore a reflective fluorescent dog jacket and a flashing collar light. My poor dogs looked like Christmas tree decorations in the winter months thanks to my neurotic mind.

We ambled along the well-worn path and round familiar bends, under trees I recognised in the half-light and we didn't see a soul. Hester and Paddington strained at their leads, excited by the scents of fox and rabbits. I felt the guilt of keeping them on the lead but I didn't dare let them off until we reached the bridleway I knew was safe. It was an area with taught fencing on one side and steep bluebell woodland on the other side where I knew from experience they could run until they ached but not risk escape. We walked just a little further around the hill and through the wooden creaky gate. The gate clacked closed, the hillside loomed overhead and we skidded down the muddy bank to the bridleway. The wild garlic had long since lost the glossy leaves of summer and overripe damsons had fallen in their place. I looked back in my mind to the weeks before when I had collected damsons from there and turned them into jam.

We rounded the corner.

'Hester, Paddington. Sit. Sit,' I commanded. They looked up at me adoringly (I had cheese) and sat promptly by my side.

They knew what was coming and Hester's bottom twitched eagerly as her muscles tightened. She was ready to run. Paddington meanwhile stared lovingly at the cheese and drooled just a little into his big woolly beard. We had been through this ritual so many times and were a well-practised team on the same wavelength. I stroked their heads lovingly with my palm, bent down and undid their leads in turn.

'Wait. Wait.' I steadied them with flat palms on their shoulder blades. I could feel the tension from them both as their excitement mounted.

'Off you go!' They sprang away and sent earth flying as they went. They ran fast and low along the bridleway, black noses to the ground as they weaved and tracked scents back and forth. Hester was always quicker and more adventurous, the one to keep an eye on. I watched as she leapt gracefully up the rocks and into the bluebell woods. She was safe there and I let her run free, happy to be alive. Paddington came bounding toward me, his thickset legs moving as fast as they could to carry him to me. He stopped, wagging his tail gently, then ambled up to me and wiped his soil-covered, wet beard all over my trousers. Just as he did on every walk, every single day. He liked to mark his pack that way, though I can't say other family members were as pleased to be stamped as belonging to Paddington by his wet beard. As I reached down to tickle his ear he suddenly bounded away from me, his ears pricked high. Something unheard to my ears had caught his attention and time slowed down as I watched him crouch low and slip under the fence into the adjacent field. The fence that was made of wire strung close and taught all the way to the ground. I couldn't believe he had found a way through so easily and I shouted but he didn't listen. It was late and I watched his fluorescent jacket disappear across the horizon. I knew there were a farm and a dark, well-used country road in that direction. I screamed his name. Nothing. Hester came back at the sound of my calls and I put her lead back on as I shouted for Paddington and ran the length of the bridleway with her. I couldn't find a single spot where I could climb over to get into the field. The hawthorn bushes were thick and I just couldn't get over or under no matter how hard I tried. No matter how much I pushed and let my skin bleed against the thorns nothing would give. I couldn't see over the top either and as darkness approached further I ran back and forth trying to find a way to Paddington.

I heard a sharp animal cry from the field and I stopped suddenly in my fear.

Oh no, what if that is Paddington? What if he has broken his leg, fallen and hurt himself and I can't get to him.

The minutes felt like hours as I shook and ran blindly back and forth. As I paused to switch my head torch on I realised this was no good. I was panicking. It was dark and Paddington could be anywhere on the hills and in the woods. Maybe he had found his way back through the fence and not headed for the road. I needed to look further afield but I didn't want to leave the spot he had disappeared from. Paddington had a terrible sense of direction and he hated being away from me for too long. For crying out loud, he had lost himself on wide open beaches before now and wandered off with the wrong person he thought was me. He just couldn't retrace his steps half the time. I remembered this as I tore myself and Hester away and ran. Strangely I didn't notice any back pain, time fell away, and I screamed his name over as we ran the entire circumference of the hill by torch light. I called my friend that lived by the hill as I ran and she raced over to help me. We split up and traced every path, every fox track and every field we could access that he may have found himself in. He was nowhere. We slumped by my car, a good 30 minute walk from where he had last been seen. It had already been two hours since he went missing.

My friend had to go and, with a look of sorrow in her eyes, she did all that she could to reassure me Paddington would be okay.

'He'll come back, he'll be just fine. But please, please let me know when he is safe. And you mustn't stay out all night'. She touched her hand gently to my elbow and with that gesture she was gone.

Hester and I were alone again, filled with dread and surrounded by thick darkness on a moonless night. 'What if' questions threatened to fill my mind as I breathed deeply and tried to come up with a plan. I hit the accelerator hard as I raced Hester home to her dinner and bed. I shakily called my parents to explain what had happened and I changed my answer phone message in case someone found my Bear and called me. They could reach me on my mobile as I searched. I left Hester safe at home and pulled on extra layers and a hat for warmth that cold night. I pulled my maps out and floored it to the village nearest the main road where Paddington may have gone. I visited each village pub and showed them a photograph of him. I left my number and asked them to please call me if any of their customers saw this dog. Please help me. I found the police station nearby and begged the local policeman to send a call out to his beat so they would keep an eye out for my Bear. Being the gentleman that he was he called his colleagues. He wrote down my details as I sat obviously distressed and holding back tears. He took one gentle look at me and proceeded to scan the village streets and country lanes in his police car that evening. I raced to the farms by the woodlands and banged on unanswered doors to ask their help. I was so frightened they would shoot Paddington if he worried their sheep. I knew this had happened locally and recently. The farm by the field where Paddington had disappeared was lit up. Hope. The old, bent farmer answered and I listened as he explained in his thick accent that his sheep had come to the barn that evening when usually they didn't. I pleaded with him not to shoot my dog if he saw him at dawn and to call me if he heard anything of him. I was embarrassed at my tears as I looked at him. He leant against the doorframe, slowly nodded his agreement and disappeared back inside.

Alone again, it was gone 10pm and nothing. The policeman hadn't seen Paddington and I had parked along the country road to flag down cars after my visit to the farms. The clouds were thick overhead and I couldn't stop picturing my dog lying injured in the field behind me, lost and unable to move. He needed me, no, I needed him, and the adrenaline pushed me into the night. I flagged down every vehicle, stood in the middle of the road and refused to move until they slowed to a halt. A woman on her own flagging down vehicles in the night wasn't safe. I knew that but I didn't care. I jumped aside at the last minute as one car refused to slow down and sped into the night. I whispered a silent prayer that other cars travelled more slowly and wouldn't fly around blind country bends towards my dog. I called the pubs at closing time, nobody had seen Paddington. My heart fell as I carried on my search; flagging down cars, shouting across the countryside and driving long into the night.

I closed my front door gently at 1am and crumpled on my stairs as I telephoned Dad.

'I can't find him anywhere, I can't find him Dad. He's gone isn't he? I can't find him and I can't do anymore. What am I going to do?'

I knew the answers to my own questions as I clutched the telephone tightly and sobbed from the bottom of my heart. I was utterly spent and knew there was nothing else I could do until the sun came up. The night had defeated me and Paddington was out there alone, maybe dead. I sat on my bed and stared out of the bedroom window across to the hill and woodlands that had been our walking place for so long. I stared at the clouds and watched the hours pass until I fell into a fitful sleep. The telephone rang at 5am and I scrambled across the room. Nobody called at that hour.

'Paddington. Do you have my Paddington?' My voice begging to hear he was safe.

The gentle voice on the other end of the telephone cut straight to the point.

'He's safe. He's with us and is okay. You must be Paddington's owner. Would you like to collect him now or wait until later this morning and get some sleep?'

His voice soothed me instantly as I wept with relief, he was safe. I told them I'd be there now and scribbled down directions to a village that was miles from where I had been searching. Poor Paddington had walked half way across Shropshire. I feared the impact on his hips knowing he had suffered from arthritis since he was a pup. But at least he was safe. Thoughts and relief raced through my mind as I drove and felt exhaustion creeping up on me. I wearily blinked my eyes open when I pulled my car onto the driveway of a stone cottage. The lights were on inside and an older gentleman appeared at the doorway in his bright canary yellow dressing gown. We introduced ourselves and all I could think of was how desperately I needed to see my boy and hold him safely in my arms. The gentleman turned back into his home with the promise of returning with Paddington.

I fell to the gravel, pieces digging sharply into my knees, as Paddington bounded and wobbled towards me as best he could with stiff hips. He was absolutely covered in muck and smelt mostly of manure. He fell into my arms, collapsed upon me and sighed deeply. He was so tired and all I could do was to whisper 'good boy' over and over as I soothed his shaking legs. He trembled and couldn't get back to his feet no matter how hard he tried. My back wouldn't allow me to lift Paddington but the gentleman in his sunshine dressing gown helped me place him on the seat in my car. Paddington lay there quietly and didn't take his eyes off me as the gentleman told me how Paddington had arrived at their house. He had been woken by his own dog barking at the glass front door and, upon turning the light on, had seen Paddington sat on the other side of the door. He let him in and Paddington had taken two steps across the threshold then collapsed in exhaustion. His flashing collar light was missing, his fluorescent jacket was no longer visible under the mud and the gentleman had felt for his collar tag to telephone me.

As I recounted this tale to my Dad the sun was coming up over the horizon and Paddington slept soundly in his bed next to the front door. He couldn't take a single step further into the house so I had moved his bed to him from upstairs. Hester slept soundly on my bed and I fell into a deep exhausted sleep. When I woke later that day I found my muddy Bear still fast asleep after his ordeal. Never again would I risk walking them off-lead. I made his dinner and watched as his nose twitched awake to the smell of food. Not much had changed overnight, he still always had food on his mind.

13

Mum was declared free of cancer. No matter how much I concentrate and dig into the depths of my mind I don't recall the moment I was told that Mum had beaten her illness and would live. That, simply put, she was not going to die. But I do remember it was a gradual realisation, like a slow sunrise on a winter's day that brings much needed warmth and relief from the darkness and bitter cold. The months of chemotherapy and Mum's endurance in the face of horrific pain had finally paid off. I had felt such acute fear when blood tests were taken throughout Mum's treatment and I recall how we waited as a family for signs of recovery, for signs that Mum's body was fighting back and finding a way to live again. Each blood test brought with it the shadow of loss and mortality or the promise of new beginnings and a gradual sunrise. I am forever grateful that the sun did eventually break above the horizon, forever grateful that each moment of pain and fear was taken away as the test results finally culminated in the cancer being gone.

The relief felt exquisitely good. It was delicious and 'shout from the rooftops' fantastic. It filled me with giddy excitement, an unquenchable zest for life, adoration for my courageous mother and an overwhelming heartfelt happiness that Mum and Dad could now continue with their lives. Nobody was going to die and there would be no heartbreaking goodbyes. Instead there would be all of us living on as a family, intact and healthy. I told anybody that would listen that we had beaten cancer, that it was an incredible life and next year was going to be amazing. No more drama, no more illness, just fun and life and happiness for all. Mum would spend the winter recovering, stronger than ever because she had survived. She was immortal and cancer could crawl back to its miserable, disease filled pit and f*ck off. My endless enthusiasm and naivety promptly put Mum on a sky-high pedestal in my mind where she wore her Superwoman outfit and was renamed God. God had beaten cancer, looked stunningly beautiful with or without hair and had a future ahead of her to enjoy. God had a lot of spare headscarves to dispose of as her lovely soft silvery hair began to grow back and she had that dreadful shredded wheat wig to burn.

I couldn't wait to visit my parents and celebrate with them. I was slowly going insane with excitement at home as the Bears and I packed our bags, closed our pale green front door behind us and headed to Cornwall. For the first time since Graham had left the previous year I was driving the familiar journey with peace and happiness in my passenger seat. There appeared to be an absolute lack of problems or heartache by my side and it was blissful. I sang my heart out to familiar upbeat pop tunes as miles of tarmac sped by, fluffy white clouds skittered past the window and Paddington snorted at the breeze tickling his wind-blown whiskers. Hester curled herself deeper into her cosy bed and I stuffed my cheerful little face with chocolate biscuits and big fat cups of sweet mocha. I plied the Bears with celebratory chunks of cheese and dog treats at every opportunity and finally arrived five and a half hours later on a pin-eyed, caffeine high.

I wish I had arrived with more grace, understanding and moments of silence rather than my outright over-excited childish enthusiasm. My parents know me well and no doubt expected me to be full of smiles and chatter but I should have toned it down. I am an adult and they had been to hell and back. The last thing they needed was my excitement and noise but that just didn't occur to me. I waded in as per usual and thought about it later. Ah, that marvellous gift called hindsight. If only I had been more prepared and had given it some thought I would have been less surprised when I found that nothing appeared to have changed. Mum was exhausted and mostly bed-ridden and Dad looked devastated in his eyes and weary in his gait. It appeared to me that the stuffing had literally been knocked out of them both and in short they looked *lost*.

Cancer does that to survivors, it leaves them lost. Not the kind of lost people experience after a few too many wrong turns onto unknown roads but the kind of lost that leaves survivors uncertain of *who they are*. A feeling that penetrates to the very centre of their being and leaves them speechless, isolated and misunderstood. The cancer survivor is at times uncertain of their very existence in the world as they trace the scars upon their body and within their heart. Scars that whisper as the survivor looks in the mirror:

I have survived, but for how long? I feel so different, somehow changed. The world makes no sense to me anymore. Who am I? Everybody is smiling, everything moves so fast. I feel empty, so tired and yet I am alive. I should be happy. But now what? What am I supposed to do next?

In my experience that feeling of being lost affects cancer survivors and their families across the globe, every single day of the year and yet nobody talks about it. Post-cancer guidance and support have a long way to go if survivors are to stop feeling lost and start feeling hopeful and whole again. We need to understand that the moment a family receives the all clear is perhaps the time when emotional support is needed the most. Survivors and their loved ones are given the all clear, told to return in a number of months to check for any signs of cancer and wished well in their future. They survived months, if not years, of treatment and the hospital doors close silently behind them. Life has turned on its head yet again and, in the blink of an eye, the survivor has lost their support network of doctors and nurses, the familiar yet awful routine of treatments and tests and is left to get on with rebuilding their life *on their own*. Job done. Family and friends fade back into their own lives and they are celebrating; happy and secure in the knowledge that death has walked away in another direction. Mortality is just a whisper on the passing breeze and nothing more. Life goes on and the survivor is supposed to be happy, delighted at being alive and high on their second chance.

With all that expectation combined with a lack of support it is no wonder that survivors don't talk about it. They are exhausted from fighting for their lives and confused as to why they don't always feel jubilant. Why everyone else feels on top of the world and has moved on instantly whilst they just want to sleep all day. The survivor needs time to grieve the loss of who they were and understand and accept who they have become. It is a time that brings questions and uncertainty for the survivor regarding what tomorrow could bring. They need patience and love to help them heal and truly feel that whilst they are changed they are no less magnificent. The survivor needs warmth and welcoming arms to help them regain their sense of belonging and acceptance in society and yes they need *us* to do that for them. They need us to stand firm by their side, not fear the big C word, gently lift them towards the sunshine and *accept every single moment of that journey. No judgement, no expectation and no criticism.* It is our responsibility as human beings, as loving souls, to do this without being asked. Yet in all our intelligence and understanding of modern medicine we seem to have forgotten and we wait to be asked. We don't know what to say or do and we fear making mistakes, upsetting people and so we do nothing. We assume everything is okay and continue with our own lives at a time when we need to start listening and caring even more.

I was as guilty as the next person of not listening and not understanding the need for aftercare when my family received the all clear. I arrived in Cornwall and was angry and frustrated that Mum and Dad were not over-the-moon-ecstatic and were not immersing themselves in celebration and dreams of their bright and happy future together. I expected so much more and felt confused and disappointed. I looked at their weary frames, absorbed the silence that permeated every corner of their home and wanted to shake them out of their lethargy and remove the dark, dank fog that had settled upon every surface the sunlight tried to reach. They had been given a second chance to *live* when others didn't get that chance. How dare they be so flat, so *lifeless* and selfish by wallowing in the past. And how dare I have thought such monstrous things about my family. I was being utterly self-centred and narrow-minded in my approach because I didn't understand, hadn't experienced it before, and neither had my parents. They didn't know any more than I did what to expect of being given the all clear, how they would feel from day-to-day yet they were streets ahead of my attitude.

The last of the autumnal days passed us by as I thought about that whilst the leaves fell and rooks caught the breeze as they swung from the treetops next door. I began to see the world differently and I realised that my family were doing precisely what they should be doing as winter approached; taking quiet time to rest, to sleep and begin adjusting to a life with cancer. Yes, you heard correctly, a life *with* cancer. For once you experience cancer it never truly leaves even after the all clear is given. With a quiet acceptance I began to realise that cancer becomes a part of all those affected, it lingers with the possibility of returning and it changes lives forever. It offers insights and lessons in appreciating every single moment of life, it demands compassion and an acceptance that we only ever have the present moment and yes it also knocks the stuffing out of people. Like the distracted rooks that were blown off their branches by the stronger gusts of wind I too had failed to prepare and was knocked sideways by those realisations.

I began to accept the reality of where we were in Mum's recovery. It was early days. I spent more time listening and observing and noticed the feel in their home was actually one of hesitant but very real peace. I allowed my own exhaustion to take me into deep sleeps and found respite and relief in the company of my dreams. Mum and Dad were taking invisible steps forward and were being gentle and supportive of one another. They were preening their feathers away from the outside world. I found myself a little space on the branch next to them and clung on tightly with my immature claws. I offered support and care as they leaned in to weather the storms and gave them the occasional nudge towards the sunshine (when it dared peek out from the Cornish mizzle that blanketed the days). They pecked me when my nudging became a little too insistent for such a youngster. It was altogether more natural, more organic than my flapping frenzy of excited wings when I had first arrived. It felt right and good; as wholesome as oats.

The moments we shared were nondescript yet precious. We ate good food, we sat in silence and Mum slept peacefully. A part of me dreaded cancer returning to haunt us and denied the possibility vehemently. I found it hard to come to terms with the idea that we would continue to experience a life with cancer in the months and years to come as recovery milestones were reached. I worked hard at acceptance and focussed on what needed to be done next. For when feathers had been preened, when sleep had been taken, we needed to turn our hearts and minds towards Mum and Dad's 40th wedding anniversary and celebrate their life together. They had created forty years of marriage, friendship, the occasional argument, family and unconditional love together. And thankfully they would both be well enough to see in the next chapter of their life. It was time to plan a party.

14

It was perfect, a silent haven of tall pine trees into which we retreated as a family to celebrate life and let our guard down after a year of uncertainty. Each of us had held our individual lives together and been strong for one another. To the world we had been stoic and had followed Mum's lead of quiet acceptance. On the inside I am sure we had nursed our wounds and felt immeasurable pain at times but we had held fast. Now it was time to rest amongst the trees.

The chalets nestled amongst peaceful pines and were far removed from the modern world and pressures of daily life. The roofs were lichen-covered and mossy where nature had incorporated them back into her gentle arms and little birds hopped from branch to branch and sang their songs to the world. It was chilly as the woodland sighed and approached a winter slumber around us. The days were still bright and crisp with the promise of celebration though and we checked into our mossy homes and stocked the fridges with foodie delights, sparkling wines and gestures of love. I could see the hesitation in Mum's eyes as she unpacked her beautiful clothes, coordinated as always in her recovery. Whilst there was an undeniable air of celebration all around us she was still living with cancer, with the possibility of it taking away her future. For every smile and moment of laughter there was perhaps the nagging thought of what if. What would tomorrow bring. *What if.* Yet in her incredible strength she carried on, pushed aside her thoughts and smiled deeply. She closed her suitcase, dropped her shoulders and walked towards her party. She walked towards her family that would do anything to keep her safe and towards her fortieth wedding anniversary with the man that had loved her without reservation, without limitation and unconditionally for all those years.

There were waterslides and I hadn't been on a waterslide in many years. To be precise I hadn't been on a waterslide since two unforgettable occasions that confirmed to me that water parks and I do not mix. There was a family holiday as a young girl when I forgot my swimming costume and was made to spend the day going down waterslides in my knickers. I was only young, it didn't really matter, but I can clearly remember trying to dissolve into myself to avoid people noticing I was lounging around in a pair of white spotty pants. It was not cool and it was my first taste of why water-related theme parks were bad news. The second occasion was a family holiday again but as a slightly older child. That time it was the dreaded wave machine that caught me out. I should probably point out that I am not a natural swimmer; I was half-drowned at swimming classes as a four year old and had a friend that repeatedly sat on my head and refused to let me surface to breathe. None the less, on that family holiday I decided to tackle my swimming demons and sat bobbing amongst the wavelets in the shallow end of the fake beach/pool of the wave machine area. Dad was by my side and reassuring me it would be fine. All I needed to do was swim when he said so whilst the wave approached and I would glide effortlessly to shore. Glide effortlessly to shore like a mermaid, like a silken seal, and not drown. Just like the other children were doing with smiles upon their faces. I looked over my shoulder as the wave approached, looked at my Dad and waited with horror in my eyes. The wave seemed enormous from my viewpoint, at least 6ft tall, but it was probably merely a ruffle upon the water's surface. With a shout Dad beamed at me to swim and I kicked like a frog, as if my life depended on it. I promptly went bum over face in the wave and tangled myself up in a knot of limbs. One half of my bikini lodged itself firmly up my backside and the other half removed itself entirely as I was dragged across the fake sand surface under the wave. It was much like being dragged across sandpaper and I thought I was going to die. That may have been a touch dramatic as I did surface a moment later gulping air. Nonetheless I pouted, burst into loud tears, pointed at my grazed and bleeding knee and have not ventured anywhere near a wave or water-related theme park since then.

As a grown adult I was well overdue conquering that fear and had invested in a bikini that I hoped would stay firmly in place. I eyed the various waterslides suspiciously and tied my bikini tighter until I felt it dig into my ribs. I comforted myself with the thought that at least I wasn't going to be attempting the slides in my knickers and get arrested. My two nephews scooted past me and, slippery as eels, flew down the big steep slide of death without a care in the world. Kids can do that kind of thing; surely it was not for adults. My older sister then ran past me and went down the big steep slide of death, as did my brother-in-law and finally my Dad. Right, so adults can do that kind of thing too. I tied my bikini a little tighter and hid behind my goggles as families ran past me. I considered my options carefully and wondered if I would be able to get away with venturing into the gentle outside jacuzzi rapids instead. I adored the look of these 'rapids', they were mostly populated by old people bobbing around like ducks on a river. They made their way lazily through wide easy bends and chatted serenely as they flopped over tiny bumps and slides into the next section of warm water. Now that was my kind of slide and I longed to be in there. I belonged with the old people. For a start I could loosen my tourniquet bikini, feel my circulation return and just relax. Alas my nephews were having none of it as they shouted at me to do the slide of death.

My moment had come; I could deny the nephew pressure no longer. I relived my childhood water slide horrors in my overactive imagination and held tightly onto the overhead rail as I sat at the edge of the slide. Apparently you are supposed to use the rail to gain speed for the descent. My knuckles however were white from resisting the flow of water that attempted to drag me down the slide and away from the comforting rail. My eyes flitted between the hand rail, the endless pit of water below me and the slide that seemed to disappear at an ungodly angle far into the distance. Why do people do this? I would rather eat my own feet than do this kind of thing. Nonetheless I have some pride and one by one I uncurled my fingers from the rail. I say 'pride' but what I actually mean is there was an ever-extending queue behind me and I was the cause of the slide traffic jam. It was time to go. With the last of my digits dragged from the rail by the water I let out an almighty array of swear words and plummeted rapidly. As per my childhood, my bikini wedged itself up my backside, I hung tightly onto my upper half threatening to escape the bikini and inhaled half the pool of water upon landing. The kid behind me kicked me in the head as I flailed. I resisted the urge to cry. My entire family watched from the balcony and promptly bent over double laughing.

Buoyed up by my survival I tried every available slide and yes, on every single slide I either lost part of my bikini to a bodily crevice or wedged my bottom on the slide and ended up rammed by the person behind me. I couldn't stop laughing at every disastrous moment as I flopped about like an utter incompetent. Pride had long gone and it was the perfect medicine after months of anxiety and tension. I felt alive (if not half drowned), I was surrounded by my family and I couldn't have cared less about the rest. It's not like people haven't seen nipples poking out of misshapen bikinis before.

After one too many slides, we huddled around hot chocolates dripping with towers of cream and sprinkles whilst our shrivelled hands and hair slowly dried. The smell of chlorine surrounded our happy family as we flopped and wedged ourselves into the coffee shop sofas and sighed. Both children and adults alike fell towards exhaustion and we headed back to our mossy chalets and drifted toward thoughts of tomorrow's wedding anniversary celebrations as we swirled glasses of thick red wine and the children slept, reliving their day in dreams. Sleep captured us all eventually in her arms as the stars came out. Tomorrow promised to be a big day for us all, we needed sleep and took it in abundance.

We had decided long ago that our party would have a sixties/seventies theme in honour of the year that Mum and Dad were married. Mum and Dad were due to arrive from their chalet in the evening and we transformed our chalet into a romance-filled nest of happy memories, family and love in anticipation of their arrival. The chalet glowed from the tea lights in red and white that covered every available surface. The light reflected and scattered as it touched heart-shaped decorations hanging from the ceiling and created tiny shadows behind glittery miniature hearts scattered across the tables. The walls were covered with old family photos from across the decades of Mum and Dad's life together and we readied the personalised cake and presents from us all. We poured our hearts into creating a room that would bring them both peace and happiness and a sense of occasion. It was absolutely beautiful and I held back happy tears as I watched my family working together as one.

Mum and Dad would soon arrive and it was time to don our costumes and pull the champagne from the fridge. I had always fancied being a redhead and purchased a glorious long wig of auburn hair to match my white plastic knee-high boots and ridiculously short swirly dress. Oh how I recall my visions of becoming a red-haired siren for the evening with long tumbling hair. Oh how I recall those visions falling flat on their faces when I tried my outfit on. There is no denying it, I looked like a man. A man in women's clothing and that was not the look I was aiming for. No matter what angle I positioned the wig at upon my head the fringe gave me an enormous face that looked much like the moon. The further back the fringe went on my forehead the more I resembled a monk with a giant forehead. The 'dress' more closely resembled a tea towel upon closer inspection and my backside was in danger of falling below said dress for all to see. I swear my backside didn't do that when I was eighteen and wore even shorter dresses. Thankfully my sister dressed as an ageing bearded hippie, my brother-in-law donned a shockingly blonde wig and dress for the occasion and my brother and sister-in-law looked hilarious in the eighties getup our parents used to wear....giant baggy t-shirts emblazoned with fake Chanel logos, tight lycra shorts, big caps and multicoloured bumbags. I positively faded into the background in comparison.

Everything had its place, everything was ready and glowing with candle light and we were all randomly dressed as one sex or the other. We heard Mum and Dad approaching and we watched as they turned open the door and took in the chalet in all its magnificence. This was their moment and their celebration of forty years standing strong together. Their moment to observe the family they created now holding party poppers and pink champagne just for them. I saw Mum take it all in. Her eyes sparkled with excitement and happiness as she pointed at the old family photos and clutched her side in laughter at Dad's old combover. She looked beautiful in a long blonde wig and crown of flowers and she held tightly onto her husband's hand. It is so easy to forget that my parents had a life before we were even a twinkle in their eyes but tonight it was apparent in the way they just held and guided each other. I could feel the love between them in the way they shared every moment of the surprise, in the gentle hand of Dad upon the small of Mum's back and in the way they danced to the music as the evening progressed. They had a world of their own that many couples long to create, they had worked hard to create a loving marriage that had spanned four decades and they gave me such a blueprint for finding love in my future. Those memories are as clear today as they were that night and I doubt they will ever leave me. Did I feel lonely being the only single member of the family that night? No, I felt humbled and privileged to be there at all. How could I feel any form of lacking when I was surrounded by such an incredible family? Such a shining example of what love is all about in its different forms.

The party was filled with laughter and emotional dewy eyes as speeches were given, a family quiz was completed and we filled our glasses with more red wine and pink bubbles. We talked, we sat, we sang and we danced with each other in high spirits. And then by 10pm the chalet became quiet and we all relaxed into the night and our own beds. We always knew the children and Mum, for different reasons, would become weary as the evening wore on and excitement turned into tiredness. We had started early, it had been magical and I lay in my bed smiling at the new beginning we had toasted that night. My family were all happy and *healthy*. Perhaps it was time for me to think about the state of my own life and consider finding a little love of my own. I glanced at my auburn wig creeping towards me from its perch atop the bedside table, shuddered at the thought of a relationship again, and quickly tossed the idea and wig aside.

15

You want me to put myself out there and go on a date? A real date, with a real person? With an actual man? No. No way. No, I'm not doing it. Stop looking at me like that. No. Stop. It. I am in my thirties and have a runaway groom to my name. I have baggage; massive oversize baggage that requires 'heavy' labels AND I have mismatching underwear. I am not cool enough for dates. And besides I'd have to shave my legs which would be akin to deforestation right now. No razor is sharp enough. No. No way am I going on a date. Seriously, stop looking at me like that. It is never going to happen. NO DATING. EVER.

Paddington cocked his head and harrumphed as I continued this conversation with myself in my kitchen and paced in my furry slippers. I paced to the hallway mirror and frowned witheringly at the part of my mind that dealt in hope, optimism and giving things a try. The part of my mind that makes me think love deserves a second chance, that skinny dipping in freezing cold water is a great idea and that eating seven desserts in one sitting is absolutely the way forward in life. She has some fantastic ideas, I can't deny her that, but still...dating wasn't one of them. Or was it? Was it about time I got my head together and took a shot at happiness? I can tell you now that it was a really staggeringly bad idea but that didn't become apparent until much, much later.

As I paced in my slippers that day it seemed that my family could be right. My sister and Mum had gently suggested after the anniversary party that I really shouldn't lock my heart away forever and that the company of a good man could be just what I needed. I pictured a tall, handsome man bringing me logs from the woods and gifts of fine chocolates and red wine. A life-size hot-water bottle of a man with a broad chest and soulful brown eyes; his sole aim in life to keep me cosy through the bitter winter and beyond with his companionship, wit and outrageously pert bottom. I sighed inwardly on many occasion as I pictured my handsome stranger, the idea evidently gnawed at the optimistic part of my mind and grew in its romantic appeal. My family and friends were encouraging me to get back on that horse called Romance and have some fun and I could see why. I really needed to get out more and stop making up imaginary men.

But seriously, a horse called romance? My horse felt like an old grey nag called Boris, weighed down with my history as he trundled along with his patchwork blanket and saddle. More of a donkey than a sleek thoroughbred and I wasn't sure he was up to the job. Besides, the only real date I had participated in up to this point in my life was when I was a chubby teenager with a perm. My male friend, that I secretly had a wicked crush on, had taken me to the cinema. I think he felt sorry for me rather than it being a date per se. Nonetheless I was giddy with excitement and nerves. He however fell asleep through the entire film and snored a little whilst I stuffed my face with a lot of chocolate. There started and ended my dating life. Graham had never taken me on a date. Could I really resurrect it some seventeen years later, in my *thirties*?? I am under the impression that dating is not something people in their thirties and beyond actually do. All of the decent men and women are happily married by that point and all that remains are perverts and divorcees. Plus there were no men where I lived anyway other than farmers and I really don't like the smell of sheep.

Shame on me for saying those things to myself but I did. I admit I was that shallow and judgemental and that was coming from *me*; the woman left at the almost-altar, the woman surrounded by dogs, a mountain of emotional baggage and wearing furry slippers. I wasn't exactly prime dating material myself. (Note to self, do not put any of that on a dating profile).

In truth I was hiding. In all of my words, bluster and resistance to the idea there lay one simple fact: I was scared, really scared to put myself out there and be rejected again. I had fresh scars on my heart that were only just beginning to heal, I was ashamed of what had happened to me and I was full of the disappointment of lost love. Oh and I was also fairly socially inept having spent the last six years of my life in a homely relationship with my now ex-fiancé. I am an introvert at heart that likes to be at home with a cup of tea and in bed asleep by around 9pm. I have no idea what to say to people and I get a sweaty backside when nervous. Again, not exactly prime dating material.

But there was a problem in my convincing argument. I was also very lonely, looking for a distraction from the past and I wanted to try and 'have some fun'. Based on that I decided that dating was actually a good idea, no, a really great idea. Yes. It would be fun and great. I felt like flying a flag from my window emblazoned with 'Bring on the men. I am single and available for dating' but decided that would be a little bit over the top. Instead I paced away from the hallway mirror, rang my sister and began exploring the minefield called Internet Dating.

Mention internet dating to people and you get responses ranging from abject horror at the thought of meeting someone via a computer through to stories of perverts and oddballs, profiles that are barefaced lies and success stories of those that found true love. Oh and a lot of raised eyebrows, rubbish attempts at concealed laughter (snorting into a cup of coffee really gives it away guys) and absolute fascination regarding how it works. I received a variety of those responses as I canvassed my friends and colleagues for their opinions and experiences. I was looking for reassurance and held on tightly to my favourite success story; that of my brother and sister-in-law. They met at a time when internet dating was brand new and mostly unheard of; that long ago era called the 1990s. They were internet dating pioneers and they are still happily married many years later. This is the best bit: they are cool people, the sort that everyone loves and wants to be like. Cool people do internet dating. With them in mind I chose to ignore the horror stories and began to explore the myriad of websites out there that would apparently bring me a happy ever after. I could picture it already. I would be the cover girl on those websites in years to come with my success story; finding true love in the arms of my imaginary pert-bottomed companion. There would be pictures of white sands, turquoise oceans and a billowing dress as my man lifts me high in true love and demonstrates how perfect our lives had become since internet dating brought us together. Or not. In all likelihood I would end up as that idiot that falls for the weirdo and gets hoisted off in a big canvas bag and held hostage for a ransom that my loved ones decline to pay. Marvellous.

Evidently I still had some work to do on balancing my expectations and fears. Nonetheless I proceeded (with a touch of caution) and explored the popular dating sites I had heard of. There are so many sites out there and I quickly learnt to avoid the free sites, the 'let's meet up just for sex' sites (really who does that?!), the slutty sites and the sites for the very young and rather old. Instead I settled upon one site that appeared to cater for people that genuinely had an interest in people beyond looks and I delved into the world of psychological and social profiling. My research was fascinating and I began to understand why people have flocked towards such sites in recent years. This generation work long and unsociable hours in offices across the world both day and night. We live in socially distant yet over-populated areas and conduct our social interaction through the instant gratification of mobile phones, iPads and twitter. We have lost the art of conversation (I never had it), the closeness of community and simply do not make the time for meeting real people in our frenetic existence. In our pursuit of 'happiness = money + success' we have forgotten to make the effort with love and expect instant results from everything we devote time to. It is no wonder we have flocked towards internet dating! It offers the promise of finding true love by ticking a series of boxes that not only describe you as a person but also allow you to describe your ideal partner and the life choices you intend to make together. And to put the icing on the dating cake this website in particular then promises to match you with an array of appropriate partners that have described their ideal person as you and who have the same aspirations in life as yourself. All whilst sitting at home in your pyjamas, drinking a glass of wine and watching television in your slippers with very unshaven legs. It is a genius idea. Right up until the moment you have to describe who you are with those tick boxes and then put yourself out there for others to judge and reject. I suspect that is the point at which many would-be internet daters quit and begin a hobby through which to find a perfect partner without the tick box torture.

Back to my tick box options which, by the way, seemed to go on forever as I scanned down the website page. There is a large gap between who I was at that time in my life and who I wished to be and so the temptation to lie about myself was enormous. Size of an elephant enormous. So enormous that on my first attempt I sat in my study with my laptop open and made up an entirely new person called me. It is incredible the qualities one can acquire instantly these days and within the first ten minutes I had become tall yet petite, deeply religious and interested in politics. I had gained an additional degree (in fashion design no less) and was elegant, patient, athletic, poetic, a sociable party animal and a successful entrepreneur. I was amazing yet entirely fictional. I soon realised that I couldn't live up to that imaginary person and I asked myself two fundamental questions late the following evening:

Who am I really?

What are my beliefs about love?

I spent days pondering the answers to those questions and still do every now and then to see if I am on track with myself and with the world around me. I can safely say there was not, and still is not, a simple answer because it depends on perspective and timing. Who I am fluctuates through the years as I age and experience different aspects of life. To be frank about it, who I am fluctuates from week to week depending upon how I feel about myself and which hormones are racing through my bloodstream and affecting my perspective or lack thereof. I am a myriad of personalities and moods all tied up in one physical body. Yet on a deep level I am essentially the same person year upon year. As testament to this I give you my obsession with muesli. I have had a mild preoccupation with the brown and dusty cereal eaten by those that wear socks and sandals since my early childhood. I cannot get enough of the stuff and witter on in excitement every time I find the cereal aisle in a new supermarket. Muesli is my Goddess. As a young child I would sit on my father's knee as he poured his bowl of muesli; I loved how it filled the bowl with a cloud of dust and sugar and exciting jewels of raisins. Those wrinkly raisins held the muesli dust in their nooks and crannies and they were striped like tigers. Raisins in muesli have always been called tigers by me. My ever-patient Dad allowed me to sit there and eat every single tiger in the bowl as I wriggled upon his knee. He never once complained as he added milk to the remaining dust and for that I believe he is an absolute legend (and no he does not wear socks and sandals).

There was no tick box that required me to admit my muesli addiction but instead those boxes asked my opinions and intentions, even my *plans* regarding marriage, children, home life and career. I was required to list my preferences about drinking (moderate; a good red wine will suffice though champagne and in abundance would be delightful), smoking (no chance, can't stand the smell), drugs (none, unless you include sugar and chocolate) and religion (it's complicated. Who is God? Am I Spiritual? Absolutely). Onwards the boxes went with opinions on children from previous relationships (could I become a mother to someone else's child? I just don't know where the idea of children sits with me), divorce (well it would be rude to judge after my experiences but I don't really want to be second best), widowers (I wish I could solve their grief and make their world a happier place to be), travel (to excess and often please), hobbies (do I include reading and piano or does that sound dull?) and education (all hail me and my two degrees. Again I am sounding bookish and dull). Why not add muesli? Now that would really complete the picture. I may as well invest in some socks and sandals and call myself Joy or perhaps Constance. It was a nightmare and I spent far too much time thinking seriously about the answer to each one. I felt as if my future love life depended upon the quality of my ticks. In spite of my anxiety surrounding this, I eventually ticked what I felt was a true representation of my opinions and composed statements that apparently described who I am: A feminine mixture of bookish intellect and charm, a drinker of fine wine, a deep-thinking spiritual person and someone that also enjoys worldwide travel, encounters with marine life and adventures. Or in other words: I read easy books, I talk to myself often and will stretch to £5 for a bottle of wine from the supermarket. I am neurotic and think too much. I like to splash about in the ocean with sharks but am too scared to learn to scuba dive and I consider a walk around the block with my dogs an adventure. I went for the first description. Though really how can I or anyone else be described by just a list of statements anyway? We are so much more than a list of qualities, characteristics and opinions. We have *soul*; that special something impossible to capture yet more real and apparent than any tick box I have ever cast my eyes upon.

Okay, tick boxes and descriptions done. The next challenge was to choose a suitable profile picture. Do I go for a sexy, perfectly groomed photograph of me looking all swish and fancy in a dress and heels? Perhaps one from a previous holiday where I look relaxed and tanned? That could work except that for the remainder of the year I do not look like that at all – my flat duck feet don't do heels and I abhor fake tan. So at the other extreme, do I go for a bushy eye-browed, wild-haired 'this is how I really look in the morning' photograph whilst wearing my pyjamas and slippers? In a word, no. After much deliberation I went for a photograph of me looking windswept during a blustery day at the beach with the Bears. I figured it was best to get the dogs in my profile early on to make it clear I had them and put off anyone that doesn't like big dogs. Plus windswept and slightly chaotic is close to my natural look on an average day i.e. unkempt.

Next up was my one and only moral hurdle about the whole internet dating scene:

I am paying to potentially go on dates. Is this like prostitution?

That thought still haunts me, let's move on and quickly. Finally I was ready and, with butterflies in my stomach, I hit the join button and uploaded my profile. I was eager to see what stunningly handsome, brown-eyed, intelligent and kind-hearted man I would be matched up with. I had high hopes of my mysterious pert-bottomed companion sweeping me off my feet any moment now. In all reality I had to wait twenty four hours for any matches to be made and it was the longest wait of my life. When finally I logged on to the site, guess what I found? My soul mate and love of my life? My best friend in the making? No. None of that. Not even a little bit. I was matched with an unemployed surfer in Cornwall called Bear. His hair reminded me of a windswept bush and he had no desire to ever leave his home county or work for a living. But he was called Bear and for that I thought he was awesome. Right up until the point my sister looked at his profile and fell about laughing down the telephone at me. I reticked every tick box I could find on my profile.

After a week of random matches with people old enough to be my father, a selection of Navy folk and political stock brokers in London I resigned myself to needing another website. I left my fate in the capable hands of my sister as she wrote a profile statement for the next site that we found. Forget psychological profiling, this one just required a variety of photographs and a statement written by a friend/family member. Perfectly simple and, judging by the recent success of the website, it would work. For the next few weeks I had a fantastic time checking out profiles and hitting the favourite button for the men I liked. I initially limited myself to the immediate geographical area but soon realised Shropshire did in fact contain only two single men: one a farmer, the other a man that lived in the woods. As an aside, I actually bumped into the man in the woods two years down the line. I recognised his face and noticed he had an Airedale terrier. A match made in heaven that was never meant to be.

Once I had widened the net to the entire UK (hell, why not), it was like looking into a box of quality street. There were so many potential favourites to choose from that I didn't know where to start. Never mind whether they would like me back, I turned into a favourite button slut and just ticked them all. Ah the thrill of when I received notifications I was somebody's favourite. Okay most of them were not, on initial inspection, my type but it was such a boost to my confidence that at least *somebody* found me attractive. There was life in the old dog yet. And then the day came when somebody liked me that I liked back. Oh my word he was hot, all blue eyes and white teeth, and I telephoned my sister immediately. He wanted to go on a date and was available any day next week.

Wow, keen. And hot.

To this day I have not forgotten my sister's words regarding Oscar's profile. Yes he was hot but she had alarm bells. He looked too polished, too clichéd handsome and it didn't make sense he was a commercial pilot yet worked on the till in a supermarket instead. She didn't like his description....*likes living the high life, very pretty women, fine dining and champagne*. My sister kindly told me that whilst she could see the attraction she felt he wasn't for me, that he was shallow and something was amiss. Obviously I didn't listen. Something had caught my attention and I messaged him to say hello. A month of conversation flowed between us effortlessly and yes I made up all sorts of hobbies in order to be seen as compatible. In the space of four weeks I became an avid fisherwoman, interested in learning to fly and a fan of Brad Pitt movies. There was definitely a connection between us, he was charming and great fun on paper but there was also my need to be liked and eagerness to be happy once again. It blindsided me just a little and made me try too hard.

Eventually we agreed to meet. Oscar had waited a month for me to be available to go on a date and we fixed a time and place for lunch in Shropshire during what turned out to be a cold and wintery December. Internet dating had been kind to me so far and, as I looked at Oscar's profile photograph once more, I wondered how it would be when we finally met one another. I was excited, curious and also absolutely terrified. I was about to go on my first date as an adult and I had no idea what to expect or what to do.

16

I can't believe I am doing this. It is a ridiculous idea. Why on earth did I think this would be a good thing to do? No. Come on Kathryn, we can do it. This is going to be fun. GREAT and FUN remember. What if he hates me though? What if I make a complete fool of myself? No one is ever going to love me and people have told me this already. No. Just focus on great and fun. Keep saying it until you believe it and breathe. I am so nervous. I can't do this.

I ran from my bedroom clutching my stomach as nerves got the better of me. I was terrified about putting myself back out there and going on a date after everything I had been through. It was just too hard to risk more hurt but then I had promised my mum I would do it and, well, nothing ventured would of course mean nothing gained.

My date had become the hot topic at work that week and my colleagues had been joking about the possibility of Oscar being a weirdo, some crazy murderer who might whack me on the head and bundle me into the boot of his car. We spent many an hour discussing this at the coffee machine and I joined in with a slightly manic high-pitched tone as my anxiety increased. Evidently it was not the type of encouragement I needed but I laughed along whilst also plotting my escape route. We decided in the end, given my track record, that it would probably be best if I checked in with a friend throughout the date. I nominated my colleague Owen; an absolute gentleman who is ever-reliable, always there for his friends in a crisis and lived close enough to our date location to be there quickly in the event of me being whacked on the head and bundled into the back of a car. This was assuming of course that I was not unconscious after being whacked on the head and so could text him for help.

Okay, this is fine. People do this all the time. People go on dates, they talk crap about liking other peoples' hobbies, and they survive. Some actually even ENJOY this stuff. It's fine, oh God I look fat and my eyebrows are bushy. Should I shave my legs? What if he wants to come back here? I am so not going to do that, I don't even want to kiss the man. What do I say? Remember he already said on his dating profile that he likes champagne, pretty women, the fast life and he is a fancy commercial pilot. I think my sister was right; maybe he isn't the best choice for me. The best plan today is to NOT be me. It is probably wisest to just make stuff up, try not to throw food down myself and escape as soon as possible. Either way he needs to meet the dogs – that'll put him off for life.

I glanced over my shoulder at my bed. Paddington and Hester were busy playing bitey face and throwing my pillows off 'our' bed.

See, that is why I will die alone. There is no way he will want a second date after seeing those two woofs on the bed.

The morning dragged by incredibly slowly, each minute like a lifetime. I felt like I was waiting to attend my funeral so accordingly I dressed in my highest red heels, tight jeans and a top that emphasised the good curves and hid the squidgy bits. If I was going to my funeral that day, I was going to look hot as I went up in flames.

1pm: I waited outside the restaurant, in my red duffel coat. Okay, it was not sexy but it was warm and I felt safe. I talked to strangers that entered the restaurant and explained I was on a date. Why did I do this? As if they cared.

1.10pm: I waited outside the restaurant, in my red duffel coat. I texted Owen [He's Late O. I am still alive].

1.15pm: I waited inside the restaurant as it was starting to get cold. I began to wonder if my duffel coat is akin to wearing a giant red carnation. Could I have been any more obvious? I texted Owen [I am still alive O].

And then he arrived. He had the whitest smile I have ever seen. I checked out his bum, his shoes, his clothes and his face – in that order. He certainly ticked my mental list of what I find attractive in a man. Yes, it would appear that on a first date I am that shallow. We introduced ourselves and he seemed normal. I texted Owen whilst Oscar bought us drinks at the bar [O, he's hot! Nice bum. I am still alive].

We ordered our food and I made a big mistake by ordering salad with dressing. I could barely eat, thanks to my nerves, and the leaves I did eat were so saturated in dressing that I mostly sprayed myself with balsamic vinegar. I must have looked like an overenthusiastic rabbit trying to eat dandelions. I excused myself to the bathroom and texted Owen [O, this is good. I am still alive. I am however covered in food]. God bless you Owen for tolerating me that day, never once did you tell me to get a grip.

The rest of the date actually went well and we talked for hours. I made up more crap about liking his hobbies (note to self, I must stop doing that) and I felt a connection between us. Something was niggling that didn't seem quite right about him but I ignored that. Instead I focussed on how well we were getting on and how attractive I found him and his incredibly gorgeous bottom. The relief at having a positive experience was incredible (with him, not his bottom). My life had been full of heartache and sadness all year and that date was a breath of fresh air. Perhaps it was my reason for the sad times; my happiness was just around the corner and he was it.

As we got up to leave I asked Oscar if he would like to come back to my home and meet the Bears. It was the moment I had been dreading. The phrase *no one will ever put up with you and your Bears* rang true in my ears as Oscar nodded a keen yes. He told me he would love to meet the Bears and had been hoping I would ask.

'Okay Oscar. Are you used to dogs? These guys are big and they are terriers. They might jump up from excitement so just relax and go with it. And it is best I go in first and you get in the house quickly after me before they run out of the front door.' I gave

Oscar his instructions, breathed deeply and opened the front door.

Now I was attending my own funeral. It was time to go up in flames. The next ten minutes were a blur and absolutely hilarious *now*. But at the time it was mortifying and I have no idea what compelled Oscar to want to see me again. With Oscar in the house the Bears went berserk. They had him pinned against the hallway wall in seconds and Paddington bounced up and down on springs to lick Oscar's terrified face. Hester meanwhile was busy burrowing between Oscar's legs for a bottom rub and practically knocked him off his feet. In panic, I was racing around the house to find my back door keys and get the kitchen door open so I could get the dogs outside. I couldn't find those keys anywhere and I clattered around in my heels trying to look cool whilst also gaining some form of control over my chaotic life.

It took me ten minutes to find the keys. Ten minutes of Oscar being headbutted and licked by Paddington. Ten minutes of having his clothes pulled at by big paws and becoming covered in dog spit. Ten minutes of me weeping internally at my life and my inability to find my keys. The worst part was that I found the keys in the bottom of the kitchen bin. To this day I have no idea why I put them there but I have never forgotten rummaging around in that bin of smelly, disgusting waste as I tried to look hot in my heels.

'I'm so sorry Oscar, so very sorry. My dogs are not usually like this I promise. Um I appear to have put the keys in the kitchen bin. Excuse me a moment whilst I retrieve them,' I explained politely.

I was so polite yet it was such a load of fiction. My beloved Bears were always like that. They were as out of control at times as my life had been and today they appeared to be on speed.

The remainder of our time went smoothly once the dogs were in the garden and I showed Oscar my home. He fussed the dogs and we chatted before it was time for him to leave. No matter how normal and easy that part seemed, I stood awkwardly in the hallway as Oscar filled the front doorway with his beaming smile. I waited for him to disappoint me, to let me down gently with a polite and permanent goodbye.

'I would really like to see you again Kathryn,' Oscar took a step backwards onto the drive.

'Oh. Really? I, well that would be...well...lovely' I tried to hide my surprise with a non-committal tone and teetered on the doorstep in my slippers. The hot red heels had long since been discarded in favour of comfort.

'I could come and visit you next weekend. Perhaps I could stay?' Oscar shuffled from one foot to the other as if weighing up which way my response would take us.

'Okay. Um, yes okay. We could do that.' I fiddled with the necklace hanging around my neck whilst I searched for the right words to fill the silence between us.

'I mean I don't expect anything and, well, I would of course, you know, sleep in the spare room and so long as I could just cuddle you, I mean no kissing, that's fine if we...' Oscar gabbled and fell over his words in his excitement. He took a deep breath to slow himself down.

In that moment Oscar stepped towards me on the doorstep and hugged me with genuine warmth; if not a little awkwardly given we had only just met and I was losing my balance in my slippers. As he drove away into the evening I felt a curious mixture of excitement at the prospect of another date and also a nagging hesitation – could I really do this? I wasn't sure my heart and nerves would handle a second date yet alone a relationship. Oscar was gorgeous and the chemistry was great but I just wasn't sure. My uncertainty followed me back indoors and the evening passed with a long telephone call to my sister to relive every detail of the date. By the time we had finished, the stars had risen and I was shattered. As I dozed on the sofa by the fire my mobile phone announced an incoming text message.

I CAN THINK OF AT LEAST TWENTY REASONS WHY YOU ARE MARRIAGE MATERIAL FOR ME. I CAN'T STOP SMILING AND I CAN'T WAIT TO SEE YOU NEXT WEEKEND. OSCAR XX

Wow. I was speechless and just a little taken aback by how keen he was. Was this normal? Probably not but my heart fluttered as I looked towards the following weekend. I can't say I had ever been called marriage material before, not even by my ex-fiancé when we were supposed to be getting married. I chuckled to myself as that thought drifted over my tired mind and I fell fast asleep to the sounds of the crackling fire.

17

By the following weekend the world was five sleeps closer to Christmas and I was five sleepless nights closer to insanity. I had spent the week reliving my first date over numerous cups of tea with colleagues at work. I had done my utmost to reassure Owen that Oscar appeared to be normal and therefore it was safe to allow him into my home again that coming weekend. I had also spent the week furiously trying to lose a few pounds of weight, which had proven to be easy given that excessive adrenaline had been lifting my heartbeat day and night. I was thin and tired by the time Friday came around. I had removed every scrap of excess body hair despite the fact I had no intention of allowing this man to see me naked in the near future and I had utterly failed to consider the date itself. It was going to last an entire *weekend*. What would we do? What on earth would we talk about for that long? And how was I going to *not* release bodily gasses or go to the toilet for a whole weekend? I suspected clenching my buttocks together for forty eight hours would be impossible and painful and so decided that outdoor activities were the order of the day. We would go for long walks in the countryside, preferably somewhere with a strong prevailing wind, and I would use the dogs as the excuse for doing so. They needed exercise and I needed to fart.

Oscar arrived early Saturday morning as I paced the house. The cheerful little red car that Oscar parked on my drive was quite the contrast to his tall manly frame and I smiled inwardly as I opened the front door to welcome him back. He burrowed into the recesses of his tiny car and produced bottles of wine and a heavy cake tin. Oscar couldn't have looked more excited as he explained proudly that he had spent the night before making me this HUGE carrot cake with thick cream cheese frosting. He had a warm open smile and a look of innocence in his big blue eyes as he talked. I opened the cake tin and my heart melted a little, as had the icing during its long journey northwards. I breathed the heavenly scent of vanilla and cinnamon and had to stop myself from licking the entire cake and shouting 'mine' (I am not a sharer of desserts). Oscar was certainly scoring points for his ability to bake. He had been so thoughtful.

We soon headed off into the Shropshire countryside for a day of hill walking. My pink wellingtons nestled in the car boot next to Oscar's green ones and his matching wellington liners (smart footwear for a country walk – another point scored). The Bears sat upright in the back seats and, with their doggy seatbelts attached, we were ready for the off. My car was only a small hatchback and I explained that Paddington may begin to bark as we passed sheep. Paddington meanwhile was licking Oscar's ear enthusiastically and beating out a tune against the window with his bushy tail. I considered that it would have been more honest of me to explain that Paddington would not bark. He would scream, howl and shriek at every passing sheep and Hester would then join in with manic, repetitive high-pitched haroo-ing because of Paddington's vocals. I couldn't bring myself to be that honest. Our wellingtons looked so cosy together. For once in my life I had a second date to go on. I laughed off the dogs' enthusiasm, said a silent prayer to the heavens and hoped there had been a large sheep cull across Shropshire the previous night.

No such luck. By the time I had driven us five minutes along the main road Paddington was shouting his head off and refused to stop no matter how much I tried to calm him down. Oscar looked horrified and had his fingers in both ears whilst explaining that as a commercial pilot he was required to take hearing tests and had to have perfect hearing to be allowed to work. My dog was killing Oscar's career and our second date. We passed beautiful barren hilltops, rolling and tumbling amongst one another into ploughed winter fields below and I shouted all about the natural beauty of the area whilst Oscar held his fingers in his ears and continued to wince. He was becoming slowly engulfed in Paddington slobber as well from his flailing head. I looked in the rear-view mirror and noticed Hester had inhaled a lungful of air from the open window and was about to start barking like a mad thing. Oh God please let this end. Onwards we went and eventually we arrived at the car park. The car came to a halt and Oscar practically fell out of his seat in a need to get away from the howling demons and spit. I strapped the Bears into their walking harnesses; regular leads were in no way sufficient for those two when in 'sheep country', and I felt like we were beginning a dog sledding race except without a sled. Oscar had recovered his senses, including his hearing, wiped himself dry and kindly offered to take Paddington as he stood tall and handsome in his green wellingtons. Good luck with that.

Did I explain that Paddington can pull like a shire horse and had caused me to slip a vertebral disc during his puppyhood? No, I didn't explain. I merely flirted and hoped for the best.

I passed Oscar the harness and attempted to be nonchalant as I trotted away with Hester by my side. I walked quickly up the nearest hillside and marvelled at the views all afternoon whilst

Oscar was dragged around by Paddington. It would appear we did have a sled and Oscar was it. The manic barking was long forgotten as Oscar was pulled to and fro and I sneakily trumped to my heart's content whilst I reminded myself there would probably be no third date. When the Bears finally stopped for a rest we talked and I listened as Oscar told me about his family and that he was living with them after his recent divorce. He told me about his young son who lived overseas with his mother and explained that he was no longer a commercial pilot; he was working at the checkouts in a supermarket. Whilst Oscar had been a successful commercial pilot in his twenties he had then dabbled with alcohol and drugs and eventually left his profession to find his way back to health again. He had gone on to spend years exploring the world and lived within an ashram in India to cleanse himself of his past. I listened to tales of his travels and his life in the ashram. I heard about beautiful ceremonies, exotic locations and some very unnecessary details regarding enemas, sores, dramatic weight loss and lentils. Oscar told me he had then moved to America and became engaged to a lovely woman. Shortly after their swift engagement Oscar had felt pulled towards spiritual work in New Zealand and so became unengaged. Onwards he went to New Zealand in pursuit of yoga and spiritual healing. There he met the love of his life and they lived together with their soul family in what Oscar described as a cult. The cult had given Oscar purpose and belonging; he had changed his name to a beautiful spiritual uttering, promptly married the love of his life and then had a son. They were blissfully happy but Oscar had lost touch with his biological family in the process and it all went downhill from there. The cult no longer filled his needs; he made the painful decision to leave his wife, grieved for the loss of his young son and returned to his parents in England a year ago. And now here he was with me on a hill in Shropshire. That was Oscar's life in a nutshell, a very big nutshell, and he told his story beautifully.

Oscar was staggeringly open, honest and non-judgemental about his own past and I had absolutely no idea what to say. It was quite something to listen to his colourful life and I didn't know what to make of his tale other than feel impressed by his absolute honesty – what else could I do with that amount of information on a second date? He was self-assured and confident as he spoke and there was no shame or embarrassment about him. My preconceptions and judgements were flying off on all sorts of tangents as I listened and I was pleased that my history seemed well, *normal* in comparison. As we walked onwards, I explained that I had been left at the almost-altar. Shame crawled up and over me but Oscar stood there and offered compassionate reassurance. Nothing fazed him.

As the late afternoon sunshine began to dip behind the horizon we headed back down the valley to the car and I pulled Oscar towards the local café for hot chocolate, tea and cake. The café was cosy with steamed windows, and muddy walking boots lined the entrance. We curled up as best we could on unforgiving wooden chairs and I warmed myself with rich sweet chocolate and clouds of cream that melted down the sides of my hot mug and onto my thawing fingertips. We finished our sweet drinks and braced ourselves for the cold outside, ready to drive home for dinner and endure another round of mad dog barking en route.

Oscar turned to me at the end of the day as I unpacked the car, and lifted my wellingtons from my hand gently.

'Let me help you honey, here let me. You know, it doesn't matter about the Bears. I can just buy ear plugs for dog walks. It's no big deal and you don't need to worry. My hearing will be fine and well, we'll manage. I'm just not used to such lively dogs as I've only ever had gun dogs but we can um find a way.'

I looked at the floor with glassy eyes as I realised that he was prepared to tolerate the dogs and me as a package. We came as one and could apparently be accepted as one. And no I didn't miss his reference to future dog walks…it would appear we were going on a third date.

We spent the evening by my cosy log burner and the Bears slept peacefully at our feet as we ate a dinner that I had prepared to impress. In true early dating fashion I hadn't known Oscar's culinary preferences and he admitted he didn't really like chocolate pudding *after* having eaten an enormous portion of thick stodgy chocolate pudding and ice cream. He slid towards me on the sofa and I knew what was coming next. He wanted to hold me, to kiss me and feel the warmth of me next to him but I wasn't ready. I practically leapt to my feet as I found the words and gestures to explain that I didn't want to rush into a physical relationship. Yes I may have shaved every inch of body hair into oblivion that weekend but I had *no* intention of it becoming apparent to anyone other than me. What if he laughed at my wobbly bits, at the go-faster stripes that sat on my hips and the red pin-prick pimples on my big toes from waxing them? Nobody needed to know about that disaster, least of all the man I was trying to impress. No matter how much I gesticulated and explained about not being ready he was just too persuasive and charming. He begged and bargained to be able to cuddle me, 'the rest could wait for a long time if need be honey', and I acquiesced. He was good-looking, he seemed innocent in his request and I had no ability to say no. I lay stiffly on the sofa next to him and tried to relax into his embrace as I reminded myself to keep my socks on all evening and not reveal the red toes.

I had never met a man that wears a full set of perfectly ironed long-sleeved traditional pyjamas before. Oscar made his way onto the landing upstairs to say goodnight before sleeping in my spare bedroom and his pyjamas nearly floored me. I couldn't decide if it was funny, quirky or sweet (?) that this six foot tall man with chiselled looks was standing there in a set of baby blue soft pyjamas and tartan slippers. It was a bizarre moment and I stifled my confused laughter as he leant into me for our first kiss. I felt like I was living in the 1950s where full bed dress was required. In the fraction of a second that preceded the kiss my mind raced.

He's going to kiss me. Do I want to kiss him? I'm not sure I can reach that high. He's wearing baby blue pyjamas. This is weird. Oh no, my nipples are sticking out. It's cold on the landing. Yep he's noticed and he's definitely going to kiss me. What if his beard is scratchy? Are those mopeds on his pyjamas? Wow, they are something else.

We kissed and his beard was scratchy but I liked it. It felt glorious to actually be kissed, to be *wanted*. I felt a trumpet salute going off inside my head as I realised I was kissing a man and he was not yet repelled by me. After a post-kiss silence, in which all I wanted to do was question him about his nightwear and hide my nipples, we went our separate ways and wished each other goodnight. I lay awake in my bed as the Bears whined and snuffled at my bedroom door. I had of course kicked them out so Oscar wouldn't think I was *that* woman in her thirties with dogs in her bed. I couldn't bear it though and sneakily let them in once I was sure Oscar would be sound asleep.

Morning soon woke us and I quickly brushed my hair and cleaned my teeth before heading towards the spare room to wake Oscar. I sat on the edge of the bed at first, unsure of what I wanted to do. Before long I was curled up next to Oscar as we watched the dawn light brighten the distant hills opposite my house.

Our second day together passed quickly with a lazy morning, more walking, food and then the long drive home for Oscar. As he drove away in his cheerful red car I reflected to myself that it had been a weekend of highs and lows but it had been good. I was unsure about beginning a relationship with anybody and Oscar was certainly one of a kind. But he had intrigued me with his charming enthusiasm and utter disregard for what others thought of him. His bold kindness and acceptance of me brought a glimmer of joy into my life that weekend and reassured me that I was attractive to someone after all. I wanted more of that feeling and to find out who this man with the blue pyjamas and outrageously camp gestures actually was. He asked me on email if he could update his Facebook profile that evening to being in a relationship with me. Before I had a chance to hesitate I said yes and was somebody's girlfriend once more. I bought new fancy underwear to celebrate and invested in another packet of razors.

Our third date was a perfect, pre-Christmas frosty wonderland at Warwick Castle the following weekend. I was wrapped in more layers than I knew existed in my wardrobe and tucked under a cosy woolly hat as I leant against the entrance and waited for Oscar to arrive. He was the picture of an aristocratic English gentleman as he strode across the flagstone paving and under the looming archway of the castle towards me. His gentlemen's umbrella swayed on the crook of his elbow in time with his footsteps, his perfectly positioned scarf lifted his chin high and his furry Russian hat billowed in the light crisp breeze. He was quite the sight amongst more casual families and couples roaming about the grounds and I felt like I was in my own version of a romantic period drama. The backdrop of our date did absolutely nothing to dispel this myth from my overactive imagination and we spent the day weaving in and out of the grounds stealing kisses from one another and supping on mulled wine. The shire horses in the courtyard whinnied as I stroked their soft noses and Oscar took photograph after photograph of me to show his parents. Oh how my ego loved that attention. We kissed in the conservatory, we kissed in the café and we kissed some more on the bench that overlooked the frosty hillsides in the distance. We were like a pair of love-struck teenagers as I sat on his knee and melted into him on that bench.

As the frost settled around us further on our bench we watched peacocks pass by and Oscar took hold of my hand earnestly. He had something he wanted to tell me. Oscar told me how since his divorce the previous year he had scanned literally thousands of dating profiles to find a woman to love. He knew he wanted to be in a relationship and had taken to his task as if it were his calling in life. He had signed up to every website, driven hundreds of miles across the country and had been on so many dates that he couldn't recall how many there were. He had met with blondes, brunettes, fashionable and quirky people, tall, short, young and older women and everyone in-between. Oscar had tried long-distance and short-distance relationships but none of them had been right, so he had said goodbye fairly promptly and moved on. He had clearly been very busy the past year. Oscar had told himself he would look at one more profile before giving up, go on one more date. And that one more date had been with me. I was not his usual type and yet I was absolutely right for him. I didn't know what to say, so we kissed some more.

More dates followed in the rush towards Christmas and I became an expert in providing fireside picnics for us whenever Oscar could get away from work and drive northwards to see me. We ate more cheese, pork pies and pickles than I thought possible and fell asleep watching films by the fire. It was quiet, peaceful and I was at long last happy.

As those future dates occurred I came to realise that dating can be wonderful but it is also a minefield. It is an explosive cocktail of social expectations, carefully chosen outfits, trying to avoid doing or saying the wrong thing at any given time and preventing the re-emergence of old neuroses and so-called issues. It is hard work trying to appear cool whilst controlling the inner-crazy, the rush of hormones and neediness that lives deep within. And I *know* it is the same for other people as they date. Teenagers experiencing their first crazy love, career-driven adults looking for 'The One' as they settle down, divorcees looking for a second chance at happiness, mid-thirties rebounds and the older generation unexpectedly bereaved. Every single one of us experiences the same nervous butterflies, the same wish to be liked and find friendship, and the same shock when insecurities and the less desirable parts of us rear their ugly heads and beg to be healed. Dates turn into relationships which turn into love, warts and all.

18

Christmas was hopeful and we had everything to look forward to as a family. Life had been kind to us in recent months declaring Mum cancer free and my shoulders had dropped as I began to look forward to a new year.

I awoke early on Christmas Day in my old bedroom and the silence of the early morning enveloped me as I listened to the Bears breathing quietly and rhythmically on my bed. They roared across the local beach that morning with their tinsel collars sparkling in the sunshine and I laughed at the beauty of the day. The skies were bright blue and the warmth of the sunshine soothed Dad and me as we walked together. The sand was soft, like blancmange, and my feet sank with every step whilst the dogs flew along the surf line chasing one another.

'What's in there?! What's in there?!' I pointed at the ground and watched them dig an enormous hole in the sand trying to find their prize. I dropped a dog biscuit or two in the hole for good measure and smiled. Life was so normal now.

We treated ourselves to real champagne in celebration of Mum at breakfast. We wore colour-coordinated outfits; by pure chance Mum and I had dressed similarly but then what did I expect? We had shared years of shopping together, of buying one another clothes and sharing our spoils. We had always been close and that day was no exception. Mum looked beautiful and dad captured us enjoying champagne and celebrating together on camera. Mum's smile was radiant as she toasted me across the old family farmhouse table. I could see the sparkle in her eyes. I knew she was hesitant to believe she was going to make a full recovery and she feared cancer would find her again but still she smiled and with genuine warmth. Her hair had slowly begun to grow back and I couldn't have loved her more.

Dad was a flurry of activity in the kitchen as pots and pans bubbled, steam rose and the oven pulsed out its heat. He was a slightly frantic magician casting his cooking spells and he made me laugh without even knowing it. He frowned in concentration as he worked and poured his heart into this special Christmas dinner as Bear noses snuffled the counter tops. They were ever-ready for a treat or a missed scrap of food and their gumdrop noses twitched in anticipation. Dad couldn't resist and passed them carrot peelings with a dash of gravy.

I sat at the family table that had been ours since I was a baby, and took it all in. I looked to my left and saw Dad cooking, sweating, shoulders hunched and wiping his brow with the effort. The Bears were falling asleep on the kitchen floor behind him like lions avoiding the midday heat. I looked to my right into the lounge and saw Mum fast asleep on the sofa under her soft blue fleece blanket. She was utterly done in bless her and slept as lunch was prepared. There was nothing to do other than celebrate and so I did.

'Dad, do you fancy a drink?' I knew the answer would be yes and we opened a bottle of smooth red wine for Dad and a bottle of cava for me. It was Christmas after all.

As the pork continued to crackle and Mum slept on in the lounge we remembered happy times and celebrated surviving the year. Dad seemed happy and the time flew as we drained and refilled our glasses over and again. Before we knew it lunch was ready. We looked to our left at the sleeping Bears, we looked to our right at sleeping Mum and laughed quietly. Now what were we supposed to do? We couldn't wake Mum, she was still recovering and needed her rest to heal. I raised an eyebrow.

'We could open another bottle?' I half enquired, half confirmed we should do so.

Of course we opened another bottle of wine and, as Mum didn't show any signs of stirring, we continued to drink our way through Christmas Day and turned the oven off. Mum eventually woke up and we ate the slightly overdone lunch with muzzy heads and fits of giggles on my part. We laughed heartily as the Bears tore open their presents, tossing paper across the kitchen and sticky tape stuck to their beards.

It was wonderful and was followed by a New Year's Eve filled with celebration as Dad and I danced around the kitchen in honour of Mum. We twirled and swirled and raised glasses high as midnight sounded and fireworks lit up scenes of London on the television. Mum slept soundly downstairs in spite of us and I truly believed the coming year would hold the promise of health, love and happiness for us all. Life was fantastic and Oscar would shortly be arriving on New Year's Day to meet my parents. I knew they would like him and, no surprises, they did. Without pomp or ceremony he walked into our family and charmed the socks off my parents. He was gentle and kind with Mum, he understood their circumstances with compassion, and ended a year that had begun with difficulties I never thought I would overcome. As a family we were okay and I was relaxing into my relationship with Oscar. Did I love him? I certainly adored his bottom, his gentility with others and his zest for life. I was certainly in lust with him and had a heady cocktail of hormones racing around my body when we were together.

We nestled down in my bed one evening and, as Oscar embraced me to say goodnight, he began chattering excitedly about our relationship. He gestured with his arms enthusiastically as he sat upright and spoke of how much he enjoyed our time together and the heartfelt connection he had with me. And then, just as suddenly, he clamped his hands over his mouth and his eyes widened in horror. I asked him what was wrong and with a pained vulnerable look in his eyes he admitted he was about to tell me that he loved me. He hadn't realised it until just then but he had fallen head over heels in love with me. He promptly hid his face in the pillow and turned the light off as I sat there in silence. Did I feel the same? Had that just happened? I thought that perhaps I did love him but recalled where that had taken me in the past. Love had hurt me so much and I was very scared to love again. I held Oscar close as he drifted to sleep and I told him I loved him. I didn't want to let him down by saying nothing after he had been so alarmed and I didn't want him to feel rejected like I had in my past.

The world around my family home ground to a halt under a blanket of crisp white snow the following day, just after Oscar had returned to his own family. I was grounded in Cornwall on the day I was due to leave and I played like a child. I built a snow lady with red heart-shaped sweets for her buttons and a fat Satsuma for her nose. I threw snowballs for the Bears, my hands froze and they ate snow to their hearts' content. The thick snowy silence and laughter allowed my mind to wander onto new beginnings and my upcoming visit to meet Oscar's family for the first time.

19

It was two weeks after New Year and I was about to meet Oscar's family. I wondered what they would be like and how would they take to me. I had come to realise from a number of conversations with Oscar that I wasn't the usual type of glamorous lady he brought home to his parents. I had seen pictures of his stunningly beautiful ex-wife and Oscar had told me that yes she really was that gorgeous in real life and also an incredibly talented singer. In fact they had owned a recording studio together and had made a CD of spiritual love songs with a picture of themselves on the cover. Good for them. Good. For. Them. I declined when Oscar asked if he could show me their wedding ceremony DVD and photographs; I didn't even want to consider how much he had loved her.

I knew Oscar's relationship with his parents had been strained because of his history and estrangement from his son. I had listened to many stories during our early dates that gave the impression that Oscar felt his parents had disapproved deeply and been unsupportive of his life choices. He disagreed with how his parents chose to live their lives and he felt they were poles apart. I had heard of his parents' hard-won professional success and of how Oscar feared women wanted to be with him because of his money rather than who he was. I didn't dare ask what he meant by this for fear of triggering a response based along the lines of me being a money-grabbing harlot or some such. I wasn't aware that Oscar had a penny to his name and I kept my silence pondering exactly what he was talking about as I drove down the motorway towards his family home.

It was dark by the time I arrived and as I drove up the gravelled driveway my instant reaction was gratitude that Oscar had not described the house to me before my visit. It was enormous, absolutely massive. There was an elegant gravel turning circle in front of the house and I hadn't the faintest idea on which area to park as I kept going around in circles on the noisy gravel. I was surrounded by BMWs and Mercedes and the largest pond I had ever seen.

Was that a tennis court I could see? A swimming pool? Yes, yes on both accounts. Oh wow.

I was suddenly intimidated as I realised just how much money the family had and how huge the mansion was that spread across the grounds like a luxurious iced cake. It was beautiful and I lived in a modest ex-council farmworker cottage in Shropshire. My house was more a dry cracker biscuit compared to that cake. I began to understand why I wasn't Oscar's usual type.

My apprehension subsided when Oscar greeted me outside and then it peaked again as I went inside and met his parents in their perfect kitchen. They were instantly welcoming and greeted me with the same warmth that Oscar had always shown. They were generous and kind hosts and I felt mostly at ease. I say mostly because I was also trying to remember my manners and choose the appropriate fork at dinner for each course throughout the weekend.

The house interior was stunning and I enjoyed every moment of the tour of each room with Oscar's father, George. The oak panelled dining room was full of history and the warm rich smell of old polished wood. The stone fireplace in the informal lounge loomed impressively around bookcases filled with adventures and the oak conservatory was light and airy for afternoon teas. I fell in love with the cheerful fox that ran across the lawn each day and the spiral wine cellar below our feet. Most of all I fell in love with Oscar's family. They were so normal and clearly adored Oscar whereas I had been expecting an entirely different dynamic.

I walked into their study one afternoon to fetch some photographs that Oscar's Mum, Alexa, wanted to show me and I saw shelves filled with books regarding God, cults and deep spiritual theories of all kinds. There were books on saving relationships, on how to cope when your loved one joins a cult and more. That collection of books bowled me over with sadness as I realised the true extent of Oscar's departure from his family when he joined the cult. It was so apparent that his family had wanted to be supportive and would do anything to make him happy. Alexa joined me when I hadn't returned, fearing I was lost upstairs, and saw my gaze upon the books. She had studied everything she could find in a bid to understand why Oscar had ceased all contact with them for two years and still she didn't understand why he always felt so lost and veered from one extreme to the other. They had eventually hired a private detective to find him overseas. I cannot begin to imagine that kind of worry and pain at not knowing what had happened. Their relief at Oscar now having a 'normal' life and relationship with me was evident from that first weekend we met. Perhaps they had their hopes pinned on me being able to bring some sense of balance into his otherwise chaotic existence. I didn't know if that was the case but I suspected so and it was all I could do to hug

Alexa and offer my reassurance that I would take care of her son. We separated and my eyes scanned over photographs of their extended family. A child that was the spitting image of Oscar beamed back at me; it was his gorgeous young son. I came to understand that he was still very much a part of the family.

I asked Oscar about his son in bed that night and listened as Oscar explained that he no longer missed him because he had grieved for him as if he were dead when he left him a year previously. But he wasn't dead and I didn't understand how that worked. His son was very much alive and both families wanted Oscar to be a part of his life. I tried to understand and to be honest I failed at that point in my life and for the rest of our relationship together. It was only later that I came to understand the complexities of loss and sacrifice for those you love. At that time I couldn't grasp the concept that to Oscar his son was literally dead and had been grieved for, so there was no further loss or pain. It made no sense to me but then I have not given up a child and no matter how much we talked about it and how much his family talked about it nothing changed. It was a no go area for Oscar, end of.

As we settled down in bed that night after talking it through Oscar suddenly announced to me that he would never have a child again. Or more precisely, he told me that he would never have children with me and it was not up for discussion now or in our future. The idea repulsed him and if I loved him I would understand and deal with it. I have never particularly wanted children but to be told I would definitely *not* have them by my boyfriend bothered me. Oscar wrinkled his nose at me, turned away and stared into the middle distance. He rocked himself soothingly and I tried to stifle tears whilst also thinking this was quite weird. Typically the more I tried not to cry the more it happened and the more Oscar completely ignored me. I reached out but he pulled himself further away from me and refused to acknowledge me. The next morning I was greeted with his frosty silence followed by a sudden change of mood into absolute happiness and joy at being together. I was a little alarmed and left for my home wondering what that was all about. It was like being with two people all rolled into one and I hoped it wouldn't happen again.

20

Life can be so f*cking cruel. That is my foremost thought when I look back upon February 2010; the time when Mum was rediagnosed with cancer, a year to the day of her first diagnosis, on Dad's birthday. Life brings incredible opportunities and happy times but it can also cut you to the quick in ways you never expect. I have scratched about for my memories of when Mum was rediagnosed but I cannot find them anywhere in the deep recesses of my mind. Yet again on a day when Dad should be celebrating, on his *birthday*, he was given the most unwanted present of all; news that his wife had cancer again. No matter how much I look inside myself I cannot find my memories surrounding that occasion or even the lead up to it when no doubt Mum was undergoing doctor appointments and tests to understand why her recovery was not progressing as expected. We had enjoyed such an exciting New Year with health and fresh starts held high whilst midnight chimed. Everything seemed to be going so well for us all. It would appear my mind has erased the worst of what followed in a bid to protect me. But it doesn't take memory to know that life was unbearably cruel to my parents that February. It doesn't take memory to know that life had given my parents a brief respite, hope in bucketloads and then whipped it away and provided despair and heavy shoulders. I often wonder how Mum and Dad found the strength to fight cancer for the second time after such a brief period of emotional and physical recovery. They had only just begun to live again.

Fifty per cent chance of success. That is my second thought when I look back upon February 2010. After the diagnosis, we were told the chemotherapy had a fifty percent chance of success and there were only two types of chemotherapy in existence that could be administered to fight that type of cancer; one of which Mum had received previously and the cancer could be resistant to. Our eggs were literally in two baskets.

What if it didn't work? What if neither type could fix this? For crying out loud fifty per cent just isn't enough. It is not enough to reduce somebody's life, their very existence, to such irrelevant stupid odds.

That much I remember. That much I can still feel now as my breath catches in my throat at some deep-buried memory I cannot, will not, access.

And so it began again. So we all walked onwards, picked ourselves up and helped Mum fight with every ounce of strength she had left. The C word became a daily fixture once more whilst old routines of hospitals and waiting on results crept back into our lives. Mum was her usual brave self, calm and accepting of every moment that came her way. Still she enjoyed the spring flowers in bloom as she began her treatment and laughed as often as life allowed her to. I am eternally proud to be her daughter though I wish I had inherited those qualities, wish I could be more like her. I was terrified, less accepting and vehemently denied the possibility to myself that the treatment could fail. I just couldn't go down that path in case I stumbled on the bricks and wasn't able to pick myself up again. I hung onto the smallest signs of recovery that I could claw into my palms. I also clung onto my relationship with Oscar as if my very life depended on it. I held on tightly, so tightly that perhaps I began to crush it.

21

Rats, a court appearance in tartan slippers and Oscar climbing out of the window on my birthday. Those are the other thoughts that sit with me when I look back upon February 2010 and the spring months that followed. They were an unlikely combination of events and some of those moments brought me light relief. The laughter distracted me from Mum's illness when I needed it most and it quickly became apparent that I was in fact dating a lunatic; a lovable, charming lunatic with hairy shoulders who had me in stitches with his antics. I also caught a glimmer of a different side to Oscar though during those early months. I gained insights into his insecurity and emotional responses far more alarming than a parade of rats marching their way across my garden.

But first the rats, all thirty five of them. In that spring my garden became a stage for amorous, romantic rats on a mission to declare their love with a riot of breeding activity. I thought the first rat was rather cute with his lolloping stride and twitching whiskers but I soon changed my mind when one morning I drank my cup of tea and looked out of the kitchen window. My magnolia tree contained a number of said rats feasting themselves upon the bird feeder contents, dangling lazily upon the branches like out of season Christmas decorations. I strode into the garden, pyjamas billowing and tea slopping over the edges of the mug I clutched tightly, in my anger and disbelief. The compost bin below had been excavated, literally emptied of contents, and turned into a rat hotel. I could *hear* the rats in there scuffling around doing naughty rat activities. I swear they were laughing at me as I lifted the bin lid and shouted at them to leave. I whacked the compost bin enthusiastically with a broom and shouted some more as pieces of mouldy carrot and tea bags ricocheted off my legs. Not so much as a whisker of a rat poked its face out of the bin. Perhaps rats didn't like water. I proceeded to give them a vigorous shower by turning my garden hose on and letting it flow through the compost bin. I was not attempting to kill them, just convince them to leave their leaking home. It soon became apparent that rats are in fact waterproof and deaf. I resumed my tea drinking and watched the rats emerge back onto the bird feeders again. This was war. A humane war on rats and I summoned my first line of defence, Paddington. That breed of dog was originally bred in Yorkshire to hunt otters. They are considered to be a courageous breed, large enough to tackle otters and incredibly stubborn. Rats were akin to mini otters and were also squeaky like a dog toy. Surely it would be a small task for an Airedale, the so-called 'King of Terriers', to scare a few squeaky rats into finding an alternative boudoir? I explained this to Paddington as I left for work and presented him with his furry, beloved soft rat toy for practice. He nuzzled it lovingly and settled down for a nap by the radiator on his favourite bed.

On my return home from work Paddington and I walked into the garden purposefully. He was on the lead next to me as we went to our battle line and I had high hopes of success. The rats would not get the better of us. I was already imagining our victory and the cheese Paddington would enjoy for being such a good dog.

'Paddington sit,' I commanded.

His heavy bottom thudded onto the grass by the compost bin as he looked up at me and twitched his enormous nose. We had already spent a good thirty minutes practising catching his toy rat as I slid it along the wooden hallway as if to mimic a real rat running. It would be easy. We couldn't fail.

'Are you ready Paddington?' I enquired.

Paddington squirmed excitedly and sniffed the air.

'What's this?! What's this Paddington?' I pointed hastily and excitedly at the base of the compost bin and hoped Paddington would pick up the scent of real rat.

He sniffed the ground expectantly and sat down again upon my command to do so (He must have known I had cheese in my pocket). His toy rat lay discarded next to him on the grass. He had real rats to deal with now.

I removed the compost bin lid and told Paddington to wait. He cocked his head to one side, knowing that 'wait' meant something was about to happen.

I shook the compost bin vigorously and watched as a single rat shot out of the bin right in front of Paddington's woolly paws.

The rat began to run across the lawn.

Paddington followed the direction of the rat with his gaze.

The rat continued to run. Time seemed to slow as the rat stretched its legs out to escape at full speed.

Paddington's head turned but his bottom remained firmly planted on the grass.

I watched as Paddington stood up casually, wagged his tail, picked up his favourite toy rat and went back to bed. I swear the real rat sniggered as it ducked under the fence and visited the chickens next door.

It was then that I admitted defeat and Oscar took over with a humane rat trap and an enormous tub of peanut butter as bait. After our dates in the early months of the year and Mum's re-diagnosis Oscar had moved in with the Bears and me, just weeks before the rats had joined us. Our domestic bliss was commencing with a healthy dose of rat removal. Pure romance. Without fuss or complaint Oscar baited the rats every day and each morning he drove them to the local woodland to rehome them. It was strange how the number of rats in my garden kept increasing despite his efforts. Well, it was strange until we found out that rats have an incredible homing device and will travel miles back to their nest. We had only moved them two fields away. I wondered if there were actually just a handful of rats enjoying a holiday to the woodlands every few days before returning to eat their fill of bird food and compost remains. I can't stand to harm animals but in the end we killed the rats as they had continued to multiply. At least they were dispatched quickly and I said a little prayer for each one.

I was surprised by how tolerant and patient Oscar had been during the rat exodus and during those initial weeks of adjusting to life with two enormous dogs and a slightly neurotic and highly stressed girlfriend. I was surprised and relieved every day when I returned from work to find he hadn't walked out of the front door never to return. For the first few months of living together my daily drive home had left me feeling sick to the pit of my stomach because I feared he would have left. Memories of Graham leaving that way haunted me and it took a long time to believe it wouldn't happen twice. At the time Oscar moved in I had very little confidence in anyone's ability to stay by my side in a relationship and I feared the inevitable would happen at some point. I was reeling from Mum's re-diagnosis and there were times when I held onto the window ledge whilst looking at the view from my bedroom window. My heart raced with anxiety and what ifs. This was now *our* bedroom, *our* home. I had let Oscar into my home willingly and into the pink, airy bedroom that was my sanctuary away from everything and anything that could hurt me. It had taken a huge leap of faith and trust to allow him to move in and yet the decision hadn't been mine to do so. It came about on the back of an argument and that bedroom was the stage.

Oscar climbed out of the lounge window on my thirty-first birthday because I wouldn't let him leave by the front door. In fact, I begged him to stay and had hidden the front door keys. I am a grown woman and yet I hid a set of keys, got down on my knees, cried copious tears and literally pleaded with Oscar not to split up with me. I was that desperate, that confused, anxious and hurt (and a little tipsy on gin and tonic) that I threw away self respect and lay down the path for Oscar to manipulate me in whatever way he saw fit in the coming years. I may as well have told him nobody else would love me and I would pay him to stay by my side. I cried so many stupid pointless tears that night as I tucked into my birthday cake alone and he drove away swearing he would never return. The cake was all pretty icing and appealing on the outside but lacking in substance on the inside – much like our young relationship it seemed. I threw most of the cake in the bin with anger and disgust at myself. Oscar had chosen my birthday as the day to announce he would never, ever consider living with the Bears and me. Which was precisely what I did *not* need to hear when my mum was unwell and I was craving stability and security in my world. Nonetheless, Oscar had stood with his hands on his hips and told me nonchalantly that no matter how much he had decided he loved me he just couldn't consider living with us *ever* and, at best, he might one day live in a house next door. Marvellous. We could be neighbours and borrow sugar from one another.

His reasons were not clear but his certainty was very apparent. He told me to just deal with it and then offered me cake before we went out for dinner with friends. I was floored by that news when I came home from work to celebrate getting even older. I had worked overtime providing lovely romantic weekends at my home to impress him. I had allowed myself to begin to hope that one day I would live with my man in our home and with the Bears at our feet. I had hoped that this time love would stay with me and I had spent a fortune on posh pork pies and cheese. We went to dinner with friends and Oscar pretended everything was normal whilst I drank gin and tonic and pretended I was having a wonderful time. On our return home I received a firm bollocking for having been upset in the first place and for having not been affectionate enough towards him at dinner. Oscar had felt ignored and I had hurt him. I tucked my drunken tail between my legs, cried and - oh yes let's not forget - I also begged him to stay. Yes, that's me and that is what I did. Oscar stood firm and eventually climbed out of the window given that I refused to pass him the keys and was a wreck of a woman at his feet. End of story. Done. I felt such a sense of relief amongst the misery. At least I would no longer be concerned with what ifs. The inevitable had happened. And yes it had been my fault. Or had it? I only saw *me* as the problem and I didn't question the other side of the story; that perhaps just maybe Oscar had behaved like a tool.

Within twenty four hours Oscar had texted to say he forgave me. *He* forgave *me*. I was so relieved that I didn't follow the path of whose fault it had been and just said thank you many times. We were due to travel to Cornwall for a romantic week together the following weekend and Oscar joined me there. I walked out to greet him with anxiety niggling in my stomach and he sat stock still in his car in silence. He looked so suspicious I wondered if I had horns and a forked tail that were invisible to my eyes. A quick glance towards my bottom revealed a distinct lack of tail, so I took a deep breath and attempted to approach Oscar as he sat eyeing me from his car like an owl within its nest. He was rigid and cold as I tried to hold him and I spent every ounce of energy I had coaxing him back to life. Oscar eventually ceased being corpse-like and held my face in his hands as he told me he loved me dearly and wanted to continue our relationship. He didn't apologise and did make it clear that he didn't trust me at all. Great. Why not just burn me at the stake whilst you're at it.

Oscar went from one extreme to the other during that week in Cornwall and ranged from not wanting to be near me to deciding upon our children's names – which was even more confusing given previously he had told me we would never have children. We were walking along the beach when we had that conversation and the next day Oscar said how repulsive female bodies were after they had children and how he couldn't begin to imagine loving someone that looked baggy and stretched. The week of Oscar veering from one extreme to the other exhausted me. On another day he was snuggled up to me one minute and the next he admitted that in his youth he had killed his headmaster's pet rabbit with his friends and put it on his doorstep. Say what?! I couldn't believe it and Oscar felt no remorse at all. He hadn't liked his headmaster, which therefore made it acceptable. Oscar was merely telling the story as an amusing anecdote of his childhood. He laughed heartily and I was furious; absolutely utterly furious for that poor bunny and the headmaster. Needless to say I didn't speak to Oscar for the rest of the day. I was, and still am, disgusted by what he did.

To complete the week nicely it was also the first of what became countless times when Oscar then didn't speak to me for extended periods of time. He didn't register my physical presence or acknowledge anything I said as he stared beyond me and I waved my hands in his face. Those times became more prevalent as the months ticked by and they were incredibly painful and lonely. For now it was a first and I fussed, apologised and fussed some more but nothing worked. He returned to his family home at the end of the week and I returned to mine for some much-needed sleep and peace. Moving in with one another was the last thing on my mind. What if he murdered my Bears and put them on the doorstep when he decided he no longer liked me?

The following week my mobile beeped a text message from Oscar as I stretched my limbs and readied myself for the day ahead.

I HAVE DECIDED TO MOVE IN WITH YOU. I LOVE YOU SO MUCH MY SCRUMPTIOUS HONEY AND WILL MOVE UP AT THE WEEKEND. O XXXXXX

I know that I thought one day we would live together but I hadn't expected such a swift sea change. Bewildered is an understatement. It was only recently he had announced he could never live with me and here he was announcing his intended arrival. He had a job and life that he would be leaving behind.

How would it work? Was I ready to live with him? Did I trust him and could I let him into my home on a permanent basis? He was exhausting but at least he wanted me; that was something.

So many thoughts ran through my mind, alarm bells tinkled quietly and yet I was excited that he loved me. My ego won over caution and Oscar moved in without any further discussion. It was only afterwards I considered that he hadn't actually asked me if he could move in. He had announced it. I shrugged the thought away and we settled into the removal of rats and an unexpected visit to court.

It was to be my first appearance in crown court, which was a part of my day job, and I paced nervously. Oscar had moved in and I had been preoccupied by that and the mammoth case at work. I had waited many days to give evidence for the prosecution and be cross-examined by the defence. My colleagues had worked on the case for two years and it went seamlessly that day for us all. Try as they might, the defence failed to confuse me and twist my statement of evidence to their benefit. They questioned, they paced and they acted out their court room drama. I felt tall and steady in my suit and heels, I knew my statement was truthful and I didn't falter. Despite my utter lack of confidence and conviction in my personal life I was adept at being in court and loved every minute of the proceedings. I would do it again in a heartbeat and I was humbled when the court clerk approached me and praised me for being precise and confident in the face of a strong defence. I left the court striding confidently and stopped short as I saw Oscar sat next to the security officer, in his tartan slippers. My boyfriend was in crown court and he was wearing his scuffed, comfy, blue and green tartan slippers. He looked ever so at ease as he sat there cross legged in his slippers, bouncing one foot gently, and for a moment I wondered if I was seeing things. It soon became clear that the security officer had refused to let Oscar into the court when he requested to see me – perhaps on account of his slippers or his lack of a coat during the unseasonably cold spring. Oscar revealed the full story whilst we walked the supermarket aisles on the way home and I laughed my way through our weekly shop. He gestured theatrically and the checkout girl warmed to him as he pointed towards his unusual attire with a hand casually held on one hip. I felt a rush of love and admiration for his ability to be so uninhibited, so unaffected by the confused glances of those around him.

Oscar explained to anyone that would listen how he had locked himself out of the house that morning when he answered the door to a delivery of new furniture. He relayed many times how we were excitedly setting up home together and how he locked himself out without shoes, a coat, money or his mobile phone. We lived in the countryside and he didn't know where I worked let alone where the crown court was. Nonetheless he had been resourceful. After considering spending the entire day sat in our tiny garden shed and rejecting the idea, as he would likely freeze, he waited at the main road in the hope that a police car would pass by. He reminded his audience of how he flagged down a passing bus (in his slippers no less) and persuaded the bus driver to let him ride for free into town. There was much begging and pointing at the slippers to make his point valid. The kind driver allowed Oscar to accompany him to the town centre, whereby he gave Oscar change to purchase a ticket for another bus to court. With his second bus ticket purchased, Oscar hopped onto the bus to court and, upon arrival, marched in with his tartan footwear and demanded to see me. The security officer refused to let him in despite hearing of the slipper misadventure and Oscar spent the entire day sitting and waiting for me on a hard and uncomfortable plastic seat. He was utterly unembarrassed and quite rightly so in my opinion. At least he hadn't spent the day making a nest in the garden shed.

22

Cheerful daffodils began to wave their faces in the morning breeze again and leant into the sunlight that poured over hedgerows and field boundaries. It wouldn't be long until the local woodlands were covered in rich bluebells as far as the eye could see and wild garlic bloomed, filling the air with its pungent aroma. The abundance of life in my garden was nothing compared to that of those woodlands and of the colourful, buzzing fiesta of life within my parents' garden. Their annual pots were prepared for summer whilst carpets of primroses and daffodils filled the borders.

We lived with cancer during those spring months and soon learnt that Mum's body had become resistant to the first type of chemotherapy. In spite of her best efforts to heal herself the cancer would not back down in the face of that specific cocktail of drugs. Doubt gnawed at me when I heard news that the treatment wasn't working, my heart fell and I clutched tightly onto hope as Mum began the second type of chemotherapy. Fifty per cent chance of success. It rang in my ears again, crawled into my dreams and I felt real fear unlike any I had known before.

It had to work, it absolutely had to work and allow my family to continue on, healthy and complete. The alternative was unthinkable and was not going to happen. How could I live without my mum? How could I continue to exist without the woman that had brought me into this world and loved me unconditionally every moment since then? She had wiped away every tear, shared my every secret, my triumphs and failures and always picked me up with loving words and comfort. I couldn't live without Mum, my best friend. She is my foundation, my everything, and being without her was not physically possible.

I buried my head deep into my pillow and left those thoughts as far from my mind as possible every day. The new chemotherapy continued its attempt at victory and spring bounced on regardless.

I only ever witnessed Mum falter once during those months and it was during our family Easter in Cornwall. We had all come together for a week to spend quality time with each other and, most importantly, with Mum. She was no doubt exhausted from her treatment and I can only imagine how lonely she must have felt at times as we all celebrated being together and she was forced to rest within her sanctuary downstairs. But then perhaps it brought her comfort to know that her much adored children and grandchildren were well and happy and by her side. As it was we all spent quality time with Mum when she had the strength and during one of my visits she quietly turned to me with tears in her eyes.

'It's just not fair,' she whispered shakily.

I held Mum in my arms and dried her tears as she leant into me. 'It's not fair' was all she said. Just one sentence of complaint and only after an entire *year* of illness. Only after an entire year of setbacks, of withstanding the horrors of chemotherapy and surgery.

'You're right Mum it isn't fair. It isn't bloody fair at all that you have this horrendous disease and it isn't fair that it has left you a shadow of the woman you once were. You are so beautiful and those big blue green eyes of yours never stop sparkling and it's not fair that cancer is trying to take you away. You are so tired, so exhausted and it breaks me that I can't fix it. I can't make it better and I don't know what to do. It's not f*cking fair at all. You are my mother and are supposed to be invincible and you never complain. You withstand every side effect, every knockback and only after a year of this have you said it's not fair. Cry and wail and let every swear word under the sun out if you need to because my God you have been the very definition of courageous. You are staring your mortality in the face and yet the worst you have said is "it's just not fair". You are remarkable and I love you so much.'

I wanted to say those words, wanted to beat the sky open with my fist and throttle the life out of whoever had brought this upon my beloved mother. How dare the world hurt her and do that to my family. As it was, all I could do was hold Mum gently until her tears subsided and she drifted back towards sleep. I knew she would find peace in her dreams and comfort in the arms of her husband as he padded quietly into the bedroom.

23

I was polite. I was polite on the telephone. I listened, I made appropriate agreeable noises and I said thank you for calling. Dad said words about results, outcomes and timescales and I said goodbye. I said goodbye as if nothing out of the ordinary had just happened. I was polite and I had just heard my mum was terminally ill.

But, how? How have we arrived here? I don't understand, I. What? Terminal. I don't understand. Breathe. But. My mum. She's, she's going to leave us.

My throat tightened.

She's going to die. I don't understand. How? How can I go on? Without my mum. Terminally ill. She's dying. Oh God. She's dying and I can't stop it. I can't change it at all. Oh no, she is leaving me and I have to face the rest of my life without her.

Slowly it began to sink in.

But I have just been on holiday and everything was fine. I, she, but

I thought she was recovering. Oh God, you b*stard. How could you do this?! But I was only away a week and everything was fine. I didn't know, I didn't realise it was this bad. I didn't know. How? How did we get to this?! I had so much fun on holiday. You can't have her. I need her. I will always need her and you can't take her from us. Oscar. My Bears. Where are my Bears?

I began to panic.

They're in the garden. I need to, to sit down. How long? What will happen? A hospice? But, I, I don't understand. I don't want this. No. Oh God no.

The telephone was wet from my tears; it slipped from my hand. I didn't know I was crying. I found myself sitting down but didn't know how I had got to the sofa. My mum was dying. The sofa was cold beneath me and Dad had been so calm.

Did I say goodbye to Dad? Where is Oscar? I have to tell him, I have to say it out loud and I don't want to. I can't, don't want this.

Walking into the kitchen, I placed the telephone down firmly on the worktop and stared at it. I willed it to be wrong. Oscar was in the garden, cheerful and full of life. He was happy and he had no idea. He was happy to be alive, walking towards me, and then he was in the kitchen smiling expectantly. Dinner was cooking and I felt sick.

'She's dying. Oh God she's dying and she's not going to get better. She's dying and she has to go to a hospice and I can't do this. My mum, she's my mum and I...'

I found myself sitting at the table in our lounge. Egg, chips and beans were in front of me. There was a hand on my back and I was being fed by Oscar. The fork tipped up as it left my mouth and I was being fed like a child. Beans and chips. I couldn't swallow.

I don't want this. I don't, I can't but I must eat. Be strong. My Mum is dying and chips taste good. My knee is wet. Paddington's head is on my leg, his beard is wet. What am I going to do? I feel sick. Empty. I want my mum, oh I want my mum. You can't take her away from me, you can't have her. Not yet. Please. No.

Moments passed, hours passed and days and nights passed. I went to work, I came home and my thoughts slowly gathered back into coherency. I tried not to fall apart and yet I ceased to exist. I heard more words about cancer, terminal illness, pain management, hospices and visiting hours. None of it was real and I couldn't find hope in any of it. I couldn't find a way out, a solution, a way in which Mum could live. I moved in bewilderment through it all. In my denial and naivety I had absolutely no idea that the second type of chemotherapy hadn't been working and Mum had deteriorated so rapidly. I had no idea that she was fading away whilst I had been talking of a happy healthy future with her when I was on holiday. I had been drinking cava and enjoying sunshine and tapas, love and laughter with Oscar.

I have been laughing when my mum had been dying. What kind of a person does that make me? How could I not have known? I am so stupid, so self-obsessed and stupid and she has been fading away from me every day without me even realising.

Before I knew what had happened, I was in Cornwall and surrounded by my family and of course my dad. My exhausted dad was still soldiering on, focusing on what was best for his wife and for their children. He was incredible. But still, I just didn't understand. How did we get to where we were? How could it end that way?

24

Mum spent her final weeks in a hospice where she received compassion, care and the very best pain management possible to make her life easier. We had all gathered to spend time with her and gradually I came to know that Mum would live for a few weeks or perhaps even a few months. Nobody really knew when Mum would pass away and I hated not knowing. Of all things, I hated that I had no control over the outcome and its timescale. I was so angry that I couldn't rationalise, adjust or come to terms with anything because there was no definite end in sight. I couldn't prepare myself for something that would happen 'at some point' and I didn't want it to ever happen. Not in a few weeks, two months or years even. It was all too soon and always would be. Emotionally I stumbled onwards every day and walked forwards supposedly alive. Every day I prayed and begged to any God or universal being that would listen and asked them to keep Mum alive. To keep her safe and alive just a little bit longer so, selfishly, I could have more time with her. More time to remember everything about her before she was taken away.

On the eve of my first visit to the hospice I tossed and turned in my old bedroom. I hadn't seen Mum since she had been diagnosed as terminally ill and I hadn't been to a hospice before. I didn't know how I was supposed to behave in a hospice. I knew they were meant to be peaceful and serene but surely they were also full of fear, grief and sadness. I wondered if I would find it frightening and overwhelming.

What am I supposed to say to my mother? How would I remember every moment of her?

I needed and wanted to be there for her and to hold myself together as an adult but I didn't know if I could. I was also her daughter, a frightened child, and I needed her comfort and reassurance that it would be okay. Which of course she wouldn't be able to give to me as life was taking her away. I needed to be with Mum; to drink in her voice, her warmth and gestures. I desperately needed to commit every single second of our time together to my long-term memory and I was frightened I wouldn't be able to remember her clearly in the years to come. I wanted to sit with Mum and apologise for the times when I had been less than perfect as her child and friend. I remembered them so clearly. I wondered if I could do that or if it would seem selfish and pointless. This wasn't about me and my stupid need to redeem myself so that I could live without regret. I sighed deeply into myself, there were so many questions flooding my mind and precious few answers. For there were no rules or expectations about how I should behave, no way of predicting the coming weeks and I certainly had no control over the outcome. All I could do was keep walking forwards and just love her.

As Dad and I entered the hospice I was struck by how quiet it was inside the small unassuming building and how beautiful the flowers in the entrance lobby were. They were a thick mass of summer flowers, no doubt plucked from the generous hospice gardens. The receptionist greeted us with a gentle smile and silent nod and I was surprised he couldn't hear my heart hammering in my chest. I could barely meet his eyes. I didn't want him to see my fear, my admission that this was the beginning of a long goodbye. I didn't want to make this any more real than it had to be.

Beyond the entrance lay the centre, the heart, of the hospice and it was light and airy from every vantage point. There were comfortable chairs, coffee tables and a self-service counter covered with homemade cakes and hot drinks for visitors. In the coming days I came to rely on those mugs of tea and sickly cakes to pull me through visits that drained me both emotionally and physically. At that time I just admired the homely feel of such an area. The hospice only asked for a small donation in exchange for any food and drink consumed. Already I began to feel they did so much and expected so little in return. Dad left me in the central area as he went to prepare Mum for her visit with me. I explored further and found peaceful art on the walls and the small hospice shop filled with blankets and tea cosies. They were knitted by local people who cared, people who wanted to make a difference. This whole area was filled with kindness, with love and generosity. I flopped onto one of the soft chairs and let it envelop me in its scratchy material.

How many people had been here before me and how many tears have been cried in this very seat?

I didn't dwell for long on my thought and instead admired the water feature outside as it trickled onto lily pads that glistened in the sunshine. Every section of the hospice I had seen so far had been designed with peace and mental space in mind. Doctors and visitors passed me quietly and disappeared behind closed doors to where the patients rested. Patients came here for temporary respite, to give loved ones time to themselves, and some came here to stay until the end of their days. To pass away somewhere beautiful, somewhere they would be assisted with kindness and where loved ones would feel less alone. I closed my eyes and drank in my first moments of how serene it felt to be there, to be in a place where people knew and understood what you were going through. I felt like I belonged.

I opened my eyes to Dad's gentle giant hand on my shoulder and walked by his side towards the closed doors. We had always been through the hard times in life together and this would be no exception. We turned right through the first set of doors and the peace of the entrance lobby followed us. I could see Mum's stocking-covered feet and the base of her bed as we approached the door into her shared room. I could recognise those small, brown, neat wiggling feet anywhere and saw that she was tucked in to her hospital style bed as I pushed through the doors. Mum looked so small. She looked so small, so worn away and hollow in stature. Her hands seemed tiny as I held them and I hadn't expected that. Somehow I had expected Mum to still look well and healthy like she had been before, like she was invincible and would always be with me. I looked upon the face of my mum, a woman in the last weeks of her life. She was physically fading away and yet I saw she was full of life. Her eyes shone brightly with love, humour and such warmth. She hadn't changed at all in spirit, in personality, and was very much the same as she had always been.

I didn't expect to be discussing funeral preferences with my mum that day and writing it all down on the back of my cheque book with an old tatty biro. In fact I never imagined a time in my life when I would be doing that at all. It was the first thing we talked about and I could tell Mum had been waiting and needing to say her piece before it was too late. Before the pain relief medication and tiredness took their toll on her memory and brought fuzziness to her mind. We talked of music and flowers with such lightness that I felt we were planning a wedding. It was a surreal and emotionless time because I didn't allow myself to think more deeply than of what was in hand: designing a celebration of life. I didn't dare remind myself that this was my mum we were talking about and she dutifully avoided bringing that up as well. I suspect she was trying to shield me in every way she could and she knew I would throw myself into being organised and creative – two things I can do with ease that would distract me when I needed it most. Mum took that time to talk with me about my life in general and I heard a few colourful swear words when it came to reviewing my failed engagement from two years before. I knew she would take that anger with her but we laughed when we recalled the happier times since and enjoyed the usual mother and daughter closeness we have always shared. Mum's usual bright laugh with a slight Liverpudlian lilt came forth with her smile. It was utter bliss and the world around us ceased to exist.

Her bedside table was covered with cards and letters from loved ones and flowers adorned every spare surface. You only had to glance once at the collection of gifts to know she was loved by all. By family, friends, colleagues and pretty much anyone that had been lucky enough to have her in their life. I can't begin to know how it feels to read kind words of thanks and sympathy from people when they know and you know you won't see them again. I can't begin to know how it feels to be fading away and surrounded by reminders of your life but I do know that the colours and sheer love of it all were wonderful to the eye and soul. I saw the soft bear

I had sent to Mum in previous months and I noticed a photograph of Oscar and me propped up alongside a card I had sent. She followed my gaze and lifted the card in her hand gently. Mum took my hand in hers, stroked the photograph delicately and told me how beautiful I was. She told me so seriously, so forcefully, as if she knew I would forget or wouldn't believe her in the first place. Mum had told the nurses this was one of her two beautiful daughters and that I mustn't forget my beauty or confidence. She stroked my hand gently with her thumb and implored me to keep going with my singing and with my art. She told me to hold on tightly to Oscar and to not worry about the future *ever* because it would always sort itself out. Without saying it explicitly she was telling me how to behave after she had passed away, so that my life would go on. She was trying to prepare me in advance and doing what mothers across the world always do; protect their children from harm no matter what. I nodded and held back my tears and I promised from the bottom of my heart to do all of those things. I also told her that I knew Oscar would look after me. Somehow I was trying to tell her I would be okay.

We talked of Dad, or more specifically that Dad would need two things after Mum was gone:

1. To be given a Welsh Terrier puppy

We had a wonderful time plotting and planning the details of the puppy surprise and it felt good to be given a task to do in the future; a way to be close to Mum and do something for Dad when he would need it most. But what caught me and had me bent double as I tried to control my laughter was the second thing Dad would need:

2. To be kept busy with DIY projects at all times

I found it hilarious that the primary thing Mum felt Dad would need in his grief and despair would be DIY and he would need it in abundance. It is the very fact that Mum was right about this which still makes me smile all the more. Mum had rightly decided that Dad would need to be kept busy and DIY should see fit to that. I came to know later from talking to my sister that Mum had also recruited her to the same cause and poor old Dad had a multitude of DIY projects to keep him busy whether he liked it or not. In the remaining weeks of Mum's life Dad had secretly been lined up to repair everything and anything that had already gone, or *could* go, wrong in my house and my sister's for the years to come. Poor Dad didn't stand a chance at objection and all I can say is thank you Mum. That was an excellent plan of yours and I am truly grateful for how lovely my house now looks.

With everything of importance said for that day I left Mum to her rest, to the kind nurses who had checked in on us throughout the morning and had brought Mum cups of tea. It had been an intense visit and I walked the gardens of the hospice to regain the feeling in my heavy legs and consider it all. I was astounded by the beauty of it all. There were curved paths that flowed like streams across one another and they took me past heavily scented roses and shrubs of all shapes and sizes. Lavenders lined flower beds and buzzed with bees; the scent was divine and suited the utter silence of the garden. Within minutes I had removed my flip-flops and was padding alone across springy grass. I was hidden amongst this secret world of nature, tall trees and summer flowers. I sat in a patch of dappled sunlight and realised just how incredible the hospice was and, I hope, will continue to be. Everything I saw around me had been created and maintained by volunteers. By people, yet again, that cared and wanted to make a difference. It was essentially a hug, a place of comfort when one needed it most, and I treasured my time there. It was a haven for many people including myself and I now know a hospice is nothing to be scared of. I was genuinely sad when I glanced at my watch and realised it was time to go home. I didn't want to rejoin the noisy outside world where people didn't know what to say and looked at me with sadness. I wanted to stay at the hospice and share in its beauty and laughter, in its sense of belonging. It had felt like a home from home. As I returned for future visits in the weeks to come I began to understand why Dad cherished his time there, why it brought him respite and peace.

Time between visits was spent at home with my family and we shared wholesome meals at the old table we had grown up around. It was a rare occasion that we were all together as adults and we laughed and recalled old memories of growing up. We talked of our time at the hospice and supported one another through it all. I heard about when my niece found one of the knitted tea cosies within the hospice shop and, before anyone had a chance to notice, she was running around the hospice with it on her head and giggling delightedly. It is such a beautiful image and I can only imagine how many smiles she brought to people that needed them the most. We were enjoying precious time with one another and building new memories to carry us onwards, yet I found those times hard. I was desperate to spend every waking moment with Mum, desperate to halt the passage of time and I couldn't stop thinking about her alone in the hospice at night whilst we were all together as her family. Whilst Mum was slowly fading away we were very much alive. It felt so wrong that she wasn't with us and

I felt incredibly guilty for laughing, for even spending a moment with joy in my heart. It was easier when we talked about Mum and recalled anything that involved her, for then she felt close and real. It was worth getting up each day when the world seemed full of darkness, just so I could remember those moments. So I could grow a little more. It has been worth it every day since then for the opportunity to practise becoming a better person by trying to be more like Mum and by living in joy. She was a truly beautiful soul and I remember when we recalled one of our favourite memories of her as we sat at that table. To me this says it all about how each of us could be a little more thankful for what we have and see the beauty in the simple things that make our lives so precious.

One New Year's Eve before Mum was ill the family were all together to celebrate the start of the coming year. We had spent an evening eating good food, laughing and sharing stories, playing games. It was noisy, fun and colourful and then one question left us all silent.

What would you choose to be reincarnated as?

The room went quiet as we pondered the most appropriate answer. What would we choose to be? We took it in turns to answer as we drank our wine and came up with choices such as 'I'd come back as an eagle' or 'an oak so I could live a long time'. Each of us went for the grand, the long-living, powerful choices. My mum, she simply said she'd come back as a chaffinch. A regular garden chaffinch, because they were pretty and had a nice life living in her garden, eating bird food from the table and being in the sunshine.

25

My wishes and prayers for Mum had started off big and full of hope when she was first rediagnosed and they had become smaller as each day passed by. I have never associated with a particular religion, I don't believe in God that a religious text defines as being 'the only God' but I do believe there is more to life than that which we see. I choose to believe we are surrounded by a universal energy that listens and guides us and I carried on praying daily to any higher being that would listen. At first I begged for Mum to live longer, to stay with us so that we could indulge in every moment, every second, every breath of her but then I didn't want her to be in pain. So I began to pray for her to pass away quietly and for her suffering not to last for weeks. I knew that 'nil by mouth' meant Mum's passing could be slow and painful and I didn't want that for her or for her loved ones. I was just devastated and torn between wanting Mum to stay and wanting it to be over so she was no longer in pain. I couldn't bear the constant expectation of that inevitable moment when she would be gone and we didn't know when it would happen. I wanted more time and yet I wanted the torture to be over. We were lost in a timeless suspended animation.

As it was, Mum's world became rapidly smaller and the simplest gestures came to mean everything to her. Mum's pain was managed with stronger doses of medication and as her strength faded she became quieter and confused. Every moment counted and we strived to bring comfort and pleasure to her days at the hospice. Mum held tightly onto the soft bear I had given her and I later learnt from my dad that she held the bear close during her final days and nights at the hospice. The soft feel of its coat must have brought her warmth and, I hope, a reminder of how much we love her. My sister and I bought Mum a body lotion that smelled of geranium and rose and we massaged it into her fragile hands and arms. Mum adored the scent, we cherished the loving touch and to this day I cannot think of a scent I prefer more than rose geranium essential oil.

Soon it was time to say goodbye to one another after our time in Cornwall and to also say goodbye to our mum. I watched from home as each family member visited Mum for their final private goodbyes. We each knew that we wouldn't see Mum again in this life and it was awful, for how do you say goodbye to someone you love that much?

26

I can't do this. Oh God I can't do this, I would do anything not to have this moment. I don't know how to let you go Mum. How do I say goodbye to you? To someone that has been there for my entire life? How do I say goodbye to the person whose love brought me into the world and protected me every single day since then? I can't do this.

Dad drove me to the hospice and I knew it would be the last time I would ever see my mother. The last time I would get to sit with her and hold her soft olive hand and feel safe from the world just by being next to her. I remember arriving, of sitting in the car desperate not to move and having to force myself towards the hospice entrance. I didn't want to say goodbye, I didn't want to lose her. I recall the beautiful gardens surrounding the car. I promised myself I would get through it without Mum seeing me upset. She didn't know it was the last time I would see her and whilst I couldn't save her from cancer I at least didn't want her to see me break.

The hospice had become so familiar and being there had come to feel normal, the one place I could find understanding without having to explain the hollow look in my eyes. But that day I couldn't find my peace as my heart raced and adrenaline coursed through me.

Just get through this without crying and remember everything, every touch and every moment. These will be your last, don't waste them.

I pushed one door open, turned right, pushed open another door and there she was. My beautiful Mum; so small and fragile in body yet bright and strong in her heart. She was tucked under her blankets as always, feet rustling as she tried to get comfortable and ready for me. The room was full of peace as she nestled into her pillows. Physically I wouldn't have recognised her as the person she used to be before cancer entered our world but as I sat and held her hand nothing had changed. She was still Mum, my best friend, and with one touch everything was okay. The drugs to ease her pain made her sleepy and difficult to understand but then we didn't need words. We had said so much during the last two weeks there and all I wanted was to breathe her in. All I wanted was to remember every detail of the softness of her skin, the freckles on her nose, her gestures and her touch. For one last time I wanted to know how it felt to be my mother's daughter.

Dad joined us and we sat quietly. Mum watched the television as she drifted in and out of wakefulness, Dad sat by her side gently holding her hand and I read a copy of Woman's Own – the magazine that had been Mum's favourite for as long as I could remember. There were mugs of tea and coffee steaming around us. It was such a normal moment between the three of us, comfortable and typical of our many years together as a trio at home and on holidays. This was what we always did; we could have been anywhere at that moment from holidays in Cornwall to holidays overseas. We had spent so much of our time together this way and it brought me a memory that never fails to make me smile. The time together passed that way until Dad quietly rose from his chair and looked at me knowingly.

It was time. Dad didn't have to say it, I just knew from the nod of his head, the touch of his hand and the sadness in his eyes as he left the room for me to say my goodbyes.

My darling mother,

I looked at you and saw all of your beauty that day. Cancer hadn't been kind to your body but it hadn't diminished you and the light and strength of you shone through. Your soft skin, your pretty eyes that opened and closed as you breathed quietly and the way you gently held my hand. Even then you were being my mum and being the one to soothe me as your daughter. I looked around you and saw your flowers, gifts, letters and cards from family and friends. You are so loved and not surprisingly so. You never complained in life or through your illness, you were always smiling and being there for everyone that needed a friend or shoulder to cry on. You were everyone else's rock. I saw your photograph of me amongst your cards and I lost track of the number of times you kept reminding me to know my worth during our time together, as if when you were no longer here who else would tell me? You had told me the importance of life and so much more. I am scared I will forget your voice as we sit silently. Your world had contracted to the smallest of gestures as you retreated into your tired body over the past weeks whilst cancer took its hold. Touch has become everything and I love that you hold the soft bear I gave you almost every day. I know his soft fur brought you comfort when the drugs inside you left confusion and unease. I looked at you again and felt my heart tear apart as I wondered how I am going to cope without you. I don't know how much more loss and pain I can manage before breaking. How can I possibly exist, live and laugh without you by my side? You have been there for every moment of my life, my best girlfriend and mum. We have shared laughter and tears, highs and lows, everything. You have been my greatest supporter and friend yet I can't save you. I am so sorry I couldn't make this go away. I am so sorry I couldn't keep you safe and well. I am so sorry for every moment I have let you down, every moment of being a spoilt child and for when I have shown you anything less than love. You deserved so much more than this. And yet here we are, just you and I for one last time. Companionable silence as I watch your eyes grow sleepy and I wonder how on earth to say goodbye. How I can apologise for everything I did wrong as your daughter and say everything that is in my future. But I know I can't.

The chair scratched harshly on the floor as I pushed back and took a deep breath. I was standing, still holding my mum's hand.

I am so tired, I can't do this. I can't say goodbye, I can't let go but I have to.

I felt the pain and tears rising and leant in close. I kissed Mum gently; her cheek was so downy and soft. I let go of her hand and placed it gently on the blanket as she drifted back to sleep. Tiny gestures but they took everything I had. It went against everything I wanted to do, every piece of me was crying out inside to just stay. I wanted to scream out my apologies for everything I didn't do, I wanted to say goodbye, tell her I would never forget her and that she is always my inspiration and hope. But I couldn't do that, she didn't know it was goodbye.

'Sleep well Mum. I love you so very much.'

And so it ended. I walked through the door, I walked through the second door, I made it outside, I got to the car, I sat inside and I fell apart. Every tear that I had held in fell, I keened with my hot anger at the cruelty, the unfairness and the loss. I was broken, spent, like a child and it all came tumbling out. I just wanted to go back inside, my mum was still there and she was alive. But I couldn't and instead I was driven home to a life without her. A life I neither wanted nor cared about for none of it seemed to matter anymore.

27

The times that followed after I returned to work were a blur of inconsequential moments but the time I received a call from Dad to explain that Mum's passing was near and when I left work are both vivid and bright as daylight in my mind. I took that brief telephone call at my desk in the open plan office, crowded with people and harsh fluorescent lighting. Dad told me what he needed to, my heart fell into my stomach and I braced myself. Each day of waiting for that call had been painful, long and full of conflicting emotions and inner turmoil. When I heard that Mum would soon be lost from this world I felt no ease or relief, I just felt like a small child left alone and frightened. But I wasn't a child, I wasn't alone and I had my father to look after. I pulled myself together, walked down the office stairs and into the kitchen. It was lunchtime and I was undone. I walked in to see my colleagues and their sandwiches, all huddled in the kitchen with my team leader. I held tightly onto the doorframe for fear of falling, pushed my emotions down and told them my dad had called. I had to go. They knew that moment was on the cards for me and they knew what my guarded words meant. I could see the concern and compassion on Owen's face and it felt very surreal. I had bounced into the kitchen many times previously and seen those wonderful faces as I waved goodbye and went on holiday or went home for the weekend. That kitchen had witnessed my highs and lows, my hangovers and coffee cravings and moments of laughter. Those people, the multicoloured walls and the giant coffee machine, that bright office; they were my comfort and familiarity. I was unable to break old habits and merely wished my office family a nice weekend and cheerily said I would see them in a couple of weeks. You'd have thought I was going on holiday but then how else do you walk those moments when nothing can make it any easier?

I telephoned Oscar, I panicked that the Bears didn't have somewhere to stay as their usual kennel was full and Oscar felt unable to take time off work to look after them or come with me to Cornwall. He had finally found some work as a pilot for a small airfield and couldn't tear himself away. I fell into a tearful telephone call with my old friend Melody late that night; she listened quietly as I bawled like a child. I keened and I was a muddle of confusion. I didn't know how to look after myself or my dogs at that moment and felt abandoned by Oscar when I needed him the most. I knew I needed and wanted to look after Dad and somehow I had to face going to Cornwall and the inevitable on my own. I was standing on a knife edge and the blade was digging into my feet no matter which way I twisted or turned when all I wanted was somebody to tell me what I was supposed to do. I slept fitfully in the spare room, unable to be with Oscar. Stupidly we had argued our way into separate bedrooms over work, funerals and dog care.

I drove to Cornwall the next day and I couldn't begin to think about where I was going and what was happening so I just took it one mile at a time. I listened to the radio, I listened to CDs and the motorway was soon upon me. The day dragged on, I missed my Bears terribly, and I felt deeply alone as I hit the accelerator hard and travelled onwards. I knew I could rely on my own reserves though and my sheer stubbornness kept me from really falling apart. I had been through crises before and I would survive one more. Eventually I arrived and Dad and I held each other tightly.

I don't doubt that Mum knew I was on my way to Cornwall that day. Dad had whispered to her that I was arriving and I know that somehow through her medication and sleep she heard him. Mum waited. She waited for me to arrive before finally easing her gentle grip on life and passing onwards during the night as we slept. A great energy was lost to us and a new star was born in the name of my mum. She lives on in the beauty of starlight and in the sunrise each day. She changed form and my sister-in-law Mia knew it. For at the precise moment that Mum passed onwards Mia awoke from a deep sleep to a flash of bright light and my mum letting her know she was okay; that she was at peace at last. I slept on unknowingly and woke the next morning to an early telephone call from the hospice. No sooner had Dad and I heard the telephone ring than we knew what it meant. We sat together quietly. It was over. Our world had changed forever, absolutely irreparably forever, and it crushed me. In the shock of it all no tears came. I realised that it is no easier to know in advance that your loved one is dying. It doesn't take away any pain, it doesn't allow you to 'say goodbye' and it doesn't make it okay, peaceful or acceptable. It is still an absolute pile of sh*t, it fills you with anger and grief and longing every single day. Every single day and it's just not fair. Damn you Universe for taking her away.

In the week that followed, everything seemed to be slow and thick like treacle and we walked through appointments with funeral directors, florists, the local authority and more. It was exhausting and we were zombies walking in a world that had no place for us anymore. Death was the main topic of stilted conversations and caffeine was our saviour. I dreaded each day as I took deep breaths and mustered the strength to hold back tears and keep moving forwards. What else could we do in those circumstances other than just keep walking? As I soon discovered, I could also laugh. My week became a mixture of grief and mildly hysterical humour and I often found myself laughing at inappropriate moments and then crying wildly the next. I must have seemed like a loon. On one such day we found ourselves looking at coffins, an actual *catalogue* of them, and it was at that point I really struggled not to laugh. It was serious, it was important to us and I take nothing away from that in my laughter. What made me laugh was that such a catalogue actually existed and that there were enlarged photographs of the most popular designs on laminated sheets. I felt like I was shopping in Argos and wondered if the funeral director would produce a miniature biro and tick sheet for our final choice. I had no idea that there was such variety in the design of coffins. Some of them were downright hideous and reminiscent of Dracula, the cardboard box designs reminded me of recycling and I wondered if there was a corrugated card coffin in there somewhere. By far the prettiest were the wicker ones; they were natural and beautiful. However, by the time I reached those designs I was tired and amused and they began to remind me of oversized laundry bins. I wondered idly if one ought to place some random mismatched socks and underwear in there to complete the image. I was silently in stitches at that thought and it was made even worse by our adorable, cheerful and light-hearted funeral director. I appreciate those are not words I would have ever associated with such a person but he really was Father Christmas dressed in black. Every time he visited us he lit up the day and provided relief from our tension. He was jolly and portly and I wanted to hug him often. At one point I felt inclined to bake him a cake. It was a strange time and that is all I can say to account for that. It was a very strange time.

To add to the madness of that week, there was a series of events that can only be described as Mum returning to provide DIY for Dad to complete in her absence. True to her word, Mum was busy encouraging the house to fall apart whilst we were busy choosing a casket that did not resemble laundry or recycling. On the first occasion of the house falling apart I found myself locked in the study (it doesn't have a lock at all). For no apparent reason the door locked itself whilst I was inside the room (seriously Mum? How? *How* did it even lock?) It would not budge until Dad literally knocked the door down with a sledgehammer and tore apart the doorframe. Next up was the exploding oven (twice), shortly followed by a repeat performance of the study locking itself again after we had repaired the damage (nice touch Mum, I liked that one) and then Mum's beloved hairdryer going on and then off and then back on and then finally refusing to work at all for a few days. We knew Mum was close and keeping us busy whilst the rest of the family arrived for her funeral in the coming days. Dad had a house to rebuild and, before we knew it, funeral day was upon us. It was our turn to shine as a family. We were determined to be strong and colourful and celebrate Mum's life but on the inside I suspect we were all riddled with emotions, tears and a feeling of wanting to just close the front door and hide in our grief. Thankfully the hairdryer had decided to work again and staying at home was not an option.

28

I woke early in my bedroom and peeked behind the blind. The morning sun touched my hand whilst family members were waking up in the rooms around me. I could hear them all amid the quiet atmosphere in the house and listened as they rose and trooped upstairs for breakfast. My family were starting the day as they meant to go on; together, loved and as one. The laughter of my niece and two young nephews filled the air upstairs. Their footsteps thundered across the kitchen floor and brought life to us all when we needed it most. I knew they missed their Gran terribly but they smiled their innocence and lived for the day. Strange things happened that morning as we moved around one another in the house with hushed gestures. Electric appliances failed time and again, switches ceased working. We just knew Mum was with us and keeping us on our toes. I could see the sparkle in Dad's eyes returning for a moment as he thought of her sending him jobs to do by causing those failures. We shared a moment and laughed. Mum knew Dad needed to always be kept busy, especially in her absence.

As I looked at my reflection in the warm, sunshine-filled bedroom I placed a silver heart pendant around my neck and pulled my new dress on over my head. The beautiful pendant sat with its pink beads just next to my heart and I knew my sister would be placing her identical pendant over her heart. Mum had asked that we wear bright clothes to her ceremony, that we make her day full of colour and celebration. So my sister and I did what we have always been taught to do by Mum throughout our adult lives. We shopped and my goodness we did that moment proud.

My sister and I had roamed the streets of Padstow a few weeks earlier during a surreal and memorable shopping trip as we searched for our dresses. The tiny back streets were busy with tourists and hugged by cottages in pastel shades of pink, turquoise, lilac and cream. The shops reflected the day with their slate edging as children pressed hands against the windows and searched for sweet delights and fudge. It was busy, bustling and seagulls wheeled overhead as we weaved in and out of every shop that sold clothing. My sister and I had spent many hours shopping together previously but this was for our mother's funeral whilst she lay resting in her peaceful hospice bed. It was confusing and tiring. We jostled with conflicting emotions yet found our joy in admiring jewellery that Mum would adore and in imagining comments that she would have made by our sides. We were enjoying a day out by the seaside being girls yet the reasoning was so sad. We visited every tiny little shop that town had to offer, browsed and thumbed dresses of every imaginable style. As we sauntered past yet another shop, wondering when we would find the right attire, we saw an inviting open door and walked in. The shop was tiny, full of ladies browsing and we grabbed every dress we could find.

My sister walked out of the changing room in yet another dress and looked me straight in the eye. She squared her shoulders back and was standing proud. Her face was deadpan yet she had the merest twitch of a smile and a twinkle in her eyes.

'Geez. Clare. You cannot wear that!' I clutched my knees as I laughed at the dress we had both loved on the hanger.

It was a fish print tea dress and we felt the fish print might be a nice way to represent Mum living by the ocean. The trouble was Clare looked like she was wearing an apron. A very pretty apron, but an apron nonetheless. We imagined us arriving at the funeral in that dress and couldn't help ourselves. The tears fell down our cheeks as we leant on the changing room door for support and tried to snigger and snort quietly. Every time we looked at one another we burst out laughing again. The other ladies in the shop began to avoid us and glance at us with disdain. Poor Mum deserved so much more than her daughters turning up in kitchen clothing. We scuttled out of the shop laughing and enjoying a moment of release from our grief. As it turned out we later found two stunning flower print, summer-style dresses that day. We would be beautiful and elegant and a tribute to the woman that brought us into the world.

My dress was the palest sky blue, covered in bright spring flowers with sparkles at their centres. A summery pink shawl hugged my shoulders as I continued to ready myself. I placed a much-loved high heel shoe on each foot and rose from my bed. I smoothed down my beautiful dress, observed the pain and strength in my eyes and breathed deeply. I heard the voices of my family in the hallway and adrenaline coursed through me.

I can do this and I will play my part to make the day uplifting. I will find a way with grace and love to remember

The hearse was shiny and black, like an enormous beetle carapace, and our funeral director welcomed us sincerely as he dipped his head to the ground. I had always expected funeral directors to be thin, hunched, with pursed lips and a yellow tinge of morbidity. Ours still looked like Father Christmas. As I looked towards him and blinked at the bright morning sunshine I was reminded of his kindness in recent weeks. Reminded of his round belly and wonderfully warm smile. He had kept us going when we felt like falling apart and had brought moments of laughter into our darkest of hours. I couldn't help but feel safe with him by my side, guiding us through this day. I sat deep into the cream seats. Again my expectations were entirely different from reality. As I huddled close in the back seat to my brother and his family, like birds on a wire, we chattered and smiled. We remembered happy times, we enjoyed the scenery of Cornwall rolling by and we found strength in our huddle. I was surprised at how uplifting the day felt so far, though I knew the hardest parts were yet to come.

The crematorium loomed in front of us as we arrived and adrenaline spiked within me again. Inside the magnificent cream building there were friends and family members waiting for us, waiting to be there for us. There were aunts and uncles that I had not seen in years. There were cousins, old friends, family friends, neighbours and more. My hand shook as I reached for the hearse door but the grounds surrounding me took my breath away. We stepped out onto a terrace backed by the cream walls of the crematorium. The land rolled gently away into gardens filled with young and delicate trees. Their glossy bottle green leaves swayed heavily with the weight of summer as insects danced around them. Butterflies drifted down to beds of rainbow-coloured flowers that hugged the trees, lifted my spirits and carried me into the welcome room.

For a moment I just stood, tense, and stared at my feet. I couldn't begin to imagine what to say to this sea of faces. How was I supposed to speak when all I wanted to do was run outside and far away from the moments ahead? And then I looked at my dad and, without knowing it, he gave me the hand on my back that told me what to do. I knew his pain like I knew my own yet he stood tall, handsome in his suit and colourful tie. He moved around the room and spoke to everyone with a smile on his face. I watched as he made genuine connections with people that loved him and could see it brought him a sense of belonging. I scanned the room and saw my sister and brother talking to cousins and dear friends. There was serenity in their movements. I scuffed my shoe heel on the floor and wondered how I could do the same. Dad must have known my hesitation for he brought people to me for introduction and I followed that lead. The kind gestures and expressions of sorrow knitted us all together for Mum.

The seats were hard and I was reminded of church choirs from my youth as we sat for Mum's service. I could feel the quietness behind us from rows of loved ones gathered together and a feeling of peace enveloped me. Peace wrapped her arms around us and quietly settled us in. Mum's casket was magnificent, an absolute artwork of spring and summer flowers and she would have adored it. Mum had always loved her garden and spent many hours admiring seasonal flowers as the years went by. She had adored the sunshine on her skin and had found peace in her garden birds, roses, lavenders and more. Dad had always been the gardener, been the one to dig and plant tirelessly for his beloved wife whilst she had happily played her part in creating pots full of pretty annuals. Mum would sit on her garden bench with a cup of tea and admire it all whilst Dad, ever busy, would dig some more. They danced that way every season and I loved it. The parts they played were familiar and comfortable. In a final tribute to Mum, she was surrounded by not just the fresh flowers filling the room but also by the flowers on our dresses and the sunshine she had given us to carry in our hearts.

I completely embarrassed myself. I poked myself in the eye by accident and let out a high-pitched squeal into the hushed room. I wanted the ground to open up and swallow me at that moment before the service began. I sounded ridiculous and, to make it worse, it also made me want to laugh. Emotions were high and thankfully Father Nicholas joined us and brought me to my senses sharply. He was much like the funeral director in that he had a warm welcoming face and a sparkle in his eyes that I admired. It occurred to me that his name was almost the same as Father Christmas as well. He guided us onwards and weaved a beautiful story of Mum through us all. He lifted us with memories gathered from close family. He brought us gently through the understanding that this was a goodbye but also a great celebration and a moment to cherish. My sister-in-law was the image of summer in her butterfly print dress and held her daughter close whilst she spoke her poetry. She had always been a peaceful and intuitive soul, just like Mum, and her words were stunning. We sang with our hearts, we let tears roll down tired cheeks, we smiled at happy memories and held hands as a family united. As the service ended I rose and walked towards Mum and her flowers. In life she had been my best friend and sunshine. In death she was still sunshine and flowers, willing me to go on. As I touched those flowers goodbye I knew I would never be the same without Mum. None of us would. But I scanned the faces in front of me and saw just how many lives she had touched. How many hearts she had lifted and cared for and inspired with her gentle manner. She was truly an inspiration.

The sunshine was glorious as we regrouped outside and dropped our shoulders. I could sense people relaxing and beginning to share their stories and memories. I walked alone amongst the flower beds and made friends with the butterflies surrounding me. Dad joined me after a short while. We had been an inseparable team these past two weeks; propped each other up from the moment of Mum passing through every step of planning the funeral and beyond. With words unspoken we admired the hills around us and acknowledged we had made it. We had given Mum a service that told of who she was and celebrated her incredible strength in life. It was time to move on to the wake and I longed for an ice-filled gin and tonic. I longed for a comfortable chair with my loved ones by my side.

The setting for the wake was meant to be, I knew that from the moment Dad and I first saw it. It was a country pub nestled amongst picture-perfect thatched roofs, surrounded by a traditional English village green in the height of its summer. Ducks padded across soft grass and quacked their afternoon stories in the breeze when we arrived and entered. The gravel crunched underfoot as guests followed us, eager to relax their grief. It was a procession of colour and life. The slate flagstones, oak beams and ash-filled fireplaces around every corner soothed us all as we propped up the bar. We found laughter and conversation in the bottom of draught beers, gin and tonics, wine and more. But the best was on the horizon as we gathered our family and friends. We led them to the sun-filled oak conservatory and I smiled.

Mum was everywhere in this room. She was in the lightly-coloured soft furnishings of rattan and cotton. In the heat from the sunshine, the flowers and the beautiful food served for us all. But most of all she was in the huge olive tree that stood at the very centre of us all. Mum had been given the name Olive for her golden skin as a baby and, like the olive tree, she had been a lover of warmth and the Mediterranean in life. I looked around to my left and saw friends perched happily on chairs, tables and window ledges. They were laughing and smiling and creating new friendships with one another. I looked to my right and saw family members bonding after years apart due to the time constraints of modern life. Everyone looked happy, relaxed and truly celebrating the day. With our love of Mum and our love of life we had created something more akin to a wedding party than a funeral. I leaned back into the soft cream chair and breathed out. I kicked my heels off under the glass table and tucked my tired feet under a soft cushion by my side. I let down my hair, I let down my defences and I admired the people around me.

Under the branches of that great olive tree, we were Olive's legacy. Under her watchful eyes across the years, she had loved and inspired every one of those people. I realised there never was a goodbye that day. There never was a real loss, for Olive continued to live on in us all. She lived on in our gestures, in the warmth in our hearts and in every sunrise that touched the freckles on our noses.

Glasses clinked on the table around me as one by one my family flopped onto cushions and brought familiarity and laughter with them. A fresh gin and tonic was pushed into my hand, the ice melting slowly. We raised our glasses and began to create the next chapter of our lives sat atop those cushions. We began the slow process of living again.

29

In the weeks that followed I was cut off from life. My head was aching, anxiety kept my heart racing and I didn't care anymore about the trivia that filled peoples' lives. I had returned to work two days after the funeral and could say with absolute certainty that nothing mattered anymore. The major news, the minor irrelevant pap that populates the media, peoples' dramas about nails and hair colour and long boring meetings at work meant nothing to me. Frankly most of that is usually irrelevant but still, it seemed even more so after I had attempted to rejoin daily living. I lost all sense of the point of this life as I sunk into my grief and felt deeply alone despite being surrounded by the support and love of my family, friends and Oscar.

I learnt that losing a parent changes you forever and I describe that loss as like being a flower that has a fallen petal. To anyone that gazes upon such a flower they would recognise it as whole, as a flower, and probably wouldn't notice the missing petal. No big deal. But to the flower, it has lost part of that which made it whole; it is changed and irreparably damaged. Bees may continue to nuzzle the flower but it is no longer complete. I had lost my mother and was still recognisable as a person to everybody that passed me by but I was changed inside and I was missing my best petal. There was, and still is, a sense of something vital missing. The person that was my history, my genetic code and who gave me my sense of belonging in the world was taken away and I am sad to say that sense of belonging never truly returned. The feeling of losing a parent is no doubt very personal and varied but for me I felt isolated and somehow different to those whose families are intact. I went from feeling young, from being a daughter with a mum to lean on, to suddenly being thrust into a world of standing on my own two feet. I no longer had a mother to telephone for advice when the world of men got the better of me or when I wanted to share stories of laughter and love. My best friend was missing and she wasn't coming back. I had been brave and strong for a long time and I was worn out by everything that had happened. I feared that if I began to cry I would never stop and that if I so much as talked about my loss or how much I missed Mum, I would fall to my knees metaphorically and never get up again. That fear, combined with the feeling I was slowly losing the plot, kept me from opening up and it kept me from leaning on anyone. I hid my weakness and I watched as life went by. I hid at work behind my iPod and slowly fell into feelings of depression and grief in the months that came. I barely interacted with my colleagues and friends and I wanted them to leave me alone to my work and tears. I couldn't bear it when people asked sympathetically if I was okay, as those were the times that I had to fight back tears and lift a tired smile as I lied to them all. I felt vulnerable and so dog-tired as I pretended I was okay.

Time passed and people stopped offering condolences as they went back to their own lives, which was to be expected. They had been extraordinarily kind with their cards, flowers and the gentle touches of understanding but as they stepped back to the living world Mum began to disappear. It was horrible feeling like she was slipping away, like she almost didn't exist because she could no longer be heard. I was frightened I would forget the melody of her voice and her elegant gestures and so I tried hard to grasp at memories and commit her face to my mind. But the more I tried the harder it became and the further I felt her slipping away. I longed to look at photographs of Mum to remind myself of her features but I didn't dare open the albums. It was too distressing to know she was gone, that she would forever be a part of my *past* and not my *future*. That thought devastated me.

Around the same time as my invisible tears and withdrawal from the world I also found myself consumed with anger, with a rage I had never felt before, and it shook me within. I have always been a sensitive soul and I can't stand confrontation of any kind. I will go so far as to avoid disagreeing upon a favourite type of biscuit with anyone other than my nearest and dearest. Yet I was so f*cking cross with the Universe for taking life away from Mum and for taking her away from us. I shouted at the heavens on many an occasion and refused to acknowledge my former belief in angels and higher beings. I *hated* every single type of energy and every invisible idiot with feathery wings for betraying us so cruelly. I couldn't begin to keep my spiritual beliefs anymore and I directed my rage at the sky. Daily.

Damn you Universe, damn you to hell and back. You can take your feathery wings and pink fluffy energy and shove it right where it hurts. Twice.

To put it more eloquently I was following that classic curve of grief that held me dancing between wild rage, utter depression and denial. One moment I was holding it together with a smile and deep breaths, the next I was on my knees crying silently in my bedroom. At no point was the passing of Mum bringing me closure or relief that she was no longer suffering. I was lost.

Relief from the madness of grief did come at times in the form of Amber and by returning to my much-loved choir. Singing at the top of my voice every week, in spite of how I felt, and being surrounded by sixty or so familiar faces really and truly lifted me. Music heals the soul and the sound of collective voices soaring through octaves was nothing short of magical. The members of that choir don't realise it but they helped me begin to take baby steps towards normality again. I adored being nestled amongst my fellow sopranos, like little birds on a branch, and their open hearts nurtured me. Amber in her gentle ways held me close and kept an eye on me at work without crowding me and without asking devastating questions. Her nature had always been similar to my mum and her gentle yet firm approach kept the torch shining in my dark tunnel. Amber was by my side and slowly she encouraged me to consider dropping my smiling mask – my performing monkey - and admit how I truly felt. She worked on this idea with me for months, God bless her patience, and yes I avoided it like the plague at first. I ought to talk about my loss, I knew that, but I wasn't ready. I was still so frightened I would fall apart and never get back up again. How could I risk *that* happening?

All of that emotion, such a rollercoaster, and yet in the traditional sense of time it was just shy of two months since Mum had passed away. As the two month mark approached I was staggered to find I had actually existed that long without my mum. I hadn't thought that was even possible. As I talked with Dad one evening he told me Mum had spoken about her children at the hospice. She had told Dad that she felt her job was done because she knew we would all be okay. She knew I had Oscar and so no longer had to cope alone. She knew that as a mother she could rest now and let life go on. That conversation pulled me up and made me realise I was the one with a chance to *live* again. Mum had been denied life and there I was doing nothing other than existing, nothing other than ploughing through daily routines without heart or courage. I had to do something, had to fight for being alive and grasp at life with a fervour as if there were no tomorrow. With that in mind I made two decisions. I looked at Hester and Paddington and told them I was going to face my lifelong fear of scuba diving and I was also going to buy a piano. Scuba diving and a piano: my two ways of coping with grief as two months passed by. I turned to Oscar and told him as much and was mildly disappointed that his initial response was asking if he was expected to look after the dogs whilst I was away learning to dive for two weekends. I knew he cared deeply for me but nonetheless I had hoped for a little more encouragement.

Oscar fell somewhat short in his abilities to support me after Mum had passed away and I suspect he was recovering from the strain recent events had put upon us both early in our relationship. I knew he was capable of listening, encouraging and being affectionate when he felt able to but there were times when he was quiet and withdrawn. He had relocated to Shropshire only eight months previously and was busy in his own world trying to progress his piloting career, adjust to this new life and also cope with my grief. He loved me and was enjoying life but he was awkward and inconsistent at times. The days when he just disappeared mentally continued and he stared through me when I tried to approach him. It was as if the world had become invisible to his eyes and he was lost somewhere in the recesses of his mind. One day I realised I was done with crying on my own and I needed some support. I took a deep breath and approached Oscar, asking for a cuddle as tears fell across my cheeks. I was scared of asking, scared of appearing vulnerable and needy, and Oscar told me to hug myself.

He gestured with his hands for me to stay away whilst he told me how I reminded him of his ex-wife and that he simply could not support me then. He felt I was being needy and should stand on my own two feet and support myself. He had a fair point, I was crying and probably looked like a child in my pyjamas and slippers, but my mum had just died. Surely that gave me rights to indulge in a little pathetic behaviour? I walked away with my head hung low in rejection and loneliness washed over me. I sat on our bed and pondered how one goes about hugging oneself anyway. Last time I looked my arms were not as long as Mr Tickle's and, without resorting to some serious yoga, I am unable to contort myself into a one-person hug without popping a vertebral disc or two.

I firmly believe that my feelings and my reactions are my own responsibility and Oscar wasn't obliged to be my rock beyond a point at which he was comfortable. But I wished he had held his arms open and welcomed me into them with love and understanding. The look of disgust on his face that evening as he retreated further into the sofa cushions was more what I would have expected if I had let out a rip snorter of a trump as opposed to asking for a hug. Perhaps we were both just too fragile to cope, too caught up in our emotional worlds and couldn't give one another what we needed.

By the time it came to my scuba diving course I had reluctantly booked the dogs into kennels. It appeared I would be giving it my all with facing my scuba diving fears and piano on my own.

30

Bring it on. Bring. It. On. I am terrified and I feel a bit sick. Why am I doing this? No.

BRING IT ON!

I shouted that last sentence at the rear-view mirror as I drove across the midlands to my scuba diving course, which was to be held in that lesser known exotic scuba diving location – Birmingham. I was going to learn to dive in a swimming pool and a cold quarry in the middle of the UK. As I hit the accelerator and drove away from Shropshire I hoped I wouldn't bottle out and turn around halfway there. I have a long history of *almost* learning to scuba dive, with attempts to do so that span across a decade.

My first attempt at scuba diving was in a worldclass location for diving; the warm tropical waters of Borneo. I made it as far as putting my mask on (whilst standing on the beach) and walked to ankle depth in the warm turquoise ocean and then went rigid and couldn't move. Every fibre in my body was begging me not to dive. I was terrified of breathing underwater and so I quit and missed out on a week of splashing about underwater with my friends. My second attempt was two years later in the waters of the beautiful Bay of Islands, New Zealand. I say *in* the waters but on that occasion I made it as far as booking the course and walking down my hotel stairs. I had spent the previous night awake in terror and on that morning I promptly turned around at the bottom of the stairs and hid, yes hid, in my hotel room for the entire day. I was convinced the dive centre staff would try and find me and so I spent a long and hungry day indoors. My third attempt came six years later in another exotic location; the Maldives. Now if I was going to learn to dive anywhere I could surely do it there? The water was absolutely flat and clear and my Instructor was incredibly friendly. On that occasion I completed the first section of diving theory and then went into the ocean with my diving kit on and my happy Instructor by my side. I slowly kneeled down in shallow water and no sooner had my face begun to sink underwater than I panicked and flailed. I tried to get my head underwater a number of times but my brain was on high alert and shouting for me to exit the water and head for the bar. And so I quit and cried quietly into my cocktail. I have a deep love of the ocean and marine life but it is combined with a belief that if I scuba dive I will die. My mind is convinced I will run out of air at depth in cold murky water and slowly sink to the bottom whilst my brain scrabbles for life and I eventually pass out. My mind refuses to be quiet and listen to logic when it comes to that fear. To qualify as a scuba diver on my fourth and potentially final attempt I knew I would have to put my face underwater, which seems fairly obvious but has so far been asking the impossible of me. I would be required to then remove my mask UNDERWATER and somehow continue to breathe through my regulator *calmly* and for an entire sixty seconds UNDERWATER. That would be followed by removing my mask again and then swimming for a distance of 15m UNDERWATER without my mask on. What kind of torture was this?

Oh sure, I can do that. It sounds no worse than putting my face in a bucket full of angry snakes.

As I continued along the motorway my mind was genuinely and wholeheartedly convinced that going scuba diving would result in certain death. I had serious work to do to overcome that particularly useless brain circuitry and I pitied the Instructors that would have to cope with me. I had diligently completed all of the dive theory beforehand and had spent a weekend practising being underwater in the local swimming pool with my dad as preparation. Yes, that's right. At the grand age of 31 I went swimming with my dad and learnt how to swim underwater with goggles on and without holding my nose closed. That in itself was a major achievement for me and took time to master. I am proud to say I even got to the point at which I could swim along with my eyes closed and nose unpinched, so long as I didn't have to breathe or do it for more than a few seconds. Dad and I were wrinkly as raisins by the end of it but progress had been made with our hard work, persistence and two very good senses of humour. I followed that weekend by having long hot baths with a scuba mask on my face and filled it with water. I thought it may help with diving relaxation as I poured water into the mask on my face from my fluorescent pink elephant watering can. I sat back, kept my eyes closed and fumbled for my glass of wine. It certainly added a new element to hot baths that autumn but I can't say it helped with my fears. It mostly made me spill my wine.

By the time I arrived at the dive centre I was beginning to regret my decision and I faltered at the entrance. Stubbornness kicked in and I remembered why I was doing this; in honour of Mum. She had demonstrated courage and grace and, with that in mind, I clutched my car keys tightly and strode into the dive centre with a warm welcoming smile and a very sweaty bottom from being so nervous. The diving Instructors were friendly and fun from the moment myself and the other students congregated in the classroom and introduced ourselves shyly. We all had different reasons for learning to dive but they centred around one main theme; we all wanted to make a change for the better in our lives. Not one of us was learning to dive for the simple act of viewing the underwater world; it was more profound than that. The gentleman in his seventies was learning to dive because he wanted a new challenge in his life and the married couple were giving their failing relationship one last chance before admitting defeat. I held up my metaphorical hand up and admitted my fear and how the recent loss of my mum had brought me to this destination, to this final attempt. At that point one of the Instructors held her hand up and admitted that prior to learning to dive she was unable to even swim, water terrified her that much. And now look at her; Dawn was a confident, enthusiastic mermaid helping others to conquer their fears. We quickly became friends.

That first day went smoothly enough and our group chatted as we reviewed dive theory, drank sugary tea and munched through many chocolate digestive biscuits. We had prepared ourselves well and learning to dive was already a tremendously bonding experience for all of us. We cheered one another on as we entered the swimming pool for the first time, practised snorkelling skills and learnt about diving equipment. As I sat there bobbing on the water in my diving equipment I knew the difficult part was just a few moments away. I was shortly going to remove the air from my jacket, sink to the bottom of the swimming pool and breathe through my regulator. Simple, except my brain read that request as: remove air from my jacket, sink to the bottom of the swimming pool and die. My Instructor was asking me to die. I tried desperately to ignore my brain as it sent adrenaline through my system, quickened my breathing and repeatedly shouted

'WARNING! IMMINENT DEATH APPROACHING'. Could nobody else hear this?!

I muttered to myself whilst heaving in great big breaths of air. Everyone else was on the bottom of the swimming pool breathing happily by this point and I was batting about on the surface like a panicked daddy longlegs. Dawn was there in a heartbeat, holding my jacket tightly and convincing me that step by step I could do it. She had done it and so could I. I took in a ridiculously large breath, squeezed my eyes shut and put my trust in her palms. We descended together; I carried on flailing, Dawn held on tightly and I hit the bottom of the pool with my knees. I was apparently underwater. My mask was on my face, I could breathe, and then I *was* breathing. And most importantly I was definitely not yet dead. I mentally stuck my finger up at my brain and did a little victory dance for making it that far. I was underwater and breathing and yes it felt terrifying but at least I was doing it.

The rest of that weekend brought about a quiet change in our group as we became familiar with breathing underwater and our confidence grew. We practised basic dive skills, the married couple helped one another with gentle gestures of support and love, and we drank more sugary tea to keep us warm after long sessions in the pool. After much practice I managed to fill my mask with water with my eyes closed and my nose pinched tightly closed. Dare I admit it, I was enjoying myself and I found myself laughing. After two months of an absence of genuine belly laughter it was such a release. As I drove home on Sunday evening I knew I was dreading the following weekend when we would dive at depth and in the quarry but I felt that maybe, just maybe, I stood a chance of doing it. Courage and determination had carried me this far and whilst the worst was yet to come I was almost there. I was almost at the point of achieving the impossible and I smiled all the way home.

The following Friday night brought with it the nerves and a sleepless night that I had come to expect. Perhaps by expecting it I had brought it all upon myself anyway. That marvellous brain of mine was interfering again but nonetheless I rose early on Saturday to beautiful blue skies and a cold autumnal morning. The air was crisp as I packed my equipment into the car and drove to the quarry for my first ever open water scuba dive. My fellow students and I huddled on the bank of the flooded quarry nervously and hid beneath cosy woolly hats. I shivered at the thought of undressing in the chill of the morning and entering the water that I knew was going to be cold regardless of the dry suits we would be wearing. I had never worn a dry suit before and found it strange to think we would be diving but totally dry underneath our suits. As I put my suit on I felt like I was being constrained within a shrink-wrap bag. My eyes began to bulge and my hands slowly turned blue from the tight wrist and neck seals. My first mental note to myself was that I MUST remember not to pee in the suit; it was not a wetsuit and I did not want to spend the day sloshing about in such a way. My second mental note was a sharp reminder that I would shortly be entering the water. I was wittering nervously with Dawn and the other Instructors as we donned our dive jackets and other equipment. Before my brain had fully kicked with its usual warning of imminent death we had entered the water and were practising dive skills at the surface. I bobbed about like a cork in my shrink-wrap bag whilst my eyes began to blur and the remaining feeling in my hands disappeared.

I don't think I will ever forget that first dive in the quarry. We descended as a group and began to breathe underwater. It was absolutely freezing cold and I couldn't see further than 2m in front of me as I attempted to move my legs in the pea soup water and stay close to the rest of the group. I quickly learnt it is almost impossible to move normally in a dry suit in shallow water as it squeezes every inch of skin to the point of being vacuum-packed. I added air to the suit to relieve the problem and found myself back at the surface within seconds. Clearly adding air was not possible until we were at depth and I descended like a vacuum-packed ham onto the shallow platform where the other divers waited for me. I don't recall any dive skills from that dive. I only recall hyperventilating with fear and finally bursting into tears within my mask. I sobbed quietly to myself as I sat on the shallow underwater platform and pretended I was okay whenever the Instructors looked my way. By the time we surfaced I knew I was going to quit and walk away from diving forever. No matter how hard I tried I could not do this. The fear was too great, insurmountable in fact, and I felt bitterly disappointed with myself as I sipped my hot chocolate at the water's edge and listened to how much the rest of the group had enjoyed the dive. I walked to Dawn with my quitting speech prepared in my mind and held back tears as I clutched my mug close to my chest. I breathed deeply, opened my mouth to speak and, as Dawn hugged me and beamed at me with pride for completing my first dive, I realised I couldn't quit. How could I after she had invested so much time and energy in me? She *believed* in me; I had to do this no matter what. I dug deep and mustered the strength to admit that the entire dive had been terrifying and I had cried in my mask. We both fell about laughing and before I knew it we were back in the water and I was reliving the nightmare all over again for another two dives and then two more the following day.

I would like to be able to say that it got easier for me as the days progressed but it didn't. I was shaking and trying to calm my mind whilst it screamed at me to exit the water during every second of every dive and during both days. My heart raced, I was so cold, I cried in my mask again and it was all a bit ridiculous. But then true fear does that to us all. It defies logic, it is unreasonable, unrealistic and paralyses us until our brain one day makes a mental leap and decides that there is nothing to fear after all. I longed for that leap but knew no such moment was on the horizon, so I gritted my teeth and carried on. I bit down hard onto my regulator as I demonstrated each of the dive skills I had learned, I refused to look at what depth we were diving as we sank deeper and I thought of everything and anything to calm me down.

I knew my moment of truth had come during one of the final dives when Dawn swam to me underwater as I sat on the dive platform. I had been watching the other students removing their masks, breathing calmly and then going for their no mask swims in the cold murky water of the quarry. My heart was racing, my mind screaming at me. Dawn looked at me with compassion, squeezed my hand and held my dive jacket to support me. She nodded gently in my direction. It was my turn. I had to do this and my years of failed attempts and preparation came flooding in on me. I desperately wanted to succeed and I thought of Mum. Somehow I found it in me to raise my shaking hands as I squeezed my eyes closed and removed my mask from my face. It was okay. It was freezing cold but I was alive and I breathed. I breathed huge deep breaths of air from my tank and pinched my nose tightly closed. I was on the verge of bolting to the surface and Dawn took my hand again. She pulled me gently off the platform and together we went for my no mask swim. I don't know where we went or what we saw but I know I did it. I know I held my panic down and I finned and breathed for all I was worth. I was swimming away from my failures, away from my grief and towards a future in which I could call myself a scuba diver. A future in which I could be proud of who I had become.

We surfaced as one that day, as a group of people brought together to achieve and conquer our own demons. We all finished the dive knowing we had passed our course and each of us was ecstatic. For once that weekend there were no tears from me; just a beaming smile of joy and a lot of leaping about at the waters' edge in celebration with the girls. I had done it! I had looked my fear in the face and was officially a scuba diver. Wow. As the group went their separate ways after a celebratory pint in the local pub Dawn asked me if I would do any further diving courses in the future. I swiftly spoke a firm and resolute no. There was absolutely no chance I would ever put myself through that kind of horror again. Dawn knowingly turned to me and said she had felt the same after her first course. She raised her pint to mine and suggested that maybe one day I would become an Instructor just like she had.

I beamed all the way home along the motorway and recalled the events of the weekend with Oscar and the Bears that Sunday evening, before stepping back and taking a moment to myself. I walked into my kitchen and leant against the cool metal of the oven whilst wearing my brand new wetsuit, hood and dive weight belt – the treats for my success. Had anyone been watching they may have questioned my sanity but I walked into the garden regardless, looked up at the stars in my neoprene superhero outfit and lifted a glass of champagne to the sky.

31

With item number one ticked off my grief management programme I mustered myself for round two; buying a piano. I have played the piano since I was a little gap-toothed child and I missed the feel of the cool ivory and black keys under my fingertips often. During my dreams I excelled at playing and my hands flowed freely across the keys as they made beautiful music that filled my ears and heart. In reality I was a little shakier than that having not played regularly in many years but it didn't matter, I longed to play again and feel the ache of my tired wrists afterwards. There hadn't been a piano in my own house before and the family piano was firmly nestled in my sister's house where it was adored and tinkered with by her family of boys. The time had come for me to bring music back into my life and there was just enough space to put an electric piano within my spare bedroom. Quite how I was going to get the piano up the narrow staircase and into the bright yellow bedroom was beyond me but that was a minor detail. One way or another my relatively small frame would get a piano up the stairs come hell or high water but perhaps with a strained muscle or two. I bought a packet of ibuprofen in preparation and tucked it into my handbag.

It felt very luxurious considering buying such a grand instrument and I pondered my choices as I drove in the opposite direction to that which I had taken for my scuba diving course just weeks previously. I tapped the steering wheel impatiently as I headed across the countryside to Chester and the piano shop that had been recommended to me. I was giddy with excitement as I parked the car and opened the shop door to the sound of a tinkling bell. There were pianos and brass instruments, guitars and sheet music *everywhere*. Absolutely every inch of the shop was adorned with potential music to be made by beautiful instruments and creative minds. It was heaven to me and I didn't know where to begin and what piano shop etiquette required of me. Was I allowed to touch the instruments? Could I play them or was I supposed to just point and make my selection based on looks? I couldn't believe my luck when a shop assistant approached and encouraged me to try the different pianos as she swept her hand across the musical vista before us. She had piano-playing fingers, long and elegant. I asked her to take me through the different types of piano available. I knew I didn't want a keyboard-style piano, I was interested in something more substantial yet still electronic. Shyly I played a tune I had always been able to recall on the first piano she recommended and immediately fell in love with its tone. That was my piano right there under my fingers and I knew then nothing would change my mind. I balked when I saw the price tag, paused for a moment as I considered it and then observed my budget fluttering out of the window with the music of other musicians playing in the store. It wasn't the most expensive piano in the shop by a long way but it was enough to make me wince as I handed over my credit card at the till with an arm full of sheet music and a wild excited grin upon my face. But then came the pertinent question...

'How are you going to get this into the car dear?'

Ah, I hadn't even considered that aspect of my purchase. We contorted the interior of my hatchback car until it held the enormous cardboard box that contained my new piano. I avoided looking at the warning on the box that told me the piano was heavy and to be lifted by two men at a minimum. I couldn't see a thing out of the passenger window next to me or the rear-view mirror as I drove away and headed for home.

I eyed my narrow staircase, I eyed the cardboard box full of piano in my car and eyed the staircase yet again. I stood on my driveway with my hands on my hips looking from stairs to piano and back again. No matter how many times I did this I could not decide how best to get the piano out of the car and up the stairs for its reassembly. I knew that box weighed almost as much as I did and there was no chance I would be able to lift it. The Bears eyed me from the lounge window and smeared their noses across the clean glass as I considered my options. The obvious choice was to wait for Oscar to come home and help me but there was no way I was going to do that. For a start I was too excited and wanted to play my piano but, more to the point, I didn't want his help. This was my grief I was trying to manage, I was a capable grown woman, and if that meant huffing a giant boxed piano up my narrow staircase on my own then so be it. It soon became apparent to me that I lacked muscle as I attempted to heave the box out of the car. After a few failed attempts and a mildly sore back I fashioned a device for dragging the piano across the drive and into the hallway. I say 'fashioned' but in truth it consisted of a number of fusty old dog blankets laid out to form a sleigh of sorts. I managed to lever the box to the edge of the car boot and cushioned its landing on the drive with a number of those carefully positioned blankets. I heaved and shoved and pulled and eventually reached the interior of my house with a sweaty red face and grimace of determination. I was a scuba diver; I was not going to be beaten by a piano. To this day I am amazed I got that enormous box of piano up the staircase without flattening myself in the process but somehow I did it. I put my shoulder into it, I slipped back a number of times but progress was slowly made as my slippers fought for purchase upon the carpeted steps and won. It may have taken over half an hour to push the piano up approximately fifteen steps but I did it and then refashioned my blanket sleigh for the final straight drag into the spare bedroom.

By the time Oscar returned home I had constructed my piano in the bedroom and was happily playing it whilst pretending I hadn't hurt my back in the process. The look upon Oscar's face was priceless as he realised that I had bought a piano and then realised I had moved it upstairs and constructed it all on my own. I suspect how I felt at that moment is perhaps how it feels to be crowned World's Strongest Man; mostly smug. I savoured the moment and swallowed a couple of ibuprofen on the sly.

Friends that have lost parents told me that six months into their grief was when they hit rock-bottom and they had warned me gently to be prepared for that moment and nurture myself deeply when it came. I recalled their wise words as autumn tumbled into November and those depressed feelings were creeping upon me like a hard winter frost again. As the winter settled in I woke every day with feelings of dread in the pit of my stomach and no reasoning behind it. I found myself low at times, truly low as if my head had been placed in a vice and squeezed until the hope and light had been taken away from my eyes. I was lethargic one moment, irritable the next and often found myself crying for no apparent reason and when I least expected it. Oscar continued his normal cycle of being ultra-demonstrative and then withdrawn and had warned me that he found it hard to find his balance in life. He knew he went from one extreme to the other and on many occasions during that summer we had sat in the garden and I had listened as Oscar explained his feelings and how he ultimately felt lost in the world. He told me with his sad blue eyes that he couldn't find his purpose and admitted he found solace in either his spiritual work or what he deemed as lesser pursuits; fishing, hunting and alcohol. I knew it tortured him to feel that way and I longed to help him. I held Oscar's hand tightly on one such day, looked into his sad eyes and promised to always help him find his balance. I promised that if he lost his way and began to veer towards addiction of any kind I would be there to pull him back. I would tell him what he was doing and refuse to give up on him. I only asked for his trust in return and that he would remember that moment and listen to me if such a time came. He promised to do so and I felt trust and commitment blossom between us.

On Oscar's good days that winter I came home to offerings of dinner, an open bottle of wine and a warm log fire in the lounge. He was thoughtful and considerate in how he surprised me and it lifted my heart through those dark clouds and towards the sunshine above. On his darker days I came home and was invisible again. At times I was living with an empty shell of a man beside me and I fell deeper into my own depression. The only things that kept me going during those moments were Hester, Paddington and my new piano. They were my constant sources of joy when the world around me kept shifting.

32

By the time December arrived I knew something needed to be done. It was time to try therapy.

Therapy, counselling, psychiatry, psychology - they are all forms of help, healing and growth, yet those words are loaded with judgement and taboo. When asked about therapy people often become uncomfortable and respond with words such as weakness, shame, denial, fear and disgust; which are most definitely not associated with that positive thing called help. All I wanted was a little help, a safe haven where I could cry it out and crawl up and away from my depressed feelings. Yet I knew there was great taboo in admitting I was going to have therapy and so I kept it quiet. Despite my open-minded approach I was apprehensive and I expected to be questioned continually about my childhood, my relationship with my parents and peers and then asked to look at blotted ink drawings to establish the workings of my subconscious mind. I expected to be told that everything was my fault, that I had a screw loose and should just get on with the task of living as best I could. In short I thought it would be a living hell except within comfortable surroundings and accompanied by a very large box of tissues for my relentless parade of tears. As it happened my course of therapy was none of those things, except it did involve a large box of tissues. They were exquisitely soft and I cried my way through a number of them, which was precisely what I needed to do.

When I first arrived at my therapist's house I shuffled nervously at the front door and was greeted by a beautiful round cat as I waited. He twirled his tail around my legs as he meandered past with his striped coat and leisurely gait. We both entered the treatment room when my therapist answered and I felt instantly at ease. The room was decorated with inspirational spiritual books, the occasional rose quartz crystal and soft plump sofa cushions. This was not a room for probing into childhood patterns and being asked to lie down whilst feeling fearful and exposed. This was a room of healing, of personal growth and understanding. It was a safe haven and I came to cherish my time there with my therapist. My first session was mostly spent with gentle conversation and tears of relief on my part for having finally had the courage to arrive and allow myself to cry. By the end of my appointment I was tired and slept deeply that night. I returned weekly from there on in and I was nervous every single time. I was fearful of being judged and blamed for past experiences and my reaction to them but that never happened. I wasn't asked probing questions or made to feel uncomfortable. I was instead allowed to just be; to sit, to talk and to cry it out. The therapist asked me what *I* thought, how *I* felt, and from that I reached my own conclusions and answers. It was fascinating and became more so as the initial exhaustion and nerves wore off and revealed a path of great discovery and healing. I began to find answers to that age-old question 'Who am I?' and I rediscovered my strength and heart. I learnt about emotional intelligence, about forgiveness, self-awareness and most importantly *love*. I used those lessons and attitudes daily and by the time I approached my first Christmas without Mum, which was also to be my first Christmas with Oscar, I was mentally and spiritually in better shape. My grief was still there, it always will be, but I carried it more easily. Importantly for me, I found I could start to forgive the world for taking my mum away. I was ever so slightly less angry and my spiritual roots began to burrow back into the ground below with strength and vigour.

Admitting I needed help and going for therapy was an incredible experience for me. It literally changed how I see the world, how I respond to others, and it helped me see who I am. It brought me peace and healing and I wouldn't change that for anything. I would go so far as to say that therapy was the good in losing my mum. I will never stop missing her but therapy at least gave me something positive in the face of such a loss.

Therapy wasn't easy but then most things worthwhile are not easy, they require grit and determination. I have since held the hands of nervous friends as they embarked on their own journey of counselling and wiped away their tears when they needed me to. It takes a great deal of courage for anyone to ask for help in our societies; where we see needing professional help as being weak and shameful. It takes heart, vulnerability and courage by the bucketload to just do it anyway and ignore the ridiculous taboo. I for one hold my hand up and admit it, I had therapy and it was amazing. I wish for everyone to have the opportunity to try it at least once in their life and open up to the healing potential of their minds. And I wish fervently that people would drop their judgement and offer a supportive hand, no, make that a round of applause, to anyone that has the strength to stand up and admit they need help.

I knew Oscar was eager to heal his own past, his own issues as he would phrase it, and he went weekly for therapy after my improvement. He walked taller afterwards, he scribbled furiously in his new journal and I couldn't have been happier for us both. He was inspired and purposeful and happily creating ideas for his future career. It was a joy to witness except for one tiny problem. As we approached Christmas, Oscar showed me occasional entries in his journal where he had written horribly cruel words about me. It was certainly a novel experience reading the words selfish, unlovable, fat, ugly and b*tch whilst Oscar appeared unaware of how it hurt me. He explained they had been written in his dark moods and so didn't matter. He explained how recently he had come to realise that he truly, madly deeply wanted me as his life partner but that he didn't like the downside of having me. He didn't want to have to work at a relationship or commit to a life together if there would be difficult times. In his words, he wanted the sweetie but not the wrapper. Oscar told his story with love in his eyes, with a smile on his face and reassurance that he would change his attitude. He told me he loved me, he was merely explaining, and that it was nothing to be concerned about. I believed him and, in spite of the hurt, we approached Christmas with hands held tightly together. I for one was determined to have a positive first Christmas in Cornwall without Mum. We owed her that much.

33

Abuse (verb): To control. To manipulate another person and strip away their self-worth layer by layer until they crumble into tiny, unrecognisable pieces. To take trust and love and use them as weapons holding the abused in place. Watch as the victim dances to the rhythm of abuse; a wooden puppet with a forced smile painted across a tired face. They dance towards their destruction; both parties trying their best to cope, to understand and never let others know their shame.

Abuse (verb): To drip feed emotional and physical pain until the abused finally falters and falls to their knees, confused and alone. To chip away at, to pick at, to criticise, to push and to mould until finally the victim falls apart. To silently destroy until both parties look in the mirror and no longer recognise who they are. Spent, they walk away from the damage with hollow eyes. The world none the wiser as to what went on behind closed doors.

How do you define abuse? Try as I might to capture it, I find it impossible to put into words what it means to be abused. Abuse is so personal, varied and hugely subjective. Is it perhaps defined by the words and actions of the abuser? Mention abuse and I think of being hit, of strong hands used to hurt another person. I think of being held against one's will, of assault, rape, bruises, burns, broken bones and of other injuries both visible and hidden. I think of verbal threats and criticism, of subtle words used to bring about tears, terror, loneliness, fear and control. I hear blame, worst nightmares being realised and of being cornered with no understanding of why it is happening. Words and actions go some way to describing abuse for me but they don't capture it completely. Perhaps it is how an experience *feels* to the victim that defines it as abuse; as the racing heart that pumps adrenaline, as the sharp fear that overtakes senses and dilates pupils scanning wildly for escape, as being trapped and the heartbreaking feeling of giving in to the inevitable. In abuse there is surrender of the worst kind; acceptance of not deserving any better. For me, the heart of what abuse actually is lies more within those feelings it generates, in both parties, than within the actions alone. For without feeling, without an emotional response, all actions are essentially meaningless.

To abuse, by definition as a verb, is *to do*. To act upon an impulse and set in motion something similar to that which I described above. But does that mean it is always intentional? Is the abuser aware of his or her actions as being abusive at the time they commit them? Do they recognise their own behaviour as wrong? I wonder if abuse is unintentional at times. I wonder if the abusive person can be an average person, unaware of the true impact of their words and actions as they commit them. A person acting out their own self-loathing and insecurities, believing themselves to be the innocent party. Maybe I have at times acted abusively towards others without even realising it, maybe we all have. I find it difficult to think of abuse being unintentional when I consider the serious acts of abuse people I know have endured. How can any of those horrific, disgusting experiences have been committed unknowingly? All I do know is that abuse is open to interpretation and blame depends upon your point of view. The abuser sees no blame within them and believes they are pushed to behave that way by their perpetrator, whoever that may be or may have been in their past. The victim sees only self-blame. It goes without saying that I am by no means accepting any form of abuse. There is no excuse.

But what I am suggesting is that abuse is often not a clear-cut, black and white story. It is an intricate web of cause and effect, can go back generations and comes with pain and destruction for both parties. It is more complex than simple definitions and judgements and I believe that to truly understand abuse, we need to start looking at it with more compassion and empathy for all involved. Listen a little more, judge a little less and try to strip away the blame and taboo. For me, abuse was a complex dance between two people, brought about by our unique interaction, our unresolved issues and fears that came to a head during the festive season of 2010. It was a vicious cycle that spiralled downwards and caused us to inflict injuries that formed deep scars.

For me, part of the healing process involved dropping the blame and looking at abuse from a different angle. It involved developing compassion and empathy and admitting my shortcomings as well as those of my partner. It involved being kind and forgiving in order to let go. I must admit that didn't exactly happen overnight…There was a period of time when I dropped it in favour of a more basic, yet effective, style of healing. For a good two months or so I went to town with enormous amounts of swearing in my journal and daily ranting with my dad over large glasses of red wine. I went on long walks with my iPod most days and stood with my face to the wind as I literally screamed and shouted at the sky from the top of Cornish cliffs. I can still picture Dad and me sat around the sturdy old family table, swearing and ranting and nodding in agreement as we went over and over the whole debacle. I treasure those memories with a laugh when I remember us spouting some pretty colourful language in the middle of the day. We were a pair of semi-drunks with ever so slightly posh English accents. God bless my steady-as-a-rock father for his patience and friendship and the wind for carrying my voice away during those times. Supermarket wine aisles I salute you for having full shelves and I thank my swear-word riddled journal for helping to set me free.

As Oscar's hands tightened around my neck just before we left for Cornwall that Christmas, just over one year prior to my red-wine-healing sessions, I remember feeling shocked. Deeply shocked and then suddenly afraid, yet also strangely free. I had a feeling of deserving it, of it being right, yet combined with fear and knowing it was utterly wrong. As Oscar held my neck and twisted my arm behind my back I recall feeling his nails were sharp and needed clipping. I remember that he felt strong and I felt utterly powerless and controlled. I gave in to his strength as he pulled the keys from my hand, scraping them accidentally along my twisted wrist, and tossed me aside. I felt heavy as my hip bounced off the edge of the sofa in the lounge and I fell to the wooden floor. I didn't hit my head. The floor was cold and dusty. To say I was shocked is an understatement but absolute indignation kicked in quickly and had me on my feet and heading for Oscar in a fury of swear words, venom and defiant anger. My heart hammered in my chest, I was full of fear yet utterly clear-headed. Adrenaline sharpened my senses and told me to get Oscar the hell out of my house. He had crossed a line; he had hurt me, how dare he, and must be removed from the premises. I don't recall Oscar's reaction or his anger. I simply don't know what he did but I do remember the feeling of pushing against his chest trying to get him out of the front door and of my socked feet sliding backwards on the wooden floor. He didn't budge. I knew if I could get him outside I could pull the safety chain across and he couldn't get back in. I knew he had his car keys, his wallet and would find warmth and safety with friends or family. Even now it staggers me that I thought of his welfare but I did. I felt so weak, powerless and pissed off as I put every ounce of strength into getting him out and it had no effect. I'm not sure if I managed to push him outside, I doubt it given my stature, but somehow he was outside against his will and I slammed the door shut. I pulled the safety chain across and ran upstairs sobbing and shaking. In one moment of violence he had ruined us, had broken my trust and my feeling of safety at home. The man I loved and cared for had hurt me, physically and emotionally. I ached from what became bruises on my wrist but I ached more so from the breaking of my heart.

I sat on my bed in shock and fell apart. I struggled to bring my breathing back under control as I stared wide-eyed and unseeing, rocking back and forth as I held myself tightly in my own embrace. I didn't understand what had just happened, couldn't comprehend it. What was I going to do? Fury kicked in again and I paced across the room, brimming full of anger. 'How dare he?' I said out loud to my Bears repeatedly as I marched across the room in my socks, hands on hips, huffing and puffing and generally being incensed. That fury compelled me to not let Oscar back in. I could hear him knocking quietly on the front door asking me to calm down and let him in. I shook and wondered what to do.

Where would he go? Was this my fault? Don't be ridiculous, of course not.

I pattered quietly down the stairs and leant against the front door. In a shaky voice that wasn't my own I said he couldn't come in until he apologised. No response. I reminded him that he had just had his hands around my neck and thrown me to the floor and I asked again for an apology. No apology came. In the same sickly sweet tone of voice he used when he told me he loved me, he reminded me I had shouted at him. He calmly explained he only pushed me and it was because I was being rude. I caused it and he asked to be let in. What was I to do? We lived together and he had every right to be there yet I couldn't let him in. I just couldn't let him in. I said no despite my concern that it was bitterly cold and Oscar would have to drive somewhere on extremely icy roads when the MET office had warned against travel. I remember that much but I don't know what happened in the minutes that followed this exchange of words. Eventually Oscar drove off. He drove off into the cold winter's night and I fell apart in the privacy of my own home. That was when the first seed of doubt began to grow within me and I questioned if perhaps it had been my fault, if I had caused it. I couldn't begin to get my head around what had happened though. In my mind the man I trusted had raised a hand to me yet apparently it was my fault. I was to blame and I wasn't to blame – depending on which part of my mind I listened to. Everything felt back to front and upside-down.

That night I went over every moment that led to his hands around my neck. I sat on our bed and clutched tightly at the duvet. I retraced every step, every word we spoke, every single movement so I could establish whose fault it was. I looked back across my recent therapy, at Oscar's black moods and those entries in his journal regarding me that he had shared. My head throbbed; instinct told me the blame lay with Oscar for his actions but slowly my self-doubt crept in and I wondered if truly it was me.

I am tired, so tired of this. He told me it was my fault. Perhaps I am the problem and I am to blame. Did I goad him to it? Did I deserve it?

I didn't know the answer then and at times I don't know the answer now. That seed of doubt still exists today and I feel shame and blame. In spite of everything, I spent the night looking at my mobile phone hoping for Oscar to contact me and comfort me. I was hoping for an apology but no word came. I expected him to turn up on the driveway as the night set in but nothing happened. I could only assume, rightly so, that he had driven back to his parents and my response to that thought was fear. Pure fear that he would reject me, would confirm it was my fault and wouldn't want me anymore. Fear that he would tell people what I did that led to him having to drive through the icy night. In reality all that had actually happened that evening was that I annoyed Oscar by being slow to pack our bags for the journey to Cornwall after work. I was apparently baggage slowing him down in life and it escalated from there. We argued and his hands reached out. As simple as that. Sleep eventually found me as I replayed the argument again and seeds of self-doubt and rejection began to bloom.

I telephoned Oscar's parents late the next day after no word from Oscar, after I had driven to Cornwall to be with my dad for our first Christmas without Mum. Life seemed a little miserable and unfair to me that day and I remember my nerves, confused as to why it was me making the first move at reconciliation. Oscar had hit me and surely he should apologise first. I wondered if Oscar had told his parents of our argument. I was close to his mum and feared the worst of her judgement. It didn't occur to me at that point that they could be angry with Oscar for his behaviour.

'But Oscar told me you shouted at him,' Alexa said confused.

That one sentence Oscar's mother spoke on the telephone that day confirmed to me that it was my fault. It was a throwaway sentence in a lovely conversation during which she was kind and supportive of us both and tried to encourage us to make amends. She wasn't suggesting the blame lay with me per se but that it lay with both of us and it was a silly argument we needed to heal. Somehow after that I spent my time convincing Oscar to give us a second chance. He never once apologised for his actions and was reluctant to try again. I apologised many times, we promised one another it would never ever happen again and that we would work on our differences. Oscar agreed and later that day he drove to Cornwall. He was distant when we embraced and I saw his distrust of me in his eyes.

Intuition told me everything I needed to know at that point in our relationship. It had been shaking me for months trying to tell me something was wrong, trying to tell me to sit up and listen. My relationship with Oscar had been full of love and laughter but it had also been full of difficult times and they took their toll. There were times when we didn't speak for days during our first year together, it happened regularly and I dreaded it. I found ways to cope as he withdrew but I began to feel as if I didn't exist. I longed to talk, to have friendship and consistency in our lives yet I felt as if I was being punished. I lost count of the numbers of days I drove home from work not knowing what to expect. I didn't know what to do to make those feelings go away, didn't know how to cope with the loss of my mum as well. When Oscar told me to hug myself as I grieved and he turned away I felt even more isolated. I assumed he was right, I should be stronger and comfort myself. I was a grown woman and ought to get on with it. I know he loved me deeply and was trying to help me in every way he could but we constantly had our wires crossed. When he pointed out the women he saw that were more beautiful than me he was trying to tell me that I was gorgeous and precious to him; that there were only a few women more physically attractive than me. Yet I felt uglier every time he pointed out one of the blonde Amazonian goddesses trotting along in their high heels. How I longed for them to fall flat on their faces or for my little pigeon legs to suddenly grow beyond their stumpy 30 inches, as I watched Oscar turn his head and admire their passing frames as we walked.

I tried to understand, tried to take the blame for his days of silence and be more stable. I ran myself ragged with self-discovery and healing for us and I look back at that period of time with deep sadness. It is clear to me now that we *both* needed comfort and support yet only one of us was getting it and it wasn't me. Between us we were a shaky foundation and I should have let go. There was a storm brewing on the horizon and I was oblivious. I should have let go.

Intuition continued to shout at me but still I hadn't listened as the months flew by toward that Christmas. I ignored my inner voice. I had been through loss and humiliation in the past two years and I was determined not to endure any more. Surely all relationships were like that anyway. Surely they all involved struggle and pain. I was helping Oscar to rid himself of his demons, he of mine and we clung to one another. Love endures and I was lucky to have him. I truly believed that to be the case, it was my turn for a happy ending and nothing would stop that. I also believed our arguments, the moods and the criticism were my fault and I was ashamed of myself. I must have goaded him to react, he told me as much, and I needed to work on myself in order to improve the situation. It was never his fault. I brought it upon myself and I would never find anyone else to love me.

Abuse: A subject not talked about for fear of judgement and rejection by others, a subject cloaked in shame. We continue to brush it under the carpet, hide it behind closed doors and pretend it never happens to us. Through shame and silence abuse finds its strength and blossoms onward; kept firmly rooted in our society for future generations to endure.

I allowed abuse to continue on in my life. Two days after Oscar had taken my neck in his hands he went down on one knee at Padstow harbour and asked me to marry him. The crisp winter air and sunshine surrounded us and Oscar looked up at me. It was absolutely stunning and as I looked into his eyes I said yes.

34

It was Christmas Eve and I heard seagulls wheeling around the house as I peeked out from under the duvet. There was a definite chill to the air and I crept out of the room to find out why. Padstow is a mild seaside town that rarely experiences crisp winter weather but that morning was something else. I stood in the kitchen holding a mug of tea close to me and admired the surrounding countryside and estuary waters in the distance. It was so beautiful. The garden plants and bare branches of the season were covered in sparkling frost and caught the orange glow of dawn as the sun rose higher. The hills were muted green and chocolate brown with their ice dusting and rolled towards the estuary dramatically. The rooks in the trees surrounding the garden cawed their early morning song and shook the cold of the night from their sleek black feathers. Footsteps pattered behind me as the Bears strolled upstairs and into the kitchen with its magnificent view. It was a perfect start to Christmas and I was glad of the peace after my recent problems with Oscar.

'Morning Dad. Did you sleep well?' I tilted the kettle towards him in offer of a strong coffee to start the day.

A routine question I have asked many times, yet I knew the answer would be no. Dad hadn't slept will since Mum passed away and understandably so. They had shared their sleep, their bed for over forty years, and now he woke up alone. Well, not quite alone. He had his lovable Welsh terrier Ollie hogging the other half of the bed most nights. All I wanted was to make this first Christmas without Mum easier for us all to endure. As Oscar joined us his festive spirit was apparent and he positively beamed with happiness at being in Cornwall. He was back to his usual self and was eager to head out and enjoy the frosty air. After breakfast we all decided upon a dog walk and off we went. As Oscar walked away from the house with Hester and Paddington in hand I couldn't help but notice he was dressed more smartly than usual, in one of his best shirts and smart trousers. It was unusual attire for a walk in the sand dunes.

We spent the morning walking amongst sand dunes that were crisp and frozen in their dells. Old seed heads stood tall on frozen stems and glittered amongst patches of pale grasses as the dunes rolled away before us. The breeze occasionally shook wisps of frosted sand into the air and the Bears happily snapped up every patch of ice they could find. It was glorious listening to the sound of waves crashing against the shore as our noses and fingertips slowly turned red and numb. Oscar found a tall pampas grass and tickled the Bears with its feathery fronds. I couldn't help but smile as they leapt and twisted with their new toy. Before long we had tired them out and turned homewards. As we walked down and onto the flat sheltered harbour, Oscar and I sat on one of the many emerald green benches and admired the pastel cottages and chubby fishing boats. It was a pretty town and I had spent many years exploring it since I was knee-high to a grasshopper. I held all three of our dogs as Dad disappeared to use the nearby bathroom and I turned back towards Oscar.

Oh my gosh, he is down on one knee before me. He is down and on...one...knee. Perhaps he needs to tie his shoe? Oh perhaps not, he is wearing those green wellingtons again. He is now holding up a wooden ring box in his hand. Oscar, one knee, ring box. He is kneeling right next to a splat of seagull poop and has narrowly missed it. That is beside the point...Oscar is holding jewellery and is on one knee.

I sat there with my mouth wide open.

'Kathryn,' he whispered as he took my hand gently in his.

'I love you so much my honey and I am really happy with you. I can't imagine being with anyone else and if I can't make it with you then who can I make it with? I love you. Please.' Oscar paused as he eyed me nervously.

'Please will you marry me?' He asked shyly.

Oscar opened the ring box and presented me with a beautiful sapphire and diamond ring that sparkled in the sunlight. It sparkled and looked familiar because it was made from the stones of my previous engagement ring. Oscar and I had talked about getting married months previously and we had discussed engagement rings with giddy excitement. He knew I had my old ring and didn't see the sense in spending money on a new one. I had reluctantly agreed that an engagement ring could be made from my old one and that yes I would design it and pay for it with my own savings. I was just so excited at the prospect of being complete, being happy and loved, that I didn't consider how ridiculous that idea was. Somehow I expected to find completeness in a wedding and marriage rather than giving it to myself from within. I was grateful at that time that somebody would consider marrying me. I hadn't expected to actually get engaged for a *long* time yet though, especially given the hands-around-my-neck incident just days before.

I continued to look shocked, mouth hanging wide open, and finally came up with this...

'Are you joking? You are, right?'

It was not exactly the response Oscar was hoping for and he looked crestfallen.

'No sweetie. No, I, I really love you. Will you?' He smiled as his confidence returned.

'Yes. Yes I will marry you.' There I have said it.

I really truly loved Oscar and we embraced. I had always expected that if I became engaged a second time (that never sounds great) I would be wildly excited and cry copious tears of joy, much like recently engaged people are supposed to do. However, at the time of my second engagement I sat there feeling mostly shocked and without tears. It took a moment for the excitement to arrive and as Dad strolled back towards us I had no idea what I was going to say. I was hoping Oscar would speak but he looked strangely sheepish. I had never associated announcing an engagement with looking sheepish but he definitely appeared that way.

Dad on the other hand was supportive and instantly excited. He was genuinely happy for us both and I knew he trusted Oscar to look after me in the years to come. We trooped to the local pub and my excitement grew as we ordered our pints and chatted cheerfully about celebrating with champagne later on. I asked Oscar if he was going to telephone his family and let them know the good news and a look of terror crossed his face. Wow, my fiancé looked sheepish and terrified. After much persuasion on my part and a look of confusion on Dad's part, Oscar finally plucked up the courage to call and exited the pub as he did so. When he returned to our table he was impossible to read and didn't say much other than his family were happy for us. That wasn't quite what I expected but onwards we went. By the time the evening had come round Dad had bought an expensive bottle of pink champagne and had been busy preparing smoked salmon nibbles to celebrate. He was in his element and I loved seeing the joy on his face as we tucked into the bubbles and found laughter in the approach to Christmas Day. As the moon sat high above the hills we walked down to the estuary, warmed by our day of champagne, and lit paper lanterns. We released them high into the night sky with wishes for Mum and for love. They looked like stars as they rose up, up and away from us. Apart from the one lantern that caught fire in the bushes when the wind changed direction.

I went to bed early that night feeling warm and fuzzy after the day of celebrations and cuddled in to Oscar. He announced he felt ill and needed to be left alone. Oscar left the room promptly without further word and I fell asleep. I awoke in the middle of the night to hear Oscar crying his heart out in the lounge above me. He sobbed and then spent hours vomiting in the nearby bathroom. I knew from his demeanour earlier that he would not want me to check on him and so I just listened and hoped he would be okay. I later found out from Oscar that it was his reaction to getting engaged to me. The idea of marrying me had effectively made him vomit. Ah, that's nice. How romantic. Oscar was scared and unsure that he wanted to get married and had only decided to ask me to marry him when he woke up on Christmas Eve. It was impulsive to say the least. I asked him if he wanted to change his mind and he said no, we'd go with it. Right, okay then.

Christmas Day was difficult without Mum but we celebrated and talked of weddings. As a family we had something to focus on in the future and I know that lifted our spirits throughout the day. I missed Mum terribly at times and it was lonely without her but Dad and I made the best of it together. We made the effort to cook good hearty food and be positive. It was all we could do and it pulled us through the festive season and into the New Year. I mentally ticked surviving our first Christmas without Mum off the list of hurdles to deal with and moved swiftly on.

35

When I casually dropped into conversation that I was getting married (read 'I announced very loudly to anyone that would listen, and often') most women responded with excited squeals, much cooing at the engagement ring followed by chatter and excitement about the impending wedding. Never mind the love, commitment and vows; getting married is all about the wedding and the excuse to get creative with bunting, cakes and outrageously expensive fluffy, flouncy ivory dresses. It is the one time in an adult woman's life that we are given permission to behave like a glossy princess and have *an entire day* devoted to us. And I for one absolutely loved that idea. LOVED IT. I dreamed of being a bride swishing in my dress for many years, which in my defence is mostly explained by being brought up on a diet of fairy tales with knights in shining armour and princesses in flouncy dresses. Loathe them or love them, rightly or wrongly, most weddings are about the bride, her whims and desires and the entire industry is geared towards encouraging that all the way to the aisle and beyond. It is no wonder some of us become just a touch high maintenance and obsessive about it all. Months, sometimes years, are spent planning what appears to be a military operation as each bride attempts to plan the perfect, unique wedding that not only represents who she is in her entirety but also suitably impresses everyone that attends or even hears about the event. I have seen many normal, wonderful friends of mine turn into over-stressed slightly chaotic brides and I include myself in this. And let's not forget that the wedding day is meant to be the best day of each bride's life – no small ask there then. No bride ever states afterwards 'oh yes that was a lovely day, really beautiful. It was probably the second best day of my life'. That *never* happens. It is touted as the best day in a woman's life and there will be no questions asked, no deviation from that, no second best. There is just the teensiest bit of pressure upon everyone involved in planning that day to end all days.

And that is without mentioning the big M word, no, not marriage...money. It costs a small fortune to plan even a modest wedding because everybody hikes up their prices knowing full well that the bride won't say no because, again, it is to be the perfect day and a few extra thousand pounds here and there are apparently no big deal. People spend hundreds of pounds on their wedding cake, which no matter how you dress it up is still made of flour, eggs, butter, a healthy dose of sugar and icing. None of which cost that much to procure from any local supermarket. But it doesn't matter because the cake, as with everything else, must be just so. There are the wedding rings to consider, beautiful hairstyles, bridal jewellery, shiny dancing shoes and suits. Then there is the venue, the one of a kind photographer, the luxurious food, the champagne, the carefully chosen thank you gifts for each guest and the entertainment for the big day. Let us not forget the hen do, the stag do, the vintage cars, the pristine flowers that adorn every surface, personalised favours, pretty stationery and expensive highly supportive underwear for the bride that is also supposed to look sexy despite being akin to scaffolding. Oh my goodness and then there is the fun of making a scrapbook and mood boards and deciding upon ribbons and bunting and confetti options. It is like being a child all over again as you get to play with glue and fabric and every colour of the rainbow. There is then of course the guest list, which is somewhat less fun. There are family expectations and social pressures galore to deal with when it comes to deciding who to invite and who not to invite. It is a minefield trying to *not* offend people when explaining you cannot afford to invite everyone and their children. As for the seating plan...it is a nightmare. Enough said. But guest list and seating arrangements aside, it is much fun planning and shopping for a wedding and the giddy excitement of it all is divine, even though it can and often does come with a hefty price tag.

As for The Dress, let's not go there. That is a whole world of excitement far too precious to discuss so flippantly and that is when most budgets really do take a nosedive out of the window. I can say from my own experience that trying on wedding dresses is akin to heaven and yes I got totally carried away and ignored the price tags whilst I pretended to be a princess with my mum by my side that first time I was engaged. It was possibly the best day in my life (I can say that, my wedding day never happened) and I spent an entire day swishing in every shape, style and colour of dress imaginable. Heaven I tell you, swishing, caffeine-fuelled heaven.

There is one downside to all that fun though and that is the dreaded bridal diet, which we all expect ourselves to commit to as if it were the marriage itself. And precisely why do we do this? Well consider that the average woman does not like being photographed or seen naked. We shimmy into the bedroom with the lights down low and dive under the duvet before our partner can notice the wibble and wobble of pouches, handles and extra curves. Yet on our wedding day we are to be stared at by everyone, all day, and then photographed thousands of times from every angle imaginable. We expect ourselves to have perfect hair, perfect skin and a teensy tiny figure that shows off The Dress. It is no wonder that most women go on a rigid diet and exercise regimen beforehand and shrink down to the size of a small Barbie doll so that the photographs are flawless and nobody will point and laugh at the merest shadow of a second chin. It horrifies me to say all of that but it is true. I don't understand what makes us think undernourished is a good look on a wedding day but most brides feel the pressure, diet like crazy and arrive at their wedding day sylph-like and beautiful yet no doubt somewhat hungry. I feel for the poor grooms who watch their beautiful, curvaceous, buxom brides morph into mini people and then turn a shade of orange for the big day itself as they slather on the fake tan. Little does the bride realise her groom loved and adored her just the way she was on an average day, make-up free, warm and cosy, curves and lumps and all. There was no need for the diet; there never is when it comes to love.

And what about the beloved grooms? It is well known that most grooms have little to do with planning their wedding beyond the initial flurry of excitement and I can't say I blame them. It must seem like a slightly bizarre female-centric, emotional, expensive circus and they steer well clear of it all. They are the wise ones. They know that precisely none of the wedding circus is needed in order to actually get married to the person they love. All that is needed is a promise of unconditional love, patience and forgiveness every single day of their married life together and someone official to hear their vows. The rest is just icing on an already perfect cake.

I knew all of this and understood the highs, lows and pitfalls of wedding planning already, having once planned my wedding to within an inch of its life and also dieted like a mad woman in order to be a skinny bride. You would think I learnt my lesson the first time around but sadly not. After settling into being engaged, which took me all of about a day of feeling shy and embarrassed to be engaged *again*, I went from hesitant and intent upon a small wedding to an unstoppable deliriously happy bridal force. I skipped through the weeks and months with bunting and ribbons galore in my wake whilst spring bloomed around me. I had been given a second chance at getting married and I committed to it wholeheartedly by ordering every bridal magazine available. In my enthusiasm I suspect I was trying to make up for my previous failure, for my shortcomings that I believed made me less than perfect as a second-hand bride and I was also trying to distract myself from the fear that it would happen all over again. That I would plan the perfect wedding and the groom would run in the opposite direction come the day itself because that is what they do. The fear niggled deep within but I had glue and scissors and distracted myself with stationery-making, paper cuts, mood boards and finding the perfect venue. Utter creative heaven for a bride to be.

Finding the right venue was the easy part, there are so many beautiful historical buildings throughout the UK, and we settled upon a rustic ancient barn that sighed and creaked with every passing breeze of the summer air as my father and I stood under its lofty beams. There was a myriad of oak beams above us that held the secrets of centuries in their whorls and splintered edges. It was the perfect venue for the celebration of our love and the day Oscar and I would become one. I smiled to myself as I realised excitedly just how much he was going to love this venue, for he had no idea about it. Oscar had requested from the start that he wanted the entire wedding to be a surprise for him since he had planned his previous wedding and he really liked surprises. Not a single detail was to be shared with him or arranged with his involvement. It was a tall order being asked to organise our wedding single-handedly but I couldn't deny his excited and child-like request as he held my hands and hoped I would say yes. I secretly relished that I could at least plan the day exactly as I chose to. No questions asked.

As the summer continued to melt upon us with unusual warmth the wedding began to take shape and our home was filled to the brim with magazine clippings, make-up samples, theme and flower ideas and beautiful homemade invitations that had been painstakingly designed and made by me. I had more paper cuts than I thought humanly possible from tearing and shaping handmade paper for over one hundred save-the-date cards and invitations and my fingers were speckled with vintage gold ink and dried glue. The newspapers used to light our fire in the winter were covered in deep cerise peony stamps from my adventures with rubber stamps and Paddington often drifted past me with glitter upon his nose. I put every ounce of love within me into every detail imaginable that summer and I couldn't have been happier. Except for one small thing; a potentially huge change for us when Oscar announced he was unhappy with his local piloting work and wanted to move away.

The news stopped me in my tracks when Oscar walked in from work one day and explained he was fed up with work. He told me with absolute certainty and frustration that he was quitting right then and was capable of much more than working for such a ramshackle local operation, which was true. He stood tall in front of my table of wedding delights and simply stated that if he had to move away without me then so be it, he would do so immediately to further his career and we could figure us out at a later date. Wrongly or rightly I was upset and felt my newly-formed roots pulled up quickly from under me. It had been such a long path of change and adjustments in recent years and for the first time I was feeling truly happy and at ease. I no longer had to fight to keep going each day and I was in a world of pink ink, feeling secure and safe. I had something concrete to look forward to and the last thing I needed to hear was that my fiancé was leaving without discussion in order to further his career. We both knew there were no major airfields within commuting distance and I knew that for his own sake Oscar needed more fulfilling work. He swiftly left his job with minimal notice and began his search for the perfect job. The sky was literally the limit and no stone was left unturned as Oscar planned his future with passion and determination and I cheered him on whilst planning our wedding with ribbons that whispered *I do*.

As someone that neither uses a hairdryer nor wears make-up, for no other reason than sheer laziness, I was really looking forward to my first bridal make-up trial that year. I had not been made-up during my previous engagement and I hadn't worn make-up for a long time. Not since my teenage years when I had thick gloopy mascaras in various colours, black smudgy eyeliners, sparkly stars for my cheek bones and eye shadows in every colour of the rainbow. I found myself daydreaming of looking perfect, smooth and somehow glowing thanks to the skills of a make-up artist and her cosmetics. I held in my mind images of me on my wedding day with flawless skin, big soulful eyes and plump lips the perfect shade of pink to complement my skin tone. The reality wasn't quite like that as I sat for what felt like hours whilst layer upon layer of expensive make-up was brushed, dabbed and dotted upon my skin. My first encounter with the eyelash curler was less terrifying than I had expected and at least the artist in question agreed not to use foundation. I couldn't begin to imagine my face without its customary freckles. By the time it came to going outside to see the finished work in daylight I was a tad bored from being still for so long and I looked, in my opinion, like a clown. A glamorous clown, but still a clown, with a very flushed face and heavy black eyebrows. Oscar's immediate response when I presented him with my clown face as he lounged outside with a beer was laughter and then he fell off his chair. When the make-up artist kindly toned it down to what my girlfriends indoors all agreed was more me and suitable, Oscar said I looked nice but still like a prostitute. Better than a clown I suppose but not quite the look I had in mind. I opted for a second make-up trial with a lady who lived closer to the venue and whose website looked impressive and not the least bit clown-like. She spent more time talking and less time applying make-up than I thought possible and by the end of the trial she had only managed to apply some pale eye shadow and clear mascara. I certainly looked like myself but I also still looked, well, a bit naked in the face department. I decided upon clown or perhaps my old sparkly stars.

The really important moment in any bride's wedding preparation is of course shopping for The Dress. It is a symbolic piece of clothing that costs a small fortune from the lowest price upwards, is only ever worn once and yet somehow is worth every penny spent upon it because it is just so pretty. I quickly cast aside various bridal shops in the vicinity of my home on the basis that they were either far too expensive or, as was the case with most of them, snobbish and wouldn't let customers touch the dresses on the display rails. There was only one place to spend my time and money and that was the very same friendly bridal boutique from which I had purchased and then returned my first dress two years beforehand when my engagement had ended. Louise the kind and gentle assistant had said to me that I must visit the boutique again when I found the man of my dreams and so I did, with great excitement and with my bridesmaid-to-be Amber. I knew what to expect, knew how much I loved being there amongst every shade of cream and ivory imaginable and the exquisite fabrics from silk satin to taffeta and beyond. I adored the rows of pointed and round bridal shoes peeking out at me from under hats galore, the dainty handbags and outrageously colourful mother-of-the-bride outfits. It was familiar and blissful walking back into that boutique knowing that this time I would absolutely, most definitely be walking up the aisle. I thumbed row upon row of dresses, pulled out more flouncy swishing dresses to try on than I knew what to do with and tried each dress with Amber by my side. It was exhausting but oh it was good. Louise quickly spotted us and, after a brief pause whilst she reminded herself of who I was, joined us with shoes and kind words. She asked after my family and of course my groom. Tears welled in her eyes as I explained about the loss of my mum and she held me tightly as she told me I looked beautiful and my mum would be proud. She remembered her from when we had tried on dresses together last time. I missed her as I always do and distracted myself with more diamanté and swishing. And then it happened. The Dress found itself upon me and I found myself falling in love with The Dress. It was perfect, absolutely perfect and left both Amber and I speechless as I turned towards the carefully positioned mirrors and admired it from every angle. The silk satin fabric clung to every curve just enough and delicate vintage flowers flowed across my hips and towards tiny round buttons that captured the curve of my back. A pool of delicious, pale coffee-ice-cream-coloured fabric covered my feet. I *had* to have that creation, that dress of my dreams, that piece of fabric heaven and then I saw the price tag. It cost more than it did to hire the venue and then some. Clearly there would need to be a Plan B when it came to The Dress and I had no idea what that would be. How would I find an alternative dress when only that one was in fact *The Dress*? It turned out I was the luckiest girl alive. My incredibly generous and kind mother-in-law-to-be took me aside the following weekend, held my hand in hers, and explained that Oscar had mentioned how much I loved that dress. She told me that my mum would have wanted me to have my perfect dress. In her absence, it was her gift to me.

It wasn't long before Amber and I returned to the bridal boutique to order The Dress and be measured up accordingly. I knew at the time that I was slim and for once my figure trundled along at a healthy size despite the fact I ate a lot of cake. I also knew the reason for this was the anxiety I had suffered periodically since my first fiancé had left and all hell had broken lose in my personal life. The benefit of a racing heart on a daily basis was being slim with minimal effort and for that I was grateful as Louise approached Amber and me with her tape measure. The numbers loomed at me as I backed away fearfully despite my knowledge that it wouldn't be that bad. I am who I am. Nonetheless, my own judgements filled every space between the inches as I imagined the perfect figure which I didn't have and the cool fabric was pressed against and around my skin. This was not fun. Meanwhile Amber lovingly tried to suppress a giggle as I stared at her with wide eyes in my mismatched knickers and bra.

'Okay I think we are done here Kathryn. Your measurements are on file, thank you.'

Louise was studiously writing down my measurements and brought The Dress to me. Oh heavens above, it really was to die for and left me weak at the knees. I tried to disguise the fact I was still half-naked by leaping into it as quickly as possible.

'So I'm a size 10 dress then? The one upside of a history like mine is the stress keeps me thin haha. I've not been a size 10 for years until now and...' I was rambling and trying to be funny but came off sounding awkward and a little bit cocky.

'Kathryn I...' Louise fussed sympathetically as she pulled The Dress up and around me, a cloud of perfect silk satin.

'Well the sizes by this designer do come up a little small Kathryn.' Louise angled the mirrors towards me as Amber helped me into my bridal shoes.

'Oh well, not to worry. So I'll be a size 12 then. I can live with that' I tried to sound cheery and not in the least bit disappointed as I waved away an imaginary perfect size 10. By the look of pity on Amber's face it was not working. I sounded broken.

'Well, actually Kathryn. It will be more of an um size fourteen.'

Louise bustled enthusiastically and then promptly left the changing room as I stood there in utter silence.

'Aw Kat, it's fine. It's just a number, it doesn't matter love.' Amber hugged me and tried to soothe me as she tried not to laugh.

'Absolutely, couldn't agree more. You're right, it doesn't matter. It really is fine. It's just a label,' I lied.

My voice dropped an octave to a throaty whisper.

'Of *course* it matters! It said fourteen! I'm not size fourteen! I can't wear a dress that says I am. And I sounded like such a tool with Louise just then with my I'm a size ten blah blah speech. Size fourteen my *arse*!'

'You can wear it sweetie, it doesn't matter and you look beautiful. Really. It's just the designer sizing coming up small. We can cut the label out and nobody needs to ever know.' Amber remained calm.

'Yes but I know. *I know* and will know it every step up the aisle as my mind shouts fourteen at me. Fourteen, fourteen, step, step, fourteen.' I deflated visibly as I realised quite how stupid I sounded and looked marching across the changing room to my numbers.

'Oh Amber. Oh for once, for just once in my life, I wanted to be perfect. I wanted to be *that* girl, the pretty one, the popular one that everyone loves with long legs and skinny arms and the perfect figure. Not the one bullied for being fat, not the one with hairy shoulders, a moon face and a moustache...oh and a fiancé that buggered off before the wedding. I so don't want to be *that* girl,' I moaned miserably.

'Kat you're being silly, come on. For a start we can pluck those shoulders and wax that mustachio right off! And besides we love you and we love you just the way you are. Come on, it's all going to be fine.' Amber lifted my chin and took my hand as she helped me back into my own clothes.

'Come on let's go and get some cake down that moon face of yours.'

Amber was absolutely right, it didn't matter at all. I was the same person I had always been, hairy body and all, and no label would change that. And more to the point there is absolutely nothing wrong with being a size fourteen or any other size for that matter. We are all unique and deserve to be loved for being who we are, not for conforming to how society perceives we ought to look. I had been a skinny child, a chubby teenager with a perm, an anorexic young adult and a buxom size fourteen woman in her twenties with fantastic enormous boobies. I stood there in that changing room as a slim woman in her thirties with stress bags under her eyes having a hissy fit over a stupid dress. I had been every single one of those people and I had been loved throughout by those that mattered to me. No matter how I looked, how many packets of crisps I ate or how many times I had sobbed at my skinny reflection when I starved myself I was truly loved through it all. I had been loved deeply for being me by everyone except, well, me. That had to change and it started right then, as Amber and I walked out of the changing room and I stuck a mental finger up at my lack of self-love and told it to do one. I was perfect as I was, and I was going to teach myself that being me was enough.

36

Amidst my wedding fever and general excitement, Oscar had continued to bury himself in his job-hunting and travelled the length and breadth of the UK in search of work. It wasn't long before one new contact led to another and he was applying for commercial piloting jobs both at home and abroad. After rejections and dead end enquiries Oscar didn't give up and flew to the Channel Islands one day for an impromptu interview with the local airline for the islands. He loved it there after just one day and pinned his hopes on a job offer. Oscar practically leapt for his mobile phone when it rang a few days later and a Guernsey number flashed up. The job was his and he had all that he wished for as he leapt around our home delighted and buzzing with excited chatter about a fresh start and a new home for us. It was music to my ears and, although I knew it would be a wrench to leave my home and career, I was eager to get going on this new adventure of ours. Not only were we getting married but we were now also moving overseas to a beautiful group of islands that had many more hours of sunshine than the UK. I barely slept a wink that night as the news sunk in and I dreamed of a little cottage by the sea.

The airline wanted Oscar to start immediately and within a few days Oscar had packed up all of his belongings into his little red car and removed every trace of his existence from what had become our home. As I looked around the house before he left it pained me to see the lack of his toothbrush next to mine and a wardrobe that no longer contained his pink shirts and woollen jumpers. My space was my own again, except this time it was only temporary for I would be joining Oscar as soon as I could find a job there for myself. I sat next to Oscar on our sofa and watched as he curled his hands around both Hester and Paddington's faces and told them he loved them. He showered them with kisses on their noses, tickled their backs and then he turned to me. I held him in my arms and told him just how much I was going to miss him and that I loved him dearly. We had not spent more than a few nights apart since he moved in and the thought of living separately left Oscar sobbing heart-wrenching tears. He was inconsolable as he looked at me and then the strangest thing happened. A moment I will never forget.

Oscar looked up at me once more and a light turned off inside of him. Every speck of emotion and love he had held close appeared to vanish as his eyes darkened. He looked at me coldly and almost without recognition. There were no tears, no expressions, and he spoke calmly and with certainty.

'It's fine. Nothing can ever hurt me like losing my son did.'

With that one sentence Oscar stood up, gently shrugged off my attempts to hug him goodbye and drove away without so much as another word or gesture. I felt the bond between us die. That day was the last time I ever witnessed an emotional response from Oscar other than anger, the last time I ever saw his tears or felt any form of love and companionship by his side. By the time I moved to Guernsey three months later to start my administration job at the airline and to move into our new home he had become an entirely different person, unrecognisable as the man I had fallen in love with. On that day however I knew none of what was to come and I was left bewildered as I stood by the front door. I shook my head as I tried to recall if I had imagined the sudden change in Oscar. It was the eve of the first anniversary of my mother's passing and my mind was awash with my own emotions. I had learnt in the year that the grieving process never truly ends but that it does become easier to manage as time passes. I had come to understand that loss changes shape as you learn to carry it more easily in your daily life and by the end of the first year I was at least able to carry mine without feeling like my knees would buckle under me. I had become engaged and I was moving overseas. I would be leaving my career, my home, my family and my friends. I thought of it all as I closed my front door after Oscar's departure and closed that first year without Mum.

The house felt empty and I noticed Oscar's absence every day when I entered rooms and expected to find him there. Paddington was his usual bustling self and took great delight in having more room in our bed at night time. He sprawled across Oscar's side of the bed like a lion and didn't seem to miss him at all. Hester on the other hand needed more reassurance and was bereft without Oscar in her pack. She was listless and held her tail low as she refused her dinner and slept quietly through the days. As she lost weight and became incontinent I took her to the vet but they could find nothing wrong with her. No bladder infections, no stomach issues, nothing. Hester continued this way for weeks, wetting her bed and leaking without even realising it every time she stood up. She was jumpy at the slightest sound and stayed mostly in her bed. I was sick with worry and returned to the vet regularly for further tests, though I suspected Hester was grieving and there was little I could do to soothe her. If only I had been able to let her know Oscar would return to her, that everything would be fine.

Meanwhile on Guernsey, Oscar was settling in to his apartment by the sea and truly loving being overseas. After his tearful goodbye I wasn't sure what to expect of him the first time he Skyped after settling in. Part of me thought he would be lonely and unsettled after moving away but I could see the happiness in his eyes as he described the beautiful island and how peaceful it was. He told me how genuinely delighted he was with his new job, how friendly everyone had been and how much he enjoyed living alone. It was a joy to see him so happy with what he had achieved and it wasn't long before on subsequent Skype calls he admitted brightly that he didn't miss us at all and there was a gorgeous leggy blonde at the office he couldn't help but admire each day. Clearly he was in his element.

37

A month later it was my turn to visit Guernsey for a job interview. Admittedly it wasn't my dream applying for an administrative role but I knew it would be the start of island life for us and I was eager to explore. I had missed Oscar, Hester had continued to be unwell and I needed to see him, to know we were still a team.

As the plane banked across the island I practically fizzed with excitement and told the air hostess that my fiancé worked for the same airline and that we were moving there. I was incredibly excited and nervous as I looked down upon a tiny pillow of an island that was dotted with cottages, winding lanes and a patchwork of fields that ended abruptly at cliffs and a turquoise ocean below. Welcome to Guernsey. Summer was certainly beautiful there and I hadn't even landed yet. Oscar met me at arrivals after his shift and strode towards me in his uniform. He looked calm and confident, more so than I had ever seen him, and it was no surprise that nearby girls followed him with their eyes as he passed. He looked fantastic and folded me into his arms before gently leading me to his car. As he drove us to his apartment I was torn between showering kisses upon Oscar's cheeks in my need to be close to him and admiring the scenery passing us by. As it was, my kisses were not especially well received and I soaked up the views of pretty stone walls covered in flowers, boxes of vegetables and honey for sale at every lane end and ponies trotting in nearby fields. It was like stepping back in time and everyone we passed seemed to be smiling and happy to be alive. As the turquoise ocean greeted us in the distance at one road junction I realised why. Guernsey was perfect, a haven from the modern world, and I could already see why Oscar loved being there.

Oscar and I had always celebrated our special occasions, reunions and time together with food and wine and I was looking forward to a night at his apartment with meats and cheeses, our usual stash of pork pies, red wine, olives and crackers galore. Oscar absolutely *loved* red wine and I had bought him a special bottle to celebrate being together again. I entered the apartment and noticed it was light and airy, perfect for our cosy time together and also ideal for Oscar living on his own. It was compact, neat and peaceful. Though I couldn't help but also notice how unfurnished it was as I wondered between the open plan kitchen/living space and the bedroom. It felt empty of life and Oscar hadn't put pictures up or adorned the spaces with the cards and photographs I had sent him. Instead the only items on view were a meditation chair and some new spiritual books. I was surprised to see these given that spiritual work had led to a painful road of addiction and loss for Oscar in his past. He just couldn't control his involvement in it if he started and had told me as much many months before. I recalled my promise to help Oscar if he lost his balance and he started spiritual work again. I was to be the person that would speak up and stop him before it was too late and Oscar had promised he would trust me and listen to me in the event that it happened, though neither of us ever thought it was likely. He was happy living a 'normal' human life and we had joked and laughed that he would be a fool not to learn from his past. Those words rang in my ears as Oscar wrapped his arms around my waist and brought me back to the present. I brushed my thoughts aside as Oscar handed me a glass of the red wine I had given him and I inhaled its dark, rich nose.

'Oh this smells amazing, try it love. Where's your glass? Are you not having any darling?' I asked innocently.

'Nah. I don't really drink anymore,' Oscar said as he shrugged off his jacket and my enquiry.

'Really? Wow, that's a huge change for you. How come?' I asked as I inhaled the scent of autumn fruits and vanilla from my glass.

'Well, you know. I just, sweetie, it's bad for me and isn't really...' Oscar's words trailed off as he disappeared into the bedroom to change.

'Oh, okay.' I shrugged.

There wasn't much to be said on the matter and I headed for the fridge eagerly in search of our evening picnic of local Guernsey cheeses and meats. No good bottle of wine was complete without cheese after all.

'Oh! Oscar, the um fridge? It's kind of empty. Are we not having a meal tonight? I thought we'd have our usual picnic. Guernsey must produce some amazing deli foods and I can't wait to try them.' I was practically salivating at the thought.

'No sweetie, no meats or cheese. I have some rice and some mung beans in the cupboard. Help yourself if you'd like to make some dinner. I'm not hungry,' Oscar shouted from the bedroom.

'Say *what* beans? Mong? Ming? Ah, *mung*. The label clearly says mung. Since when do you eat mung beans and rice? And apparently absolutely nothing else other than peppermint tea,' I muttered under my breath as I searched the cupboards for anything resembling food. They were empty other than one can of chick peas, a packet of vegetable stock cubes, a carton of juice, herbal tea and various spices.

This was weird. Of course they were only a packet of beans and quite lovely looking beans at that. All green, round and shiny like bald heads. I love vegetarian food, having been vegetarian for fifteen years until bacon seduced me, and lentils, rice, herbal teas and vegetables in abundance were always a staple of my diet. But this wasn't about me. Oscar was a carnivore to excess ever since I had known him and thought meat should be eaten with every dinner if possible. He was about as far from vegetarian as I could imagine yet now he apparently only ate cheerful-looking green beans. Oh, and rice. Something wasn't right and I felt anxiety rise within me but I ignored it. They were just beans and perhaps he hadn't been paid for his work yet.

We passed a very quiet evening together as Oscar told me about his time on the island. I waited patiently for the right moment to mention the changes I saw in him and listened as he told me soothingly that it was nothing to worry about. Yes he had started spiritual work again but it was okay as he was also working full time and so wasn't losing his balance. He placed his hand on my knee and assured me that he wasn't becoming addicted or withdrawn, he had it under control. He was merely meditating daily and enjoying reading some new spiritual books that he felt helped him find his balance. Yes he had decided to stop drinking and yes he was also restricting his eating but it was no big deal. He stroked my hair lovingly as he spoke and then proudly stood up, lifted his shirt and pointed to himself whilst exclaiming about the weight he had lost. He beamed at me and said he had never been happier. I couldn't deny that Oscar did look very healthy, was making sense and didn't seem withdrawn other than being a little less affectionate with me than I was used to. I let it go as we went to bed. I was hoping for a night of passion, we hadn't seen each other for *weeks*, but Oscar took up his spiritual book almost immediately and then promptly fell asleep. I lay awake staring at the ceiling.

'What the f*ck is that?!' I exclaimed as I sat bolt upright in the early morning light and peered through my sleepy eyes.

'Good morning sweetie, it's my alarm for meditation,' Oscar chimed in response.

'Alarm? What the...' I mumbled in my confusion at being awake during what felt like the middle of the night.

'*Oscar!* It is still *dark*! What kind of time is it?' I reached for my mobile phone.

It was precisely 5am. There was only one thing worth being awake for at 5am and that was not meditation. I wiggled my way under the duvet and snuggled closer to Oscar.

'Well you know we could always cuddle a bit first, maybe show me how much you've been missing me...' It was impossible to sound seductive at 5am, I sounded like a pervert.

'No thank you. Time to meditate,' Oscar chimed yet again and leapt from the bed eagerly.

I was just a little bit annoyed that Oscar was putting meditation ahead of our sex life and swore quietly into the pillow that I would talk to him later about it. Being 5am, I then promptly fell asleep until Oscar woke me an hour later by leaping back into bed just as eagerly as he had left it earlier.

'Honey wake up. Wake up sweetie, I need to tell you something,' Oscar said excitedly.

'What is it darling?' I smoothed the hair from his forehead lovingly despite my earlier annoyance.

'Well, first you have to promise not to get annoyed and not to say anything. You just have to listen. Okay?' He sat cross legged in front of me like a child, wide-eyed, smiling and innocent in his tone of voice.

'Okay, that's a little strange. Can I respond afterwards? Can I speak then?' This felt like a game and I giggled at what on earth he was planning.

'No. Not really, no. You just need to listen and then take it in and own it. Don't react or respond in any way at all.' Oscar furrowed his brow to make the point clearly and held his hand palm up in front of himself as if to set a boundary between us.

'Oh. Well, okay love, if it's that important to you I can do that. So what's going on?' I propped myself up with pillows.

'Well I have been having such incredible times meditating, this journey is blissful. Something really important came to me during my meditation just now that I *have* to share with you. Wow, it's amazing and you must hear it and own it for yourself. It's not about me; it's about you and you must not react at all. Oh this is all so revealing and great for me,' Oscar exclaimed as he clapped his hands together and his smile returned.

'Okay.' I couldn't decide if he was going to say something good or bad. His light tone of voice suggested good but the reminder not to react and furrowed eyebrows suggested I may not like it.

'So, I had this profound moment where my mind and heart were so clear and I realised that I *really* don't want to live with you or be with you anymore. There is a *huge* part of me that doesn't want you at all in my life. I don't need you and I love being on my own. I don't want to marry *you*! But it doesn't matter, because the other part of me loves you so very much my sweetie. So it really is amazing realising all of this within me and I couldn't wait to share it with you! Wow!' Oscar was practically brimming over with excitement and looked so proud of himself.

I took a deep breath to respond. How could I not say something, anything to that revelation? I was absolutely devastated at hearing those words. He didn't want to be with me? Since when? Oscar quickly lifted his hand up in front of himself as if to stop me.

'No sweetie. Remember not to say anything,' he reminded me in a sing song voice.

'This is yours to own and you must not allow yourself to react, remember. Oh it'll be so good for you! Ugh, are you upset?' Oscar pulled himself up and away from the bed and looked disgusted.

'You *must not react* Kathryn. Get a grip of yourself. You know it's good for you and for me as well. Stop over reacting like a child. You're pathetic and you always do this. This is why part of me doesn't want to be with you, you have to stop it.' A more serious and exasperated tone of voice this time, as Oscar stared at me.

I tried to keep a calm face and hold the tears in my eyes. I just wanted him to hold me and soothe me yet I was angry, deeply upset and so confused. What was I supposed to do? Apparently I should feel nothing at that revelation because there was nothing to be upset about according to Oscar. I tried harder to hold my emotion in and I said nothing until my tears faded away inside of me.

Oscar was delighted with my lack of a response and leapt back in to bed telling me that *now* we could snuggle. As he nestled in behind me and drifted back to sleep I cried into my pillow.

In stark contrast to the confusion and misery I had felt that morning, Guernsey was full of sunshine that day as I explored every nook and cranny of the island within walking distance. I expected Oscar to be quiet and withdrawn given his frustration earlier on and I was hurting inside but he was excitable once more and took my hand as he pulled me along pretty lanes towards the coast. I touched my hands to pots of golden honey perched on top of ageing stone walls and tomatoes bright and shiny as buttons, tucked amongst boxes of eggs and punnets of strawberries. Every corner we turned had more of those goods for sale with honesty boxes for the small change it took to purchase the locally grown food. The hair whipped away from my face as we turned yet another bend in the lane and then stopped in front of the ocean. It took my breath away seeing that vast expanse of ocean and I longed for the time I would live here. We explored the coastal path shaded with old oak trees and came upon a hotel and restaurant in our wanderings. It was the perfect spot for lunch and I discovered from the friendly manager that this hotel allowed dogs to stay in their rooms. I wondered if perhaps one day the Bears and I would be there together. In the meantime Oscar had decided he did drink alcohol after all and ordered us a bottle of prosecco to go with the lavish meat dishes he ordered for both of us. I said nothing.

After a glorious day of sunshine and bubbles together everything was normal, nothing had changed with Oscar and I felt the comfort of that familiarity as I drifted towards asleep. Perhaps he was just adjusting to a new chapter in his life and I was overreacting, being too emotional? Oscar had said as much and I trusted him to always be truthful with me. Perhaps I needed to change? My mind wandered to and fro with a lack of answers and eventually settled on thoughts of my job interview the next day. I wasn't especially nervous until the time of the interview and I needn't have been at all. The people at the airline were friendly, keen for me to join their warm and caring team and seemed impressed with my skills and experience. I walked away knowing I could settle in there and that the job was mine. The rest of my short visit was spent exploring the island, revelling in knowing I would soon be living there and, most importantly, house-hunting. We needed somewhere to call our own and we visited apartments nestled in the town, cosy cottages tucked away down quiet lanes and windswept stone houses alongside sandy beaches. We couldn't for the life of us afford any of them just yet but it was a dream to at least be looking together and thinking up plans for the future.

As we walked through one cottage that I particularly loved for its pretty garden I realised just how much I had to look forward to. Within the space of one visit I had fallen in love with the island, had a job lined up and was looking at houses with the man I loved.

Life didn't get better than this and that feeling followed me all the way back to Shropshire.

38

My bubble burst back at No.8 when I realised that Hester was still suffering from the stress of Oscar being away and that, during the days and weeks since my return, Oscar had gradually become distant again. He no longer Skyped and was distracted and agitated whenever we spoke on the telephone, which wasn't often in any case. He stopped telling me he loved me and spent his time at home alone whenever he was not at work. And then one weekend he announced he was visiting us and that he couldn't wait to see us all. By which point I just didn't know how to feel anymore. I was strung out from trying to keep up with his mood changes from one day to the next.

In spite of everything that had been happening recently I truly loved Oscar and was fidgeting with excitement and nerves when I met him at the airport in arrivals. I practically ran into his arms only to be pushed away as he looked around embarrassed. I had hoped he would be pleased to see me, though sadly he was cold and looked blankly at me whenever we talked as I drove us home.

On the other hand his reunion with Hester was perfect. I watched as Oscar walked into the garden to meet her, he had managed to sneak up to the back door without her realising his presence, and I watched as Hester went berserk. Oscar crouched down low to greet her with his arms held wide open and she ran into them, letting out what I can only describe as squeals of delight as she twisted and turned in the air and licked Oscar's face. She made sounds of pure relief and joy that I had never heard from her before as she wiggled through his legs and stamped her back feet when he tickled her thighs and rubbed her back. And as if by magic, her incontinence and stress were finally cured. By the next morning she was well again and symptom free.

I was eager to chat about the progress I had been making with our wedding plans that weekend and share with Oscar my thoughts on writing our own vows for one another. We had always planned to do so and I had written a draft of mine to share with him. No sooner had I approached the subject than Oscar sat me down on our bed and told me he felt wedding vows were meaningless and he wasn't bothered about them anymore. He told me that he wasn't just marrying me, he wanted to marry the whole world with his love and he didn't need vows to express that. Whilst he loved me he didn't need me and would never share his money with me (not that I had ever asked for any) and he would never allow me to work anything less than full time unless I earned more than him, which was fairly impossible given he was a pilot earning a small fortune. He explained that he was reading an incredible book concerning a yogi who hadn't eaten for a year whilst living in a cave and he was working towards doing the same. Instead of a honeymoon he thought we could both go on a month's silent retreat.

'It will be good for me, for us Kathryn, so why can't you just understand all of this and support me? Why do you look so bewildered and dismissive of it all? Why did you have to keep disappointing me this way? For crying out loud why can't you just rein yourself in and stop being so, well, you?!' Oscar shouted angrily.

Because I was terrified I was losing the man I loved to an addiction I knew was creeping up on him just like it had in his past. He was changing boundaries almost daily, he wouldn't listen to me or believe me when I voiced gentle concerns and I didn't honestly know if it was okay, if it was right for me, to be told all of those things and yet again be expected not to react. My voice, my part in our relationship, had gone. I was supposed to just trust that my beloved knew best for me and was right when he told me how our future life would be but it didn't seem right. He loved me, so surely he wouldn't manipulate me or lie. Yet everything he was telling me and doing of late felt very *wrong* to me. Life didn't taste of love and certainty anymore and doubts began to niggle at my mind.

Before Oscar returned to Guernsey we had our leaving party and friends from choir and work came out to raise their glasses and see us off. We all huddled into my favourite local pub for dinner and I looked around at the smiling faces of the people that had seen me through tough times and celebrated milestones with me for the past eight years. I couldn't believe I would soon be without my friends and I knew I was going to miss them very much. I couldn't help but notice that Oscar was no longer the person they had known before he moved away. He was withdrawn, quiet and sat in the corner sipping his sparkling water all evening as we tucked into bottles of good wine, hearty food and conversation. He barely spoke to any of our friends, those very same friends he had previously held close to his heart and spent hour upon hour talking with and laughing. They began to ask me if he was okay and all I could say was that I didn't know. As more questions came I began to ask myself if I could I live with him for the rest of my life. I was packing up my entire life to be with Oscar, I had handed in my notice at my current work after almost eight years there and I was due to move to Guernsey in a matter of weeks. I just didn't have time to think, it was full steam ahead and I had to trust we would be okay.

In the final weeks my dad and I packed up my life in Shropshire as I left my work and said goodbyes to friends. We found tenants and I couldn't believe that someone else would soon be living in my home, sleeping in my bedroom and making it their own. On my final night at home I placed a present for the tenants on the kitchen sideboard; a little something for them to celebrate the beginning of their next chapter, as I started mine. I walked around empty rooms and corners piled with boxes and furniture ready to be moved. Those rooms had been my home with my first fiancé and the Bears until just four years ago and then they had become my fortress, my place to hide when he left and my mother faded away. I had cried against those walls and slid down them in moments of despair, I had leant against them admiring the view and the Bears had wiped their noses across the windows more times than I could remember to welcome me home. I had made jam in that beautiful sage green kitchen and celebratory cakes for my loved ones every year. I had sung my heart out to the radio and the bird song in the early mornings as I leant over the stable door that led into the garden, with a cup of tea and homemade marmalade on toast in hand. I had created my beautiful garden of curved flower beds and shrubs when I first moved in and the house was being renovated after it had flooded. That same garden had been overrun by real rats and by two enormous Airedales that turned it into a mud pit as they grew up and raced across the lawn. There was the dry patch of lawn from too many BBQs with friends and the fence panel that

Paddington had chewed through to see the chickens next door. I had celebrated every stage of my career with bottles from my little wine rack and I had hauled my piano up those narrow stairs in defiance of limitations and sad times. I had sung choir songs, Christmas songs and happy birthdays and fallen asleep by my log fire time and again. Dad had created a miniature library in my spare room, I had the pink bedroom I had always wanted and I had a lemon tree that I adored. Whilst it only produced one lemon a year, which was dry and tasteless, I sliced it lovingly into a gin and tonic every year and relished it. I had let my heart breathe again and had welcomed Oscar into that home to create more memories within. Before I knew it, my life had come to this and I was leaving it all behind. I peered out of the window at my tiny car piled high with belongings for the Bears and I, all we would need for our long journey across England and the ocean to Guernsey. I had loved my home so much, it was everything to me, but I knew it was time to go. I was as ready as I ever would be to pull my roots out of the ground and take a leap of faith towards what promised to be a wonderful life by the ocean. And so I tucked in the corners of a box labelled Books and quietly made my way to bed for my last night at home.

I awoke very early the next morning to a cup of tea from my darling dad, my ever faithful friend, and together we had a last breakfast at No.8. Dad kindly unscrewed my favourite pine cone door knocker, a reminder of where I had lived, and replaced it with a new one for the tenants. It was time to go. The Bears leapt excitedly into the back seats of my car and quickly they squirreled about and found the treats I had hidden for them under the covers as I turned to Dad. We took one last look at the house, spoke fond farewells and waved to each other from our respective cars. Tooting horns briefly, we drove away as the sun came up and moved towards the next chapter of our lives.

39

I had hoped to be met by the loving arms of Oscar on the day we arrived at Guernsey but he was flying his passengers between the islands and had sent his friends Tim and Ali to meet me instead. My first taste of Guernsey that day was following this couple along tiny lanes I recognised from my previous visit and to the hotel that accepted dogs, which was to be our home for the next month until we moved into our new house. Whilst I had been busy in Shropshire Oscar had found us a cottage to call our own and we would be in before Christmas. Tim and Ali welcomed me as they helped me unpack my belongings into the hotel apartment and I was truly disappointed when Oscar messaged to confirm he wasn't going to visit me that first evening after work because he wanted to meditate at his home, which was all of a three minute drive away. Eager to find some good in the day I accepted the inevitable and took the Bears along the coastal path next to the hotel. The sky and ocean were bright blue all around us as we dipped down paths and along jagged cliffs that framed the beaches. As dusk finally set in, a barn owl flew overhead and we rounded the path to the hotel. There was Oscar sitting on the doorstep, looking tired and cautious of us. We embraced, us eager, him not so much, and then after a brief hello he drove back home.

My first few weeks living on the island were mostly filled with one of life's greatest activities, eating. I couldn't get enough of the fresh produce and the incredibly rich and delicious Guernsey butter. It was butter heaven and I devoured pound after pound of it on crackers. Like a child in a new sweet shop, I was overexcited and eager to try everything. Oscar was soon caught up in my excitement and, whilst he didn't go to town as much on the butter as I did, he seemed to enjoy himself when he stayed at the hotel and I presented him with novel food delights. Between all the eating and exploring the local beaches I found time to start my new job and soon settled into my administrative duties and felt a part of the team. They allowed me to visit the Bears each lunch time and on a Friday evening we all went for drinks after work. I was included, just as I had been in Shropshire, and before long I became a member of the Guernsey choral society, I found two wonderful friends in Tim and Ali and discovered the delights of the local three-tiered honey cake at the garden centre. That little green island dotted between England and France had it all and by the time Oscar and I moved into our new house a month later I was settled with my new life and also at the hotel. It was time to make a home with Oscar and for him to leave his much-loved peaceful apartment behind. I knew leaving his solitary existence behind was causing him distress and tension. In the weeks since I had arrived and explored the island, he had mostly busied himself with his work and whatever it is he chose to do at his apartment. I saw glimmers of the old enthusiastic Oscar when we went out with friends or explored a new beach together but his mental absence was always apparent to me if not to anyone else. The light in his eyes had mostly vanished other than when he talked about his spiritual pursuits and the joys of his yoga and daily chanting.

By the time moving day arrived Oscar had already unpacked his handful of boxes at our new home whilst I was busy admiring our cute little cottage for the first time. He had chosen well and I liked the garden that sloped steeply upwards and afforded us a view across the other rooftops from the top area of lawn. I couldn't help but notice how beautifully curved the old walls were upstairs and how my piano would fit perfectly under the staircase. I also couldn't help but notice how little Oscar had brought with him and I soon came to realise he had completed a ruthless clear out of clothes and belongings prior to moving; in order to grow spiritually and let go of attachments to belongings and sentimentality. The pile of boxes that arrived from England was enormous in comparison to Oscar's empty collection and they filled the lounge like oversized beige Lego blocks waiting to be unpacked. I immediately began to empty them whilst Oscar waved goodbye to the removal men and Hester poked her nose into every available box to find her toys. I eagerly pulled out favourite photographs and furnishings that would turn the cottage into our home. As I turned to Oscar to show him a particularly beautiful photograph frame we had chosen together and asked for his help unpacking he dismissed me with a wave of his hand saying he didn't want to be a part of this. He was going upstairs to meditate and chant and we could unpack in a month or so.

And so that was how the unpacking proceeded in the coming weeks. Every day Oscar studiously avoided each box and eyed them suspiciously before retreating upstairs to meditate for hours on end whilst I unpacked alone and admittedly turned my music up a little louder to disturb him when I was feeling childish. I began to wonder yet again who this stranger was that I had chosen to live with. The excitement of making a home together had disappeared and we were getting married in less than six months' time. I had six beautiful red wine glasses and yet there was now only one person to share a glass of wine with anyway, me. It wasn't about the wine so much as it was about companionship and shared moments. By the time I finished the unpacking Oscar had made his disgust clear at the number of mugs, glasses, cutlery, plates, books, clothes, shoes etc we had and reduced the contents of the kitchen by half. The wine glasses remained well-hidden as did my favourite tea pot and ridiculous knitted tea cosy. They were the must-have items of a thirty-something year old woman and I would not be parted with them for love nor money.

After I had hung the last picture I paused to look up at our home and realised how lonely I felt there each day despite the familiarity of my possessions and paintings on the walls. It looked cosy and yet felt empty. I hadn't really noticed initially but the second bedroom was slowly being turned into a meditation room and Oscar had replaced his entire wardrobe with expensive new clothes we couldn't afford. He was no longer sharing a laundry basket with me and instead insisted that he store and wash his clothes separately. I was told not to touch them. Oscar barely spoke to me and often when I approached he gestured me away with his hands as if I were an unwanted seagull trying to steal his chips. He began to encourage me almost constantly to give away my beloved books in order to improve my spiritual energy and asked me to try meditation as well. He was worried about how stressed I appeared to be and thought it would bring us closer. When I explained my concerns that he was becoming addicted to his spiritual pursuits he began to put his hand in front of his face and tell me to stay away for I was bad energy and he didn't want me near him. Every day I came home from work I was greeted with The Hand and ordered to stay away from him with my bad energy until I learnt to control myself and change. The concept of me having anything worse than bad flatulence, let alone bad energy, was new to me but before long he ignored me entirely and when I tried to greet him each day he looked through me as if I didn't exist. It was horrible and on one such day I walked in and overheard Oscar on the telephone telling his mother he was worried I was going to have a breakdown and perhaps needed to be committed to a mental hospital. He told his mother he wanted to help me. I was so embarrassed and hurt that I didn't mention what I had heard and instead I quietly wondered if Oscar was right about me. Perhaps I was the problem and, as Oscar had told me many times since my arrival, any reaction on his part was my fault because I had behaved so dreadfully in the first place.

Should I be committed? Had I really caused all of this?

By the time I asked myself those questions I was riddled with anxiety and didn't truly know my own mind anyway. I found myself constantly apologising for existing, trying to be as small as possible in the presence of Oscar and yet still trying to voice my concerns about him when I found the courage to speak up. It was to no avail, he merely held his hand up even more to quieten me, and eventually I agreed to do three things he asked of me.

1. Go and see a hypnotherapist
2. Give away my books
3. Take up daily meditation

It is my deepest regret to this day that I didn't have the strength to stand up to Oscar and say no and walk away. Whilst those requests were not exactly extreme, I didn't want to do any of them and yet equally I loved Oscar and so felt I *had* to. Those beautiful books of all shapes and sizes were my link to my childhood, my prized possessions that I had collected and had been gifted to me over many years. Some were given to me by my mother and reminded me of her in many ways. I still cannot believe I gave them away so lightly and that I didn't at least tell somebody what was happening in my life. Maybe they could have stopped me from making such a mistake. My books went the same way as all of the other items Oscar didn't want us to have, off to the charity bins, and I then went to the hypnotherapist. The therapist was a lovely elderly gentleman with soft eyes, fluffy white eyebrows and a firm handshake. He asked me gently why I was there.

'Because apparently something is wrong with me but I don't know what it is. My fiancé is worried I am mentally ill and I know he wants to help. I truly love him. Please help me,' I begged.

I assumed in my confused state of mind that Oscar was right and completed my therapy session and practised with the hypnotherapy CD daily. Despite alarm bells constantly making my ears ring, or perhaps that was tinnitus, I tried my hardest to become a different person. One evening Oscar walked in on me sitting in the bathroom sobbing into a towel as quietly as possible after my shower. I was deeply distressed at the turn my life had taken and was trying not to show my pain. Oscar briskly shouted at me to stop being pathetic and such an attention-seeker. He told me to stand on my own two feet and stop being needy and disgusting. He ordered me to get dressed and go to bed, as if I were a naughty child. After that humiliation I went running often, I walked for hours, I sang my heart out and played the piano until my fingers ached as much as my heart. I made an effort to lose weight, to be glossy and beautiful like the air hostesses I knew he admired and to always smile. During every dog walk I held a rose quartz crystal in my hand and constantly repeated to myself a mantra Oscar had suggested.

It is okay. I am loved, I am a good person and Oscar loves me so much.

I am calm and happy and there is nothing wrong. This is just me overreacting and I can change who I am.

I cried throughout my walks when it didn't change anything about who I was as a person and Oscar encouraged me to just try harder. As for the meditation, that didn't go very well. I practised both morning and night but every single time I began I nodded forwards and fell fast asleep. On many days I awoke to find Oscar in the spare room chanting before dawn and meditating deeply. The look of ecstasy in his eyes when he emerged was quite something and I could only liken it to how I thought someone on drugs would look. He was glassy-eyed, had dilated pupils and appeared drowsy after every session. His practices gave him a high like no other legal substance could. No wonder he had no time for me. I barely made him smile.

By the time we approached Christmas I realised I had been living on Guernsey for almost two months. We were still due to be married in less than five months and my mind drifted towards the final stages of wedding planning. As fate would have it that was also the time that Oscar's mind did the same and he announced he was no longer going to wear a wedding ring because it would interfere with his spiritual energy. He had always wanted a ring and I loved the idea of seeing my husband with a wedding band; a silent declaration of our commitment to one another. I was disappointed by his news and lack of discussion but I was even more flummoxed when Oscar made his second announcement; that we would never have sex again. Ever. I almost laughed out loud but then he explained sincerely that it was a waste of his spiritual energy and there was no place for it in his life. He could orgasm just by lying next to me – now that I would have liked to see except I know I am not that good. Of course I tried to change his mind, for what young(ish) red-blooded female wouldn't want to have a sex life with their husband-to-be? Nothing worked and eventually I gave up. Oscar's third announcement pre-Christmas was that the only thing he wanted to cuddle in bed was a soft grey toy cat a friend had given us. When I tried to cuddle Oscar (with the assurance it was for affection purposes only) Oscar outright refused each day unless the grey cat could be cuddled as well and positioned between us. When I said no he refused to even put his arms around me. I acquiesced and so began a bizarre ritual of cuddling that always involved the grey cat and often didn't involve me at all.

I made one last attempt to bring some normality back to my life after that and asked Oscar to take an additional day away from work before our wedding so we could visit family. I thought the time with loved ones would be a blessed relief from what my life had become on Guernsey and it would help bring Oscar back on track. As I leant on the spare bedroom doorframe and put forward my request I watched Oscar turn visibly angry and listened as he shouted at me because he had already submitted his annual leave form for that year. As I began to step sideways out of his way and towards the landing he slammed the door hard on my outstretched arm. Oscar leant on the door with his body weight whilst shouting for me to go away and I yelped that he was hurting my arm. No sooner had Oscar opened the door than I slapped him across the face as I backed away fearfully and found myself pushed to the ground with force. I lay on the soft carpet in a heap of tears unable to believe I had actually slapped Oscar and I realised this was the second time in our relationship Oscar had been physically abusive towards me. He had promised a year before that it would never happen again and yet there we were.

I sat on our bed in shock and whispered to myself *this isn't right, this just isn't right*. I needed to be anywhere but at home and I had nowhere to go. Even though I knew what had happened wasn't right or acceptable I thought maybe it was my fault again. After everything that had happened in the previous weeks with Oscar I thought I was to blame even if I couldn't understand why. At precisely that moment, Oscar walked into our bedroom cheerfully.

'What's the matter my honey bunch? Why are you crying?' Oscar chimed in his sing song voice as he pouted and sat down next to me. He clapped his hands on his thighs theatrically.

'You...hit....me....Oscar, you...' I gasped.

'How could you?! You...promised...but...you...you hit me' I could barely get the words out between my tears as I leant away from his attempt to hold me. I didn't want his hands anywhere near me.

At that pathetic attempt to explain how I felt, Oscar laughed out loud heartily and looked at me seriously. He lowered his tone of voice and with a smirk he explained.

'Really sweetheart? You are really going to blame *me*? You should stop picking fights with people that are bigger than you darling. I will *always* win.'

You would think that was the moment that finally broke us but it wasn't, for that came with Oscar's fourth and final announcement after the New Year.

40

'I am leaving you. I am leaving you to find God and your bad energy is stopping me. I am going to become a celibate and live in an ashram in India.'

Oscar stood in the lounge in his fluffy baby blue dressing gown and tartan slippers, clutching his favourite spiritual book close to his chest, as he announced his departure from my life. He looked vulnerable and his eyes shone with unshed tears when he spoke and then he went cold. His face turned stern and then into a broad and happy smile. In that small fraction of time he had set himself free, admitted his truth as it were, and the relief was visible on his face. I had walked in from work just moments before and barely said hello before Oscar made that announcement. To say I was shocked is an understatement. I know we had our ups and downs but just three days before he had told me how much he loved me, how he couldn't imagine ever being without me. I couldn't quite believe my ears.

'You're what?' I said half smiling and with a look of confusion.

'You are leaving me to find God? You are going to live in an ashram as a celibate? Wow, well you might want to tell you parents all of this, as I'm sure they'd be just delighted to hear you are running away again.' I said sarcastically.

The hurt was rising within me as I started to suspect that perhaps it was true. Reason and logic told me that surely it was a sick joke and perhaps Oscar was having a bad day. It sounded ridiculous and there was no way he would go through with it.

Oscar strode confidently to the telephone and called his parents immediately. I couldn't believe it. He was actually going to speak to them and do this. Had I not been as distressed and involved in the situation I would have pulled up a front row seat and watched the moment unfold. I listened with my mouth wide open like a goldfish and felt both my heart and my life crumple around me as Oscar relayed his intention to his mum and dad. Without so much as any hesitation or apology he told them he was leaving me to find God and that yes he was going to live in an ashram as a celibate for the rest of his life. I could see his happiness and relief overflowing as he told them, his excitement at the prospect as he relaxed onto the sofa and leant back stretching easily. Oscar joked and laughed with his parents as they chatted about life in general and his plans. Of course I do not know how the conversation went at the other end but I knew then that Oscar was being serious. He neither looked at me nor acknowledged me when he mentioned my name and I walked away to the bathroom and focussed on trying to breathe.

As I sat on the cold toilet seat I realised that Oscar leaving me meant I had to leave Guernsey immediately because I was on his visa to live on the island. Without Oscar I had no right to be employed or living there and the rules were enforced quickly within such a small population. I telephoned my employer in between tears and explained I would not be coming back to work and that I had to leave. They knew the rules, they also knew Oscar had been erratic lately at work, but they were still shocked by his announcement. After I had spoken to my sister I calmed down enough to think clearly about what came next. I wondered if I could persuade Oscar to stay or if that was it. I left the bathroom and found Oscar sitting comfortably on the sofa reading his book again.

'Please don't leave me. Please Oscar, I can't do this again. I just can't do this. I love you and we can make it work. You don't mean this, surely you don't. You told me you loved me and *you* asked me to marry you remember. Please stay.' I begged.

My dignity climbed out of the window and I clutched at false hope one last time. Tears fell fast down my cheeks.

'I am going to bed now.' Oscar said coldly as he stood tall and walked past me towards the stairs.

'So that's it? That's *it?!* You announce you are leaving me, without so much as any warning or discussion and *THAT IS IT?!*' And there came my anger after and in between the tears as I shouted up the stairs after him.

Oscar ignored me and went upstairs as I paced in the kitchen angrily with the Bears at my feet. I eventually followed him and walked into our bedroom to find Oscar sitting serenely in our bed reading that God book of his yet again.

How dare you be so calm after what you have just done to me. How can you even find the clarity of mind to read after what you have just done?! And, most importantly, where the hell am I going to sleep?

Oscar had thrown the spare bed out the day before; in the name of spiritual cleansing apparently. Fantastic, what a great idea that was of his. I calmed myself before I spoke.

'Please Oscar. Please will you stay in a hotel tonight? I have nowhere to go and you threw our spare bed away.' I spoke as an adult, trying to reason with him.

'No Kathryn. This is my home. Stay in a hotel yourself, it's *your* problem not mine. Now if you don't mind I am trying to read.' He dismissed me with a wave of his hand.

'How dare you do this to me?! How dare you treat me so damn appallingly and expect *me* to be the one to find somewhere to stay. I have NOWHERE TO GO AND NOBODY TO GO TO you cruel, cold-hearted b*stard. Since when did I deserve any of this, any of the abuse you have doled out to me over the past few months? Since never, you piece of cr*p. You can shove your book right up your arse and rot in hell. Oh, and by the way, cuddling that damn soft cat toy instead of me? Really. F*cking. Weird.'

Those are the words I wish I had said at the time and yet it took me two and a half years to be able to write them out. I was hurting too much to speak when Oscar dismissed me with that wave of his hand. I just looked at him blankly, slammed the bedroom door after retrieving a change of clothes and walked away. That was the last time I ever saw Oscar. I stumbled down the stairs in shock and called the only two friends I had on Guernsey, Tim and Ali. Within minutes they picked me up and took me back to their apartment where I spent the night on their sofa. I lay awake all night as my mind churned and tears fell. For the second time in my life I had been left just before my wedding. How humiliating and shameful.

What is wrong with me? I have no trouble getting a man but I can't seem to keep one. Am I really that dreadful? Did I cause this just by being me? And how am I going to face the shame and judgement of telling everyone? I can't do this again; I don't have the strength anymore.

Oscar had left me in much the same way my first fiancé had; without talking about it, without letting me know gently or trying to fix what we had. He knew how long it had taken me to get over that first time and yet he did exactly the same thing both knowingly and ruthlessly. I contacted Amber in Shropshire when I couldn't bear to think anymore and she hit the roof at Oscar's behaviour. My dad was away from home and so I didn't let him know what had happened. It could wait until the next day. Unknown to me though, Amber contacted him immediately and before I could say 'left at the almost-altar not once but twice' he was driving through the night to come to Guernsey.

As the sun rose overhead I lay on the sofa glassy-eyed and uncaring and slumped deeper into my own mind. Despite my lethargy I was desperate to get home to my Bears. I had hated leaving them with Oscar and didn't trust him not to hurt them. By the time Tim drove me back home I knew Oscar would have left for work and my mobile phone confirmed I hadn't heard from him overnight. As I walked in to the cottage nothing had changed. The wedding acceptance cards were still lined up on the piano as I ran my fingers over the ivories, our photographs and tokens of time together were still on display on the walls and coffee tables and the house was peaceful and still. It was as if last night hadn't even occurred. I walked into the kitchen and, as I tossed more tissues into the bin, I saw that Oscar had thrown away the final wedding invitations I had given him just the day before for his colleagues. His beloved journal was also in there as well. It had taken me hours to make those beautiful invitations, I had been so happy with my ink and peony stamps, and already he had thrown them away as quickly as he had discarded me. I was nothing to Oscar anymore. He had walked away and would never look back, that much I knew about him.

How dare he throw those invitations away! And he hasn't even apologised! How could he....

On it went as my mind coursed with rage that early morning in between fits of crying and grief for what I had lost. I was absolutely furious with Oscar and barely kept myself in check when his parents rang and asked me kindly how I was coping.

Almost immediately they both apologised for Oscar and told me it wasn't my fault and that it was what Oscar always did in relationships. He couldn't cope with commitment and ran away chasing one addiction or another. They went into more detail and I only wished they had warned me two years previously. They asked if I felt Oscar had become addicted to spiritual work again and lost his way. I answered yes, absolutely, and that I had been trying for months to make that clear but nobody listened to me. They asked me for signs and I explained about his beloved book that encouraged him to starve himself and renounce all links to family and friends. I told them about his behaviour and about his journal that was now in the bin. Alexa asked me to take both the book and journal and post them to her in case they could find a way to help him. I felt deeply sorry for them and, despite my anger, did what they asked of me. And yes I also looked in his journal, which I should never have done, because I was desperate for any answer I could find. The contents shocked me with page upon page of references to being lost, broken, of being an angel and a demon and a clear need for help. He spoke of good and evil and there were pages of unlinked words I could barely understand. It was wrong of me to read any of it but I admit it gave me comfort, a way in which I could point and prove to myself I wasn't the problem. Well I thought that until I read the pages of insults towards me as well. That wasn't so comforting and left me doubting myself all over again.

I only had a few short hours to collect as many of my belongings I could fit into my car and leave the house before Oscar returned home. It is interesting what you choose to pack when you know you have limited time and space and in that panic most people chose valuable and sentimental items to save. I didn't even know what mine were until they were the first three things I reached for hastily and angrily.

1. Every single bottle of expensive champagne we (Oscar) had been given at Christmas
2. Toiletries for the bath
3. My favourite cheese grater

I never knew I had such an attachment to cheese and toiletries but apparently I did. After filling the car I took one last look around the cottage that had been the stage for much hurt and drama and I left without looking back. My heart raced as I sped away from the house and towards the hotel I had first stayed in when I arrived on Guernsey. I checked into that old familiar apartment and met Dad there later that day. The devastation washed over me again as I sobbed into Dad's arms and I realised that within the space of twenty four hours I had lost my fiancé, my home and my career. I had myself and two dogs to look after and yet I had lost all means of being able to do so. I didn't know if I was ever going to come back from that. I had thrown everything away to be with Oscar and now I was left with nothing. I drowned my sorrows in cheap hotel food and red wine.

The next day Dad and I boarded the ferry and hunkered down with our hangovers for a rough crossing back to England. It was horrendous, I felt seasick and numb, my eyes were raw from crying and I just lay on the dirty cold floor all the way there. I wasn't allowed on the car deck because it was unusually rough and I was miserable not knowing if Hester and Paddington were okay. I felt like giving up, then my rage at Oscar washed over me again and I resolved, with swear words, that I would not quit. Oscar was not going to be the end of me and somehow I would regain my life and sense of self. I had done it before and I would do it again, I was tougher than that. I talked all the way back to Cornwall with Dad as we drove more miles than I care to remember. I couldn't return to Shropshire, I had no job or home there anymore, and so Cornwall was to become my new home. We arrived, tired but in one piece, and so began another chapter of my life. As I pulled myself wearily into bed I logged onto Facebook and saw Oscar's profile picture had already been changed to one of him smiling and holding up a glass of champagne.

41

News of our separation travelled fast and I was overwhelmed by bouquets of flowers, cards and gifts of hope that arrived in Cornwall within a matter of days. People are kind when life throws a curveball and I was deeply touched by lovely words and the ways in which they made me feel less alone. Such compassion and understanding propelled me onwards during the difficult days where I grieved and wondered what to do with my life. I had lost so much in the past few years and I just couldn't cope with fighting back yet again to rebuild my life. I knew I needed to pull myself together enough to apply for jobs though and so I applied for everything going including my old job but based in Cornwall. It took all the strength I had left to telephone the office with the vacancy and explain my past experience in the role and also my circumstances when they asked why I had left the company and now wanted to return so soon. It was humiliating but the prospect of finding a job gave me something to focus on. I also knew early on that I needed to limit any further pain upon myself. I couldn't handle much more stress and I recalled the damage Graham and I had caused each other when we separated with our angry emails and fighting over possessions. With that in mind I cut all contact with Oscar. It was a relief to no longer have the threat of him over my shoulders and afterwards I slept for days. My dad dutifully banned me from answering the telephone in case Oscar tried to contact us and in those early weeks and months Dad stood metaphorically in front of me and protected me from it all. He was immovable and strong in the face of a situation that must have hurt him deeply.

I was however caught out once when I answered the telephone expecting my sister to call and was greeted by Oscar's voice, which flooded me with fear. He took up the opportunity to speak almost immediately.

'Was it worth it Kathryn? Really worth doing all of this and sending my journal to my parents?! I really don't know why you are complaining and crying - *you* got an expensive wedding dress out of it. And when are you going to accept it was your fault anyway? You did it *again*, you pushed away yet another fiancé with your crazy behaviour and constant need to destroy everything. Are you going to spend the rest of your life doing the same? Make it third time lucky hey Kathryn and push away the next fool that falls in love with you?' He whined cruelly at me.

As I put the telephone down I felt like all he said was true.

Both sets of parents handled the wedding cancellation and the sale of our house whilst I searched for jobs and went on long walks to try and find my sanity and rid myself of my tears yet again. I heard from my friends on Guernsey that Oscar had washed his hands of everything and moved back into his apartment immediately. It angered me deeply that during his contact with Dad he didn't once apologise and merely carried on cheerfully as if nothing had happened. I spoke to Oscar's parents often in those early weeks as they offered continual words of support and encouragement. They were going to visit Oscar just weeks after our separation and I had warned them of his unusual behaviour, fearful of what they may find and how it would upset them. They returned and told me happily that he was like a new man. Long gone were any connections to spiritual work and Oscar was in fine fettle. He had joined a gym, made new friends, become the party animal of the island and had taken up sport hunting, smoking and champagne to excess. They were delighted and yet confused as to why he hadn't mentioned our separation or asked after me during their visit. At the end of their time together Alexa had prompted him and Oscar merely shrugged and laughed. Apparently I had wanted to leave Shropshire anyway. I was of no concern.

That was confirmed to me when, on Valentine's Day, all of our furniture arrived from Guernsey. Oscar had taken nothing, absolutely nothing, and left me with his own belongings and boxes full of the letters, gifts and photographs I had given him as a couple when he lived on Guernsey alone. He had thrown it all in the removal van without so much as a thought to how that would affect me.

In spite of my efforts to move forwards as quickly as possible I couldn't stop chewing over everything and talked for hours with Dad about what had happened. I constantly questioned if there was something wrong with me. I was mentally broken and Dad watched me hang my head and apologise for everything I said or did. He wondered where his bright, strong and opinionated daughter had disappeared to under the influence of Oscar and asked me why on earth I had stayed with him and not told anyone what was happening. I was barely recognisable amidst the tears and constant chatter of my addled mind and Dad later told me he wondered if I would ever return to my old self, I was barely recognisable as his daughter. He refused to give up on me and listened as I talked on and on about the same things every day and then he repeated the same words of comfort, tough love and swear words directed at Oscar every day as well. It was a routine that allowed me the freedom to get it all out of my system rather than keep it in and it worked, it truly worked. Dad was my hero, the reason I didn't give up, and by the end of that first month in Cornwall the beginnings of my self-belief remerged like a tiny flower in spring. It was my thirty-third birthday and, whilst I was still deeply hurt and had baggy tired eyes, I ate my chocolate and orange cake with genuine joy. I stabbed the cake with my fork in conviction and announced to myself it was time to take responsibility for me and I was going to do it in style.

I will show the world that this woman is not going to quit, that I am going to find a way to let go of Oscar and emerge from the ashes of my past as a bright and slightly dusty phoenix. I may have two runaway fiancés in my past, which I admit is both rare and embarrassing, but I also have courage and strength by the gallon. I have not survived that much crap in recent years to give up now. I will not give up on myself.

We opened a bottle of Oscar's champagne and raised a toast to a brighter and better future as I made my first decision.

I am going on my honeymoon and I am going to take my sister. Screw convention and tradition, we are going on a Sistermoon.

42

Turquoise; The colour of warm inviting oceans and exotic locations filled with sunshine, cocktails and cloudless skies. The colour that is thought to have a calming effect on anxious psychiatric patients, that is used to soothe in holistic medicine and, as a gemstone, is meant to encourage open communication and clarity of thought.

As my sister and I boarded our flight to the Maldives looking somewhat bedraggled and pale from a stressful English winter I could think of nothing I needed more than a soothing dose of turquoise. I held that thought close as we travelled across countries and boarded our final sea plane to the island that became our home for the next two weeks. I wondered what people would think seeing us together at a honeymoon resort and if they would assume either a failed wedding or that we were a couple. My sister and I are so clearly related. I thought that much would be obvious and hoped the resort staff had remembered to ensure we had two single beds and had removed any reference to Oscar from our 'honeymoon suite'. The last thing I needed was to be referred to as his wife. As we banked around to land upon the water I peered out of the window and forgot my concerns and became mesmerised by the view below us. There amongst the endless atolls lay a tiny round island with thick lush greenery at its centre and a fringe of palm trees along its shores. At the far end of the island lay a string of exquisite beach huts on stilts that followed the curve of the house reef. It was idyllic, the beaches appeared to be mostly unoccupied and light sparkled upon the waves lapping at the shore. We disembarked at the floating jetty and our first taste of the island was fresh iced cocktails served with cool scented facial towels and a view of paradise. I thought to myself I could get used to that, it was turquoise on steroids.

For the first three days of our Sistermoon we lay on our beach hut sun loungers, pale and tinged pink from the glorious sunshine above us, and I talked until my sister probably felt like weeping. I went through *everything* to do with Oscar and what happened on Guernsey and I didn't know how to stop. I chewed over the same topics every single day on the beach, worried about what would become of my future as we swam in the turquoise, warm waters and I gnawed anxiously at the doubts within my mind that it had all been my fault. I am amazed that Clare didn't throw her cocktail in my face, slap me with her straw sunhat and tell me to get a grip and move on. She lay on her lounger every day, sipped her rosé wine and listened to me until finally, one day, I stopped. I had nothing more to say, I was done with talking about Oscar and his abuse and it was time to try moving on. I had talked about it constantly for two months and enough was enough. When I made that decision, it was as if a cloud were lifted even though there were no clouds around that island in the first place, just pure sunshine. I woke up the following day under my beautifully draped mosquito net and I no longer needed to think of what had happened quite so much. All I wanted to do was have some fun with my sister.

Our adventure began and we discovered the luxurious spa and the restaurant with more desserts than I knew what to do with. We ate like queens every night in that airy, sand-floored restaurant and, as

NO DAMAGE

we began to talk to the honeymoon couples around us, we realised they thought we were a couple. Once we made it clear we were not, one of them kindly pointed out they thought I was the husband. A local waiter who overheard and knew us then admitted he was going to ask me if I went to work all day as the man whilst my wife Clare stayed at home with the children. I almost choked on my dessert at the realisation I was the manly one in this 'couple' and Clare decided my name would henceforth be Moonface The Dude. To this day she still always calls me Moony. There was one downside to the staff and guests' realisation that we were not a couple; we became fair game for the local staff. The male staff lived on an island that was mostly only frequented by couples and they were all far from home and perhaps lonely at times. There was the wide-eyed chef at the restaurant who spent every night staring at us obviously and occasionally pointed at himself and his dishes and asked us 'You like?' He followed us daily around the buffets as we chose each item and on many an occasion I saw him breathing down Clare's neck from behind as she leant in for some curry and came away with the fright of her life. I am sure he was just trying to be helpful and attentive but it came off a little creepy. There was also one of the island groundsmen who leapt out from the bushes every time we passed his work area and showed us half-naked photographs of himself on his mobile phone. We had no idea what to say to him and in the end we crawled through the undergrowth to get home without seeing him – which was no easy matter in flowing dresses and flip flops.

Then there was Basile, the island diving Instructor. I had myself a little rebound crush on him from the moment his French accent appeared on the scene. Clare and I decided to try scuba diving one day and, both being terrified of diving, we spent the night beforehand lying awake all night under our respective mosquito nets. We were exhausted before we even boarded the boat the following day with Basile and lay sleeping in the sunshine all the way to our dive site. The dive itself was hellish, with a current so strong we were swept downstream onto urchins, coral and stinging sea creatures whilst all of the other divers clung to the reef with grapple hooks. I see where we went wrong there. Basile did his best to look after us but spent a lot of his time singing at the passing manta rays, which made me develop an even bigger crush on him. I wasted no time in making my intentions clear as he applied ointment to my coral grazes and I spent the remainder of that day flirting so obviously that he took the hint and I had my official post-separation rebound. It was such a cliché but so good to be wanted again, to be touched, right up until the point he asked me after our passionate encounter why I was at the island. I explained I had been left by two fiancés as we lay in the moonlight listening to the surf and, in his delicious French accent, he turned to me and spoke.

'Two? Wow. What is wrong with you Kathryn?' He asked earnestly and without the merest hint of sarcasm.

Having two ex-fiancés turned out to be a passion-killer.

As the first week rolled on Clare and I became ever more bronzed and relaxed and decided that every woman on her Sistermoon needs a daily dose of afternoon tea and a glamorous photo shoot. We had a ball exploring the different areas of the island each day with our cameras and posed for each other in our various outfits. We went for the classic beach look in bikinis, the 'look at me frolicking in the surf' shot, the 'I am walking serenely along the sand with flowing hair' look and the occasional 'I have a coral willy' photograph as well. It was soul healing and made our afternoon cakes all the more enjoyable for the amount we had laughed in our own sisterly world.

Heady from our new-found confidence, we decided to enter the island crab race one night. We were told that the guest who chose the winning crab would receive ten per cent off the cost of their holiday bill, which was a lot of money when you consider it was a honeymoon resort. We were so excited that we spent a small fortune on crabs and told ourselves it would be worth it for the return. We assessed each crab for its speed, size and shape with great care and eventually settled upon our winners. There were a lot of guests present that evening, crowded around the crabs, and the race itself went well. As we watched one of our crabs win the race Clare and I went absolutely crazy. We leapt, screamed, whooped and hollered as we hugged each other and then realised everyone was staring at us. When we exclaimed that we had won, we had won all that money, the staff member running the race explained it was only the first round. Oh. Two more rounds passed and one of our crabs made it to the final. We geared ourselves up for the final race to being winners and watched as our nifty little crab came last rather than first. We were devastated, absolutely gutted, and didn't understand why the guest who had won seemed nonplussed. It was only later we found out that the prize was $10 not ten per cent off the bill. We had spent at least three times that buying crabs in the first place. To add insult to injury we went handline fishing the next day and Clare caught a remora, which emptied its bowels all over her face and front as she tried to release it. I caught a beautiful, enormous tropical fish and felt awful that we could not release it because I had hooked it incorrectly.

Everyone else was catching sensible edible fish whilst we were destroying and traumatising the local population of the coral reef.

It was an incredible experience spending those ten days with my sister and it healed me tremendously. By the time of the last day I was asking myself what I wanted to do with my future, what I had dreamed about before all of the past few years happened, and I realised I still held my dream of working with the oceans and marine conservation. I still had a zest for travel and wanted to explore the world in the future and live overseas. I knew it wouldn't be possible in the lifetime of the Bears, I had a commitment and responsibility to them and would never abandon them, but one day I would do it all. As we flew back to the cold UK winter that was beginning to consider spring, I knew it was time for me to continue building my life. I knew it was time to step up to the mark and find a way to let go of all the anger and anxiety I held somewhere deep within. I needed to come up with a recovery plan and it began on that flight home.

It is exceptionally difficult to let go of the anger and hurt associated with someone leaving you. We all have egos and they get bruised to the point that we rage about it and vow never to love or trust again. I knew that wasn't the solution though, that for my own sanity and health I had to find a way to rebuild my life but I wasn't sure how to go about it. I knew it started with rebuilding *me* and I considered the idea of self-love, which was something I clearly lacked. My self-esteem was about the size of a small pebble and all I knew how to do was survive the knocks of life, not carve my way through them with esteem and a sense of worth. In all my adult years I had been so busy making a career and ensuring my partners were happy that I had forgotten to also tend to me. Firstly

I needed to address wellness and so I ate properly and did an enormous amount of walking along the Cornish coastal paths every day. I plugged my iPod into my ears with motivational music and marched out my pain every day with the dogs. There were times, many times, when I wanted to sit down on the nearest rock and cry but I refused. I would not be that person anymore and I forced myself onwards with tears falling as I walked if need be. I honoured my feelings but I didn't let them destroy me with their weight. Without fail I drew a hot bath every night and repeated to myself everything I had to be thankful for. My mind tried to wander onto anger and disbelief often but I gently reined her in and told her to do one. I kept saying my thanks to the Universe as if my sanity depended upon it and spent the little money I had left on luxurious bubble baths to help me along the way. Those rituals put me on an even keel in those early days and gave me a sense of purpose when I needed it most.

By day I had to find a job and I continued to apply for everything I could find in Cornwall. The most humiliating part for me was my weekly trip to the Job Centre to sign on for benefits. I cannot put into words how angry I was at Oscar for having caused me to lose my career and that weekly visit brought it all up within me. I was absolutely furious as I put my favourite boots on, held my head high and marched through it every week with a forced smile upon my face. That centre was one of the most grey and miserable places I had ever been and I hated being forced to go there by circumstance and I am sure the other unemployed people hated it as well. Thankfully I was lucky and, by the time spring arrived, I had been successful in getting the job I had first applied for with my old company. I was thrilled to finally know I had a way to support myself and the Bears and decided upon the next part of my recovery plan; more scuba diving to continue working on that fear.

Many sleepless nights and cold sweats followed as I joined the local scuba diving centre and completed two courses, the second of which gave me the title Rescue Diver. I really did not enjoy a moment of those courses, I was petrified, but I am truly proud of my achievement. Yes I cried my way through it and was convinced I would fail especially when I had to rescue an unconscious diver from underwater who was twice the size of me. My knees buckled time and again as I tried to lift him onto a small pebble beach whilst the waves hit us from behind and I fell on my face. In the end he couldn't resist shouting words of encouragement whilst pretending to be unconscious as I fell on my face during my six rescue attempts. When the less than encouraging Instructor turned to me and rolled his eyes at my efforts I explained that I had a good set of lungs for shouting help and that the emergency services would have arrived by now anyway. The Instructor introduced me to a new and terrified diver the following day and told her not to worry for she would never be as bad at diving as I was. I knew I was perfectly capable, if not very nervous, and as per my recover plan I no longer had time in my life for people that put me down. I walked away feeling even more determined on the back of completing my Rescue Diver course and booked a diving holiday in Tenerife. It was time to put my new skills to the test in the water and take some time alone to breathe before rejoining the working world.

All of those moments within my recovery plan helped me to regain a fragile but growing sense of self-worth and identity that I continued to work on and probably always will. I was beginning to get to know me at last. Before I left for Tenerife I knew I had one final task in hand; to let go of Oscar and every emotion that came with him. Whilst on the surface I was finding reasons to be superficially happy, truly letting go of the hurt and forgiving someone that had physically and mentally destroyed me was no easy task. I *hated* him with a passion but I didn't want to become one of those people that carried their hate forever and lived in its shadow. I had every reason to feel betrayed and disgusted at the way both Graham and Oscar had treated me but I knew that those feelings would ruin my future unless I let them go. Anger had no useful place in the life that I wanted to create. I found forgiving Graham was the easy part. So much had happened since our separation that I barely even grimaced when I sent him an email to apologise for the ways in which I had hurt him. We hadn't spoken in three years and I offered an olive branch hoping we could reconcile our past. Graham's quick and sincere response with apologies and regrets of his own was the push I needed to attempt forgiving Oscar. I had no intention of getting in touch with Oscar, his mind games filled me with fear, but I found my own way to forgive without his help.

It started with two journals that I filled daily with every emotion, sentence, word and paragraph of anger and hurt that was within me. I wrote so fast that my hands barely kept up and I scribbled my fury with abandon until two journals were filled with my hate, disappointment and utter disbelief that he could have been so cruel. By the end of those journals my arm ached but my mind no longer throbbed. I began visualising forgiving Oscar every day and I offered up a wish of peace and my forgiveness of his actions. I asked for Oscar to forgive me for the hurt I had caused and I wished him well in his future. I honoured and acknowledged our past and then I mentally cut the ribbon that held us bound. I watched him metaphorically float away and I repeated that practice every day for a long time. It was a gradual process, I stumbled at times and it was hard, but it worked. I began to feel peaceful inside and, as I walked Padstow harbour one day, I threw my angry journals in a public bin and never looked back. Whilst the thought of Oscar still hurt me I was no longer angry for the hand I had been dealt in recent years and, if anything, I actually pitied him. It was time to go to Tenerife and I packed a new journal I intended to fill with hope and inspiration for the life that would be mine.

43

I met a man. I had absolutely no intention of meeting anyone in Tenerife and my holiday was supposed to be a time of self-discovery and retreat for my soul. Fate clearly had other ideas though and pushed a man right in my path when I least expected it. When said man walked past me in the local dive centre all I managed to do was look at the floor and I spent the rest of the week avoiding him whenever our paths crossed. I hid behind wetsuits, I sat as far away from him as possible on the dive boat and I brushed off his random attempts at conversation with me. He was so handsome and tall I couldn't even look at him. As his perky bottom and broad, tanned shoulders meandered past me I was tempted to just grab him and see if he was real but instead I gazed at the floor and hoped he would disappear, a figment of my imagination. That man was a stunner and I was absolutely not going to talk to him then or ever.

I spent a lot of time scribbling in my journal as the sunshine beamed down upon my balcony and, thanks to a cold, I didn't do much in the way of scuba diving that week. Admittedly that cold was a blessed relief because I was still terrified of diving and didn't really want to do it anyway. Being ill was also handy considering I was avoiding the handsome Divemaster at the dive centre, who I discovered was called Nicholas. Whilst recovering, I spent hours gazing at the ocean from my balcony and formulated dreams of my future and wrote down everything I still believed in and hoped for. One evening I sat outside and touched upon the topic of love and realised how regretful and sad I felt at the prospect of never allowing myself to love or be loved again. I realised I had a choice to make; I could renovate my heart, work on trust and allow myself to be loved or I could close the doors permanently and fester in bitterness for how love had treated me so far. It was not an easy conversation with my mind and I was desperately torn between never risking the warmth of a human touch and love again for the sake of being safe from hurt or having the courage to heal my tatty heart and open its doors in the future for the right person. As I sat considering both I knew what I would do. The idea of playing it safe and never trusting again felt lonely and defeatist, a way to ensure I would be safe but forever missing something vital. The idea of falling in love again and being with someone felt terrifying in my mind, queasy in my stomach and yet right in my heart. That night I chose to listen to my heart and scrawled my prayers to the Universe in my journal.

I begged and prayed for help to heal me and learn about love. I knew I had my own lack of self-love to deal with, which of course contributed to the demise of my insecurity-filled relationships, and I knew I also wanted to be more accepting of others and the love they offered rather than it coming with conditions on my part. Less 'if you do this I will love you', more 'I love myself always and I will love you just the way you are.' It wasn't so much about asking for true love, my man of the sea, to come to me, than it was about asking to be shown how to truly love – warts, hurt, risk, joy and all. I needed to learn about unconditional love and I was ready to begin walking that path. As I drained my glass of cheap red wine I sat on my heels that night, admired the stars, and whispered my prayers to the sky. I begged from the bottom of my heart for the world not to give up on me but to show me the way forwards instead, to teach me about love for the rest of my days. I spoke seriously, I felt serious, and then I finished by asking lightly if I could start with the hot Divemaster Nicholas.

The very next day, my last in Tenerife, I walked tall into the dive centre and found Nicholas alone cleaning the floor at the end of a busy day. Determined not to lose the opportunity I made some random conversation about diving and propped myself against one of the benches hoping he would respond. He was very quiet and seemed in a rush, perhaps to get away from me? I offered him my email address on a piece of scrappy paper just in case I was reading him wrong, just in case there was a possibility of something there. He took the paper and backed away to the rear of the dive centre and then hurried past me to another room down the corridor. It wasn't until two years later I learnt he had disappeared because he was looking for a pen to write down his contact details. At the time his response wasn't entirely how I had hoped it would go and I walked out of the centre feeling embarrassed. But then I stood at the end of the corridor and felt something within me tell me to turn back and go and say hello to Nicholas again. Without my permission, my legs started walking and then I was opposite Nicholas in the room he had entered. We spoke an insignificant and awkward hello, talked idly about the work he was finishing and I attempted to say goodbye whilst suggesting it would be nice to see him again. As I leant in to hug him and leave he scooped me up into his arms in a close hug. Shocked is an understatement and I stood there with my feet dangling above the floor and my eyes wide open. Nicholas put me down, closed up the dive centre and told me he was going for a beer. He didn't exactly invite me but his hint seemed obvious and I offered to join him as casually as possible. We enjoyed beer after beer and non-stop conversation as the sun sank towards the horizon. We discovered our shared love of the oceans, science, music and much more. My mental tick list was already double ticked and flying high above us when we arranged to meet in England and walked along the beach towards my apartment for dinner.

I have never felt chemistry and an instant bond like I did that evening. We talked for hours, interrupting each other, gesturing and smiling as we excitedly shared our loves and ideas about life and it felt natural, normal. By the time we left the bar I felt as if I had known him a lifetime and it was no surprise to either of us that our date lasted the entire night and, the next morning, I didn't want to leave. We had much in common and I felt there was something special there, dare I believe it could be so, and I didn't know what to do with that feeling. Nicholas was moving overseas permanently after a brief return to England and, well, what exactly did I hope would happen? I wasn't ready for, or wanting, a relationship yet I was reluctant to leave without confirming the possibility of seeing him again. We stood in the doorway to my apartment and I offered my telephone number, which looked perhaps a tad desperate given he already had my email address. Nicholas joked that he hadn't even emailed me yet or given me his number.

I thought I was coming off over keen and that it was just one night but when I touched down in England I couldn't get him out of my mind. I knew it was a stupid idea to consider meeting this man, whom I barely knew, and I suspected he wasn't going to get in touch anyway. If he did it would only end in disaster with another broken heart on my part. I questioned if I had learnt anything in recent months and I knew I should walk away but I didn't. Instead I opened my emails to find a long message from him thanking me for a lovely evening and confirming our plans to meet upon his return in a month's time. Against my mind but perhaps in favour of my healing heart there was a man on the scene *again* and it turned out much further down the road that it was just the medicine I needed. But at the time of reading his email I was confused, cautious and overwhelmed at the prospect of being hurt again.

No good will come of getting involved with a handsome man who was moving overseas Kathryn. No good at all.

In the month that followed I started my new job and celebrated beforehand with a bottle of champagne from the stash I had kindly removed from Oscar when I left Guernsey. On my first day at work I was hoping to make a good impression but failed when a blackbird flew into the glass office space just as I was being introduced to my new colleagues. In my confidence I told everyone not to worry, I would handle it, and attempted to usher the blackbird out of the office through the open door. Sadly the bird had other ideas, panicked and flew into the window next to me and then dropped dead by my feet. I had to spend the next thirty minutes standing next to the bird, which by now had a traffic cone over it, to ensure nobody tripped over it whilst its disposal was arranged. I was affectionately known as the 'Kat that killed the bird' from that day forwards. Whilst it was comfortable and easy slipping back into my old role and my colleagues were all warm earthy types, I struggled to balance long days at work with looking after Hester and Paddington. It was a juggling act and I didn't have the freedom of long walks each day now that I worked farther from home than I had in Shropshire or Guernsey. After the Bears' needs were met as best I could, any spare time I had was spent chatting online to Nicholas or sleeping. Our friendship was blossoming quietly behind closed doors and I didn't mention him to others or think too much about it. We were just friends, nothing more and that was right for both of us. When my sister questioned me as to who this mystery man was I tried to play it down and hoped one of us at least believed it meant nothing and would go nowhere. Whenever Dad asked who this man was I poured him another glass of red wine and ignored he had even asked me.

I also visited Shropshire and faced seeing my friends for the first time since I had moved to Guernsey. I was awkward and apprehensive as I walked the familiar streets of my old town and memories of my time there filled my mind. So much had happened since I had left high on the prospect of new beginnings overseas and I missed my friends. Without exception they welcomed me back with smiles and condolences and I put on a brave face when necessary. Amber didn't so much as let me slip into Performing Monkey mode and she kept my heart open when at times I felt like closing up. I met up with my old choir friends and I shared numerous dinners, coffees and peaceful times with them all. Nobody laughed at me for having two ex-fiancés and my friends were resolute in their belief it had just been bad luck and that it was absolutely not my fault. When I opened up to Amber about exactly what had gone on with Oscar she was horrified and angry with him in a way I hadn't known was possible. I didn't know hippies could get so angry.

The last thing to do during my visit was to return to the bridal boutique and collect my wedding dress. For the second time in my life I drove there to collect a wedding dress I would not be wearing because of a failed engagement and yet that time it didn't matter to me. It was less painful for being a familiar experience and I was beginning to understand that it had been a lucky escape from a marriage that would probably have sent me insane. Louise was kind as always when we met, I was slightly ashamed as always, and I squashed that beautiful dress into my car and drove home to Cornwall. The dress gathered dust under my bed whilst my engagement ring sat in my bedside drawer and my wedding shoes perched within the wardrobe. I was thirty-three, living with my father and had a wedding dress under my bed. It was soon to be my wedding day and I was logging onto the computer to chat with a man I barely knew. I couldn't escape the feeling it was all a bit tragic and clichéd.

The perfect antidote to being that person was surprisingly my wedding day the following week. My family all gathered in Cornwall and we celebrated my escape in style. My brother unexpectedly flew over with his family from Australia, my sister arrived and we had an incredible sunshine filled weekend of laughter and food. There was not a tear between us as we laughed, sang and danced in the garden and stuck our fingers up mentally at all that had come to pass. We were united, we missed Mum terribly but we were not going to fall apart. As I sat in a local pub with my sister and sister-in-law that weekend we promised each other that we would work on following our dreams in the coming years. We had learnt that life was unpredictable, too precious and short and we wrote out our wildest dreams:

> In a year's time I will be working towards a life of marine work overseas and becoming a qualified diving Instructor.

I knew that dream was impossible for me, for both practical and fearful reasons, and it was asking too much of me but I tucked my promise away in my journal. I promised myself I would somehow make it all happen, whether it took six years or ten, and thought nothing more of it as I prepared to visit Nicholas. Since my holiday we had talked online most weeks and our initial plans had developed from one day into an entire week together in Bristol, Cornwall and London. As I began the laborious process of plucking my eyebrows and packing my best shoes, I had no idea what to expect from this new-found friend.

44

As I sat on the hard bed in my box-shaped hotel room in Bristol I thought seeing Nicholas again was perhaps the most stupid of all of my recent ideas. I was meeting a man that I barely knew beyond a holiday fling and computer chat and who no doubt had no intention of us being anything more than a passionate fling before he moved overseas. I had travelled halfway across England to meet him, I had a heart that was only just healing, I had just escaped a random frisky man in the spa sauna downstairs and I was sat on my bed potentially leaping into the arms of Nicholas the next day knowing that it would go nowhere and mean nothing to him. I may as well have offered my heart up on a platter with a grater for shredding it with, it was that stupid an idea of mine. I honestly do not know what I was thinking, very little at the time it appeared, and I stared out of the window at the pouring rain and wished to be back at home in Cornwall. I longed to be anywhere but the place I had brought myself to but it was too late. I jokingly asked the Universe for a sign that I wasn't making a huge mistake, flicked on the television and was greeted with the start of the film Serendipity.

Serendipity (noun): The occurrence and development of events by chance in a happy or beneficial way

I snorted derisively at the coincidence and eventually fell asleep.

I walked out into the rain the next day, took a deep breath and committed myself to the inevitable as I walked along the busy city streets in search of Nicholas. I had spent the morning in the Bristol museum drinking numerous cups of tea whilst picking at cheap napkins anxiously. My mind had been on overdrive and I was already running on adrenaline. I looked up from the puddles as I walked and there he was, his tall frame ducked under a bus shelter and frowning. Nicholas was definitely frowning and not smiling at me as I walked towards him, which I suspected was not a good start. But then he said hello, leant forward to kiss me gently on my cheek, took my arm and walked me under the umbrella whilst he became soaked to his skin. It seemed I had found a gentleman.

We spent the day exploring Bristol aquarium and paused under exhibits for swift kisses and touches that ignited our already roaring chemistry. We laughed our way past tanks of jellyfish, lingered around a leopard shark exhibit and weaved through the dark corners of the frog display. Time flew by and we made our way to the theatre that evening for a performance of The Phantom of the Opera. The last time I had seen Phantom, my favourite musical, had been during my ill-fated hen do and I hoped this performance would be better for the improved circumstances. We had a wonderful time and before the clocks sounded midnight I lay in Nicholas's embrace at the hotel whilst he fell asleep. As I watched his rhythmic breathing I shook my head at the prospect of falling for him and already I knew I was going to get into trouble one day. Not only was he gorgeous but we also got on incredibly well as friends. I pushed my thoughts aside and told myself to focus on just having some fun and enjoying it for what it was; a week of passion and adventure with the best looking bottom I had ever set my eyes upon.

I did just that and we took our laughter and passion from Bristol to Cornwall. We didn't exactly go outside during our time by the sea and spent one evening sharing the final bottle of champagne from Oscar in a candlelit bath. It felt such a fitting tribute to an epic disaster and I explained my history to Nicholas, fearing the worst as usual. He didn't so much as bat an eyelid at my revelations and just listened intently as he poured us more champagne. He was nonplussed, he told me we all have history and he looked sad on my behalf rather than wondering if I were to blame. He was quiet and self-assured and enjoyed our time together without demands or questions. The Bears were in kennels but he wanted to know all about them as we drove the motorways to London, he adored dogs. We sang Foo Fighter songs together at full volume in my tiny car and, as he fell asleep in the passenger seat, I kept nudging the brakes and laughing when his head fell forwards and he snorted awake. Our ease uplifted me and the time exploring London was perfect. We ate good food, charged around the Natural History Museum, talked for hours on end and Nicholas laughed when I couldn't keep up with his giant strides across the underground station. We also had more sex than humanly possible. When I stood by my car and we embraced to say goodbye I knew exactly what I was leaving behind and that we would never see each other again. I had found a connection with someone that went far beyond trying to impress one another with fake hobbies and being agreeable to all he said. I had found a genuine friend, chemistry and companionship and yet it was not meant to be. Nicholas was moving overseas to pursue dive instructing and had no plans to ever return to England. He too had his heart broken by his ex-girlfriend and was moving abroad to follow his dreams and fly free. It was the end of the road for us as we walked away from one another.

Nicholas had set the bar high in my mind and I intentionally focussed on getting over him in the coming months. I tried to convince myself I could be attracted to other men that were interested in dating me but the chemistry just wasn't there. Eventually I convinced myself that none of it really mattered, I would forget about Nicholas in time and could just enjoy our friendship. However, as we spoke online after work one day, Nicholas asked me what I had told Clare about him and I decided to risk being honest.

17:52 TeamAiredale: to be honest I actually said how great I think you are and how annoying it was you were moving overseas

17:52 Zone: funny you should say that. I'm more relaxed around you than just about anyone else I've ever met.

17:53 TeamAiredale: really? Likewise

17:55 Zone: I'm generally a relaxed person physically, but with you it's a mental thing too (and I mean that in the line above, not that one of us is crazy :P)

17:55 Zone: Actually, scrub that, you're mental too :P

17:56 TeamAiredale: heheh mental? yeah I like to think we're both like minded :P

17:57 TeamAiredale: Tell you something you'll probably think is weird but hey you can't laugh too hard from over there....of everyone I have ever met you're the only person I could happily sit with all day doing nothing/not speaking as I just love your company regardless of what we're doing. Okay I'll shut up now ;)

17:59 Zone: I'm good at just sitting silently and cuddling :)

18:00 TeamAiredale: I know and I miss that bit the most, your company and cuddles are the best in my eyes :)

18:04 TeamAiredale: oh I feel like such a tool after telling you stuff

18:05 Zone: why?

18:07 TeamAiredale: because you didn't need to know how I really feel, probably the last thing you wanted to hear but heyho you're still my buddy :)

18:07 Zone: Not at all, you'd be surprised how similar my own thoughts are

18:08 TeamAiredale: really? I genuinely had no idea you felt anything towards me to be honest

By that point I was perched on the end of my bed, staring at my laptop, and my heart racing. I had no idea Nicholas had feelings for me beyond friendship with benefits and I waited for his response.

18:16 Zone: penny for thoughts? Well despite the fact you're so much more ancient than me, I do slightly regret the fact that we're not living in the same general area. Would have liked to see what might have been.

18:18 Zone: even despite your tragic history with permanent relationships :D

18:20 TeamAiredale: Oi cheeky! Okay fair play it is a touch tragic but I am actually a good girlfriend. I just made some errors in judgement and ended up with losers. Likewise though I do regret the circumstance to be honest, as I have a feeling with you and it would've been something

18:22 Zone: well who knows. After your next failed attempt at marriage, and my failure to separate the pretty women from the lady boys in Thailand, who knows where we'll end up :P

18:23 Zone: now less typing, and more card clicking!

18:23 TeamAiredale: stop distracting me then!!!

By 11pm we signed off for the night and I lay awake considering what Nicholas had said. He had feelings for me but had also said we were not going to happen. I didn't know what to do with that information. I definitely didn't need to fall for a man yet again in my life, it was the worst thing I could do and yet I couldn't help thinking about him. As I said, I knew I was going to get into trouble one day and that day was it.

I buried myself in work, tried to forget about that conversation, and the summer passed by in a blur of work, dog walks and ice cream. I struggled with balancing my work, home life and time with Nicholas online. I was exhausted from long hours at the office after a recent promotion, the dogs were not getting the attention they were used to and I began to wonder how long term I could make all of this work. It all came to a head when I put my back out at home one day and found myself lying on the floor unable to walk. I managed to crawl to the telephone to alert a neighbour I was alone and spent the next three weeks lying in bed with no mobility. It took months to recover, to regain my strength, and the Bears suffered from a lack of walks. They were incredibly bored. As I lay in bed it niggled at me that it would soon be time to move out of Dad's house and, on my wage alone, I didn't know if I could afford a home and the expense that came with my dogs. That hadn't even occurred to me previously and the realisation was a huge shock to me. I wondered how, with the long days at work, the dogs would cope alone. They always had company at home with Graham and then Oscar and needed so much more exercise and time than I was able to give them alone. I wondered what I was going to do and realised I didn't have any clear, obvious answers. I brushed my thoughts aside quickly, assured myself we would be okay and focussed on the good. I effectively buried my head in the sand.

Nicholas and I couldn't keep away from each other and spoke for hours on end as I lay recovering; playing games and listening to the same music whilst miles apart. We came to know everything about each other and yet we never mentioned becoming more than friends. I knew he was committed to being overseas and I had a life and commitments in England for many years to come with the Bears. No amount of sensible talk from my sister or Cornish ice cream helped me forget my feelings though and I kept trying to push them back down.

By the time summer was over I was due for my last holiday of the year. It was the final part of my Recovery Plan and I had booked it before visiting Tenerife, to finish the year off positively before the gloom of winter began. I had been determined to have a holiday that would complete my healing and give me hope for the next chapter of my life and another impending New Year - surely I was at last due a memorable and positive New Year? Before departing for my holiday I told Nicholas about my plans and we discovered that he was living just around the corner from my destination. Fate was pushing us together again and this time our rendezvous was to be in Egypt. Yet again there was to be more leg shaving, more nerves on my part and reminding myself no good would come of this. It was an emotional rollercoaster but a delicious one at that.

By the time my flight landed I had a sweaty bottom from nerves, the shakes from too much sugar and looked my usual post-flight mess. It was not the ideal look for meeting with the man I had feelings for and I was so excited I couldn't sit still in the transfer bus to my apartment. Nicholas was going to meet me at the beach bar and he texted to confirm he was waiting for me. All I had to do was get through reception and check in to my room so I could freshen up. There was no way I was going to meet him looking bedraggled and dehydrated from aeroplane air conditioning. As I swiftly changed into the shortest skirt and prettiest top I owned I asked myself why I was doing this if we were supposedly just friends. I didn't have an answer I cared to admit and made my way to the bar.

As I walked along the soft, golden sand towards the bar my heart was hammering and I could hear it above the gentle waves lapping up against the jetty and shoreline. My flip-flops kicked up a small cloud of sand in my wake and there was Nicholas, tall and smiling as he stood up from his seat and beamed at me as I approached. He looked so happy and for the next hour I was so nervous that I barely stopped talking while Nicholas kept smiling at me as if I were a lunatic. That description, in fairness, was probably close to correct given my verbal diarrhoea. I did eventually calm down and, like naughty teenagers, we sneaked up to my apartment and welcomed in the night with a bottle of champagne and fancy underwear to celebrate our reunion. It was fantastic, pure escapism from the realities of my life in England, and it thrilled me. I was rapidly running out of money to be able to afford the bubbles and holidays but for now I didn't care. I was having the time of my life with this man.

As Nicholas had work, I spent my days lounging in the sunshine all week and listened to the water lapping at the shoreline. It was peaceful, rejuvenating and gave me a chance to reflect on all that the year had been and how far I had come in my healing. I mustered the courage to go scuba diving off the beach and *almost* enjoyed it. My healing back was soothed by the water and I relaxed enough to admire the colourful coral reefs that looked like underwater forests with trees of all shapes and sizes. I watched as small tropical fish dipped in and out of their coral hideaways whilst we swam by and clown fish nestled amongst the anemones they lived with. There was every colour, shape and size of fish I could possibly imagine and they reminded me of sweets with their humbug stripes, candy colours and glossy scales. A blue spotted stingray passed me on one dive and I squealed in delight at the dive guide. The lemony-coloured disc of a ray glided past effortlessly and displayed its electric blue spots as it settled on the sand. I hadn't known that diving could be so beautiful, so peaceful, and then I remembered I was under the water and my old fears attempted to kick in. I had by no means won my battle with scuba diving but a glimmer of light had appeared and it reminded me that I wanted, *needed*, to do more diving and work with the oceans. It was staggeringly beautiful and peaceful underwater and I was hooked in spite of myself. I spent the rest of my holiday wondering about the next steps in my life and how to make it all happen. I felt like I was asking the impossible but a seed had been planted and was beginning to grow in my mind. Could I do this?

I scribbled out ideas in my journal and decided roughly upon my path. As Nicholas joined me one evening we sat down on my balcony and I talked it all through. I felt guilty admitting that I wanted to move overseas, that I had dreams I wanted to pursue and that becoming a diving Instructor was what I thought I had to do next. I felt like I was letting people down by admitting that actually I wanted more from my life than to follow everyone else's path and society's expectations of me. What would my family think? Would they be disappointed in me and think I had utterly lost the plot this time? I rattled on with Nicholas and convinced myself it was a plausible idea and would be the final way to rid me of my diving fears and achieve something positive after the horror of previous years. I didn't know where it would lead me to, I thought it was asking the impossible, but I had to try. I had to do it.

I knew it couldn't happen for a number of years and that it wouldn't involve Nicholas because I had my Bears to consider. Thankfully they had plenty of life left in them and, whilst I wondered if they would cope overseas, I realised it was asking the impossible. I couldn't afford to move them overseas and they would hate it. The dream I admitted to on the balcony would have to wait until after their lifetimes because I would not desert them the way my ex-partners had deserted me. They came first, they had been my rock and I would wait.

The remaining nights of my holiday passed with local food, cheap beer and time with Nicholas. We were at ease together as always and by the time my last day came I was wondering when we would see each other again. I didn't dare ask but then Nicholas suggested I visit in February and within the space of about ten minutes we had a two week holiday planned together in Egypt again. Quite how I was going to afford the holiday I didn't know but I brushed that concern aside. I couldn't resist the invitation to see his delicious bottom again. We were playing a dangerous game letting ourselves get closer both physically and emotionally and we both tried to keep it in check with flippant statements about not becoming a couple. My feelings were growing in spite of my trying to ignore them and I began to lose my hold on reining them in. Little did I know that Nicholas was also feeling the same way.

45

After returning from Egypt I took the lid off my favourite pink pen and every week I wrote down my dream in my journal. I never once looked back at previous entries and I always did it at a time when I felt free in my mind, relaxed. I sat down and said this to myself before starting:

If money were no object, if you knew you would succeed, if you had no fear and could do it all....What would be your dream?

That thought changed my life. It gave me permission to write down my dream as if it were a game; a game where I could be anyone I wanted to be. I chose to be a woman free of limiting self-beliefs, a woman with courage and inspiration and the talent to make her world beautiful. I wrote and wrote until I needed a new pink pen and then I wrote some more. Sometimes I cried as I felt my dream and still couldn't see how to make it a success. But I kept on writing it out regardless and I did that most days. I started to write down what it was that really mattered within my dream, how each component made me feel and how my ideal day would look. By feeling my way through my dream I came to learn what my priorities were. I discovered new passions and listed what was not negotiable in my dream and what I could compromise if need be. Importantly I discovered, wrote and felt exactly what it was that lit up my heart and that I couldn't wait to share with the world.

My mind changed with that writing. I started to believe that actually I could do this. I could succeed at anything if I put my mind to it and the only thing stopping me was fear and circumstance. I began to write down ways to achieve my dream. I wrote down practical changes I could make both small and large so I could start to live my dream NOW. I started painting pictures of sharks again to express my love of them and my love of art. I booked that diving holiday with Nicholas for February and I started to connect with people living their dreams. Importantly, I also listed my limiting beliefs about who I thought I was and started to make changes to my mental attitude so that I would set myself free. The only person stopping me in the past had been effectively me. Now the only person that was going to stop me from quitting on my dream this time around was me. I became my greatest supporter in my journal – I didn't have the courage to say it out loud or admit what was going on for me internally to anyone at home. I felt guilty and ashamed that I had this dream, that I was indulging my own potential happiness, but still my seed of a dream began to bloom. My attitude changed from *it will never happen* to asking myself *how will I make this happen?*

The one thing I said to myself that helped me the most was True Love. I wrote those two words in the sand in Cornwall, in my journal, on rocks I tossed into the sea and on paper I burned into ashes.

True Love.

By that I meant the ability to love myself truly, unconditionally, and to nurture my dreams for me, for the love of life and so I could give my passion and love to others. I honestly felt that it all came back to learning true love and never giving up on the pursuit of it in all its forms. Those two words helped me through the good days and the ones where I felt like throwing my pen away, squashing my seed of a dream with my boot and giving up.

Somehow my writing, my mental work and my dreaming were the keys to my changes on a practical level. I put one foot in front of the other without even knowing it and I started opening doors to new opportunities and saying yes to everything that felt right. Yes to anything and everything that took me in the right direction and no to everything else. I think the reality is that it was the moment I believed my dream would one day come true that actually made it real. We all have the practical tools, the imagination and the ability to do whatever it is we dream of but we have to believe it is possible first. You can't grasp your dream if you don't believe it can exist. You can't grasp your dream if you don't believe you deserve it.

I flew to South Africa six months later to start a new life and, at the time of my dreaming, I had no idea that move was on the horizon. I had no idea whatsoever and I wouldn't have believed anyone that told me it was going to happen. My plans were to stay in Cornwall for the foreseeable future but, with my journal and pen in my hand, this is what I wrote word for word during my flight to Cape Town:

Never again will I underestimate myself. I am so much more than I led myself to believe. I am beautiful, I have gifts and talents to offer this world. For crying out loud just do it! Make it happen!! SING, PAINT, TEACH, SHARKS, DIVE, LOVE. Don't settle for anything less than what I truly deserve and am capable of. Shine like you were born to do. Step out of your shadow. This is your time girl. Go. Fly. Show the world who you are. NOW! GO! DON'T FEAR, DON'T DOUBT YOU KATHRYN.

NEVER AGAIN GIVE UP.

46

I made my decision to rehome the Bears and the weeks after doing so were incredibly hard on us all. They broke my heart all over again. Every day, I came home from work and pulled my car into the garage. I closed the car door, kicked my shoes off and felt sick as I approached the door into our home. I knew my Bears would be waiting on the other side. They had waited for me every day since they came into my world and always greeted me with such enthusiasm. It would start with Paddington's low woof and snuffle snorting on the other side of the door, as his tail beat out a bold and lively tune against the radiator. I could hear Hester's paws tapping on the floor as she danced in excitement. I knew her bottom would be wiggling in anticipation as she pranced on the spot trying to contain her delight. Every day was the same; every single day had held this perfect greeting for the last six years every time I entered their world from wherever I had been. It had always been my greatest joy at the end of a working day, my support when life dealt a bad hand, and now it had turned into my nightmare.

In the months after my holiday in Egypt, whilst I had been busy writing my long-term dreams, I had also worked tirelessly to find a new home for my woofs and I but it had been impossible. I discovered that nobody in their right mind would consider renting a house to two enormous dogs left alone all day, bored and contained, and I could only just afford a matchbox house with a tiny garden. After fruitless searching I realised there were no rental properties that would take us. I searched holiday homes, caravans, considered us living in my tent and investigated selling my house but it was pointless. None of them were possible and I couldn't sell anyway thanks to the non-existing housing market and my tenants at No.8. I was rapidly being pushed into a dead end with a conclusion I didn't want to acknowledge. It slowly began to dawn on me that there was in fact no way I could house or afford to keep the Bears unless I remained living with Dad and I knew I couldn't do that. I looked for jobs elsewhere that might pay more but there was nothing suitable. I lay awake at night in tears often and kicked myself for being so naive that I hadn't realised the inevitable before now. Still I couldn't imagine ever being without Hester and Paddington and searched harder for anywhere we could call home, anything I could do keep us together. I applied for promotions across the country at the company I worked for but it was to no avail. I tried to find a dog-sitter I could afford. I tried everything and anything and nothing worked.

As a single dog owner with a limited salary I was finally beaten and realised I only had one option. It was almost Christmas and I had to do what was right for my Bears; I had to let them go, and give them the life and home they deserved. I had to forget how much it would crush me to be without them and put their needs far above my own because I loved them that much. I would do anything for them, anything at all. I will never forget the moment I stood in the kitchen and told Dad what I was going to do. I barely managed to stand up as I told him, through my sobbing, that I was going to find them a new home. The Bears and I had always come as an inseparable package and I felt like I was ripping apart my heart and everything good I believed in. Everyone who knew my dogs loved them, we had always been Team Airedale and now I was admitting we would be no more. Those two woolly dogs meant that much to me that I could barely speak.

I wanted to cherish every moment with Hester and Paddington all the more because I knew that one day they would be gone. I knew there was a day on the horizon when I would wake up without them by my side and I dreaded it. I never wanted that day to come. I hated that it would eventually arrive. Yet there I was pausing at the door, not wanting to go inside after work, as I didn't want them to feel my sadness. I felt extremely guilty that I was letting them go, I had failed them, and they had no idea. They just went on loving and trusting me every day. How could I do that to them? How could I be so cruel? I took a deep breath, opened the door and fell to my knees to envelop myself in their cheer and unconditional love. As per usual Paddington poked me with his nose and I fell over backwards with a laugh. He always was so strong and enthusiastic and never knew when to stop. Within seconds I was covered by them both and I couldn't stop laughing. For a moment in time they were still mine.

It didn't get easier as the days went by. I jumped every time my mobile phone pinged and I expected the message from my friend and Airedale owner Millie or the Bears' breeders to say they had found a home. All I wanted was to find their forever home but I never wanted to let them go. I prayed for the right home to come to them, I prayed for the strength and courage to put them first and not crumble when the moment came. I prayed relentlessly, I cried my tears alone and prayed some more. I wrote feverishly in my journal.

Dear Universe,

Please bring my Bears their perfect home. Please don't let me have to separate them or let them go anywhere other than their true home. This is breaking my heart, what am I doing this for? All I want is for them to be cherished, to be adored and given everything in life. They are so bored here with me, I see it in their eyes, and I can't cope any more with this pain. I beg you please listen and give them what they deserve and need. Please don't give up on us now. Please find their home and show me what to do. I will do anything for them, anything so long as they are happy and homed together with the perfect family. Please show me what to do. Don't let my heart fail me now.

Days later, my mobile phone pinged. It was a message from Millie. I felt sick inside. Was this it?

Sweetheart, I know this is going to break your heart into a thousand pieces but the time has come. I have found their forever home with my sister's friend Mary. It's time to let go now sweetheart. And I know this is real soon but they would like to have Hester and Paddington before Christmas. Can you do this? All my love, Millie xxx

Before Christmas. So that's next weekend.

I crumbled and fell onto my bed. I knew it would be their perfect home. Millie had mentioned Mary before as a possible home and told me how much she would love them. My tears were both joy and sorrow. They had their perfect home; they would be living together with a family and all of their dreams were coming true. Yet all of my dreams, my dreams of a future with my Bears were breaking apart. I was so tired of having to say goodbye. I walked up the stairs to share my news with Dad. I couldn't put my emotions or thoughts together or into words. This was good news but I felt like my world was collapsing again. I couldn't get the words out. I made it to the lounge, Dad read Millie's message and simply cried by my side. After all the anguish and heartache this was really happening now. The day on the horizon had arrived and I knew that in a week I would be turning my Bears' lives around. I would be breaking my heart all over again except this time I knew I was doing the right thing for them. No matter how much it would hurt me, it would give them a future to cherish and enjoy. That thought kept me going through sleepless nights.

In the days up to that weekend I could feel myself withdrawing from the Bears unintentionally. I didn't want the re-homing day to arrive but I also couldn't cope with letting my heart connect with them anymore. It reminded me of when Mum was in the hospice and I knew I would have to let her go. I became an empty shell, a walking ghost, as I made our plans and ensured they had everything they would need. Emails went back and forth between Millie and me and the final arrangements were made. I would drive straight to Millie, who would drive us to Mary's home and then stay overnight with Millie. It was the five hour drive I was dreading.

How could I prepare myself for that? How could I ever do that when my journeys with them had always been full of howling, cheese and adventures? They would have no idea and yet I would drive every mile knowing I would never see them again.

I couldn't prepare myself but I decided to make sure that the Bears had a wonderful last few days with me and I invented No Rules Day. On that day I decided that all rules were out and I would give them the things I knew they had wanted for years but hadn't been allowed. Hester slept IN my bed that daytime; fully under the quilt and with her head resting on my pillow. I cooked her favourite meal of chicken and rice and gave it to her in vast quantities. She was in Hester Heaven. Paddington ate more marmalade on toast than you could possibly imagine and tried many types of cheese. All of his gastronomic dreams came true and I laughed at those moments. I laughed at how we were finding light in a difficult time, how we were doing it our way – the Team Airedale way – and it was blissful.

'Dad, you don't have to say goodbye but I'm going to bed now. I'll be off very early and, well, you might not be awake when we go,' I touched Dad gently on his arm as I spoke and looked at the floor.

It was the night before the re-homing and my eyes glazed over as I shuffled my feet awkwardly and hinted that this was the last time Dad would ever see the Bears. He had loved and adored them as much as I; he had raised Paddington as a puppy when my back injury prevented me from doing so and I knew this would be hard on him. I left the hallway and occupied myself in my bedroom as he gently patted them both and walked upstairs to the kitchen before his tears gave him away. I knew it would always be too hard for him to say goodbye; that the words would never come. The words would never come between Dad and the Bears and they wouldn't come between Dad and me just yet either. I was resolute that I would see it through alone, I spoke to no one, and my resolve couldn't crumble.

For one last time, I looked at Hester and pointed to her beloved cat bed nestled at the foot of my bed.

'In your basket, in you go sweetheart,' I encouraged her enthusiastically.

Hester curled up on her bed and waited to be tucked in by me with her favourite pink blanket. I lovingly wrapped her into her bed and wondered if her new family would know this about her. I vowed to tell them. Paddington sat dutifully next to my bed and waited for his command.

'Up up Paddington,' I commanded and patted my duvet.

Paddington leapt silently and flopped onto his side of the bed. I reached over and turned off the bedside lamp, listened to their breathing until they fell asleep and pulled Paddington close in my arms. I lay awake all night staring at the ceiling. *What have I done?*

47

I knew I was taking them home, to where they belonged, the moment Mary opened the door and welcomed us into her home. I was terrified, my heart was racing and all I wanted to do was hold it together until the deed was done. I was met with a warm, kind face.

'You must be Kathryn. Come on in.' Mary held open the door to her beautiful dormer bungalow and I saw the faces of her three adult children waiting expectantly. They looked so friendly yet unsure of how to handle the situation with me, understandably.

The Bears strained at their leads and bounced on hind legs in their excitement to explore this new world and greet their audience. Mary gently unclipped their leads as I stood there bewildered in the hallway. I watched as they roared upstairs and straight onto the beds.

What if she changes their mind once she realises they are not like your average obedient dogs? I have tried my best to explain their characters honestly but what if?

I was brought back to my senses as the lead clip hit the tile floor with a sharp clank. I was left standing with two empty leads, my dogs no longer my own. The adrenaline flew through me and it was all I could do to hold back my tears and focus on the happiness this would bring to the Bears and that family's life. I couldn't understand my combination of feeling so heartbroken yet also peaceful. Intuition was telling me then that I had brought them to where they truly belonged.

The house itself was immaculate and warm; a family home full of love and Christmas preparations. I noted it was open plan, perfect for big Bear bottoms, and there was plenty of sofa space for Hester and Paddington to explore. I eyed the Christmas tree in the lounge with a pile of beautifully wrapped gifts in shades of gold and cream. Millie caught my eye and whispered in my ear.

'I don't think they're used to Airedales, those presents won't last long under the tree.'

I smiled wearily as the Bears thundered down the stairs, through the lounge and skidded on the kitchen tiles en route to the garden. I cringed at the scratch marks I envisaged them leaving on that beautiful floor and hoped Mary and her family would learn to love them in spite of their giant paws. The garden was incredible, more than I could have hoped for. It was huge and more than enough for the Bears to run around in circles playing bitey face whilst ruling the roost. I leaned heavily against the back doorframe and smiled as they charged around and barked their presence to the neighbourhood. The sun was shining and Paddington flicked his paws through the grass to leave his scent whilst Hester raced into the distance, bunny-hopping in joy.

I had written a list for Mary of the dogs' preferences and essentially a history of who they are and what they knew. I took Mary aside and pressed the list into her hand awkwardly and explained I wanted her to know everything about them. I told of how Hester had had problems with other dogs in recent times. I explained how Paddington liked to be held for hours on end and enjoyed howling if you howled with him. How Hester would steal socks from the linen basket and present them to me because she liked to be mock-chased around the house and how Paddington would do anything for marmalade on toast. The commands they knew, the foods they preferred, the cat bed that Hester insisted on sleeping in despite being half her size. Paddington liked fireworks yet hated lamps and metal gates and couldn't work out how to get through partially open doors. Hester liked bottom rubs, laying in the sunshine on her back, disliked Collies and knew every word and emotion I expressed. She liked to be tucked in at night and would only walk on my right hand side. Say the word 'Granddad' and she would go crazy looking for him. I told Mary everything in that list, far more than she ever needed to know. But then I was pouring my heart out in the hope that none of the little details would be forgotten, that I wouldn't forget the little details once they were no longer a part of my life. I was desperate to imprint every moment on my brain let alone theirs and I knew it gave Mary the best chance of understanding.

'They're going to be fine Kathryn, so very loved with us. You see that low gate by the fence and bushes?' Mary pointed across the back garden.

'That leads to their adopted Gran and Granddad next door. They adore dogs and have been waiting for them to arrive. I promise we will look after them and love them with all our hearts. They will have company every day and we are trying to organise taking them on our beach holiday next month. I can't tell you enough how thankful we are to you for bringing them into our world.'

The Bears were having a grand old time in the garden with Mary's family and they bounced high as the new Gran and Granddad appeared from the low gate into the garden as Mary spoke. Paddington was on hind legs and licking faces for all he was worth within seconds. I watched from the door whilst the elderly couple were all smiles and soft talk to their new babies. Their soft white hair bobbed in the breeze as they fussed and tickled Hester and Paddington in turn. I couldn't resist smiling at how perfect their life was going to be with that much love and affection. I couldn't have asked for more.

I had to leave. I knew the moment was coming, it was the culmination of weeks of heartache, months of decision making and I couldn't let myself falter. For the love of my Bears I wanted them to see me happy, to slip away quietly from them and not put them through a painful goodbye with me. I asked Mary if she could keep them distracted in the garden as I left. Typically they ran indoors just at that moment; full of enthusiasm and tails wagging, they ran straight towards me. Hester parked herself between my legs and looked up at me lovingly. I looked into her beautiful brown eyes, those eyes that had kept me strong through every tough moment we had shared. I recalled moments from her puppyhood and beyond and how she had always been with me every step of the way and loved me unconditionally. I gave them both an enthusiastic command I knew they loved.

'Hester, Paddington! What's in there?!' I exclaimed, my voice faltering, and pointed to the back door.

Out they raced in search of whatever it was I had pointed towards. Mary went with them and I knew that was it. Hester and Paddington were no longer my own and, although I had given them a new start in life, a happy start, I just died inside. I looked one last time at them playing in the garden, made it to the front door through glassy eyes and, under the gentle arm of Millie, I fell apart at the car. I felt sick inside and only shock kept me going.

I don't remember the journey back to Millie's; only the whisky and wine she gave me and the cuddles with her two Airedales Delilah and Murphy as I cried myself to sleep. I woke often in the night, desperate to hear from Mary.

How have they settled in? Has Hester been okay without me?

I knew that Hester was neurotic and fearful; she adored the familiarity of me and I had been her one constant in life as others left her so easily. I couldn't imagine her coping well without me just as I wasn't coping well without her. I woke early to Murphy snuffling in my bag for socks and asking for a cuddle. I thought it was Paddington and for one sweet moment I forgot my new reality; that I was no longer a team of three, it was just me now. I didn't think I could ever get used to that, get used to waking up alone and having nobody to care for. My family had simply vanished overnight. I checked my mobile phone for emails and was relieved to hear from Mary. They had settled well and she had hand-fed Hester to help her feel cherished. They had slept on the beds upstairs and they were off for their morning walk as she typed. Thank God they were okay. I knew that if the first night was peaceful they were going to be okay. My heart lifted momentarily as I dressed for the journey home.

The drive home was long, five hours, and I was exhausted and shocked. I kept looking into the rear seats expecting to see two big woolly Bear beards and black noses. Leaving the rear windows open was instinctive after so many years of dog adventures in that car and I opened them automatically. Instead of noses snuffling at the air, woolly beards occupying the rear-view mirror, I just saw traffic and watched as the miles clocked up. I have never felt so alone yet I knew the feeling of heartache well and I knew this was just the start of my grieving, that it was going to be hard to adjust. I was brought back to my senses as an enormous sheet of ice fell from the roof of a lorry in front of me, heading straight for my windscreen. I swerved hard, braked and was lucky to right the car and continue on my way as the ice shattered where I had been moments before. I was exhausted and knew I needed to get home and sleep yet I was dreading facing Dad upon my return. How could I possibly hold it together with someone that knows and loves me so much? We had been through everything together but this I couldn't even talk to him about. It was just too hard and as each mile ticked by I was closer to a moment I desperately wanted to avoid. My pain was my own and I had so far stood by my decision that I needed to do this alone.

Maybe the heart and mind try to protect us from the greatest pain, as I don't remember the rest of that journey or what happened when I arrived home. I can't recall those first moments or when I spoke to Dad. I only remember being comforted in his arms and my desperation to also speak to Nicholas and just be soothed by his words. For once I wasn't even nervous about logging onto the computer to speak to him. My emotions were shot and I felt like I had been struck by a train. His familiar typed 'hey hey' and companionable silence were all that I needed. Nicholas was gentle, he didn't ask too much and he didn't pester or push for information. He just waited patiently as I tried to find the words to explain. When no words came from me, it didn't matter. I knew he was there by me. He knew exactly how I felt and there was no need for me to speak.

22:01 Zone: I'm tearing up. I know how much you loved the Bears :(

That line of text broke down the barriers I had held in place all those weeks as I toughed it out for the sake of my dogs. I cried my tears, typed until my hands ached and then I laughed. Laughed when I felt so broken? Yes, I laughed. I let out a ridiculously loud, life-affirming, laugh as I realised it. It was at that moment I recognised just how much I loved Nicholas. I had slowly fallen for his solid companionship and unwavering acceptance of me (and his bottom). Someone nudged me that night as if to say 'There he is, the one for you sweetheart. Don't let him go'. Of all the times to realise it, I would never have picked then. Something changed for me that night and amidst my sadness the next chapter began to take shape.

48

Three weeks later, on New Year's Eve, I held a meeting with my manager and nervously announced that I wanted to hand in my notice at work and move overseas. I was shaking as I explained to him that, whilst I was thankful for my recent promotion and had been enjoying the work, I needed to move away and being a new chapter of my life. After everything that had come to pass between 2008 and 2012 I no longer wanted to stay. I had been through more ups and downs than I ever expected to and I wanted to have a bite at the world, to create something positive for me and in honour of those I had loved and lost. I fiddled with the sugar sachets in the café nervously as I spoke and expected to be told to drop my stupid ideas and stay. I had already raised the idea with a few friends and acquaintances and they mostly thought I was as mad as a box of frogs for wanting to give up a well paid and permanent job during a recession and move overseas. A part of me agreed with them but I had spent nights awake scribbling in my journal whilst missing my Bears. I was lost and heartbroken without them and needed a distraction. I had written page after page of positive affirmations that I would make my dreams come true. I had written my dreams on that scrap of paper with my sisters in the pub in May and I would make it happen even if I was doing it alone. After everything, life would not stop me now.

Thankfully my manager was incredibly open-minded, a good friend, and he told me to go for it. He said he had always known I could and would do more with my life elsewhere. He grasped my hand tightly in his and said I had to take a leap of faith and do it, whatever it was, whilst I had the drive and passion to do so. He told me he wished he had my courage. I told him I had no idea what I was doing and smiled.

As I drove home along the rain-soaked roads after that meeting, in the dark of the evening, I pulled over and messaged Nicholas.

I am doing it! I have told my manager I am leaving! Oh wow, breathe, I can't believe I am actually doing this....Happy New Year you...watch out world here I come :D xxx

I felt sick with anticipation, excitement and nerves as my mind ran ahead of itself and tried to stop me with fearful reasons of why not to leave and how I would fail. With my fears and abilities it told me I would never become a diving Instructor. It told me I would never survive overseas with so little money in my savings and I should stay safe, keep my job and settle down. I chose to ignore those voices though, they would only hold me back, and instead I focussed on my plans. Nicholas and I had spoken at length before handing my notice in and I knew I had to do what was right for me and not follow my heart all the way to Nicholas. This was to be my time to fly free and grow as a woman whilst living overseas and I wanted to achieve that on my own. It had been my dream for a decade and I wasn't about to ruin it now. Nicholas and I talked, I researched where to do my Instructor training, and we talked some more. Of course in the end I decided upon Egypt and I tried to balance my hope we would one day get together with being certain I was going there for the diving opportunities and location that was right for me. It was a fair mixture of both in my mind, though we danced around the subject online most days and drew our emotional and practical boundary lines from the start. I suspect we were both trying to protect ourselves.

13:58 Zone: I just wanted to check we're on the same page really. I know how you feel about me, and I also have very strong feelings for you. However, I'm really not in the place to be in an 'official' relationship at the moment. I just wanted to be sure that if you're going to be heading out here for more long term plans, that you're not expecting us to get together straight away.

14:05 TeamAiredale: I understand where you're coming from. I hadn't expected us to get together when I'm out that way but I won't lie, it had crossed my mind that I would like to if all went well. But I totally respect you saying that's not an option.

14:06 Zone: I'm not saying it's not an option as time goes on, if you do end up here more or less permanently, but I just didn't want you to expect it :)

14:06 Zone: And so much deja-vu...

14:06 Zone: Maybe because I've run this conversation over in my head a couple of times already :P

14:14 TeamAiredale: okay, here is where I am.....I'm about to make some big changes to my life and yes my plan is to head out to Egypt and be an Instructor and then travel the world whilst diving and teaching people all about sharks and conservation as I go :) It's a huge change for me and I have to be certain that Egypt is the right place for me - which I intend to do by spending some time at the dive centres in Feb and just being there quietly figuring out how my heart feels to be there (call it intuition). The attraction of Egypt rather than Thailand (that's my second choice) is a mixture of the work, ease of access, amazing sea life and yes also you are there. I won't lie, that is one reason I am drawn towards Egypt as I enjoy spending time with you and would like to see how that goes. BUT I need you to know I'm not expecting anything from you at all.

14:17 Zone: The only bit I want to really clear up is that my current thinking is it's a 'not going to happen' unless we both end up in Asia. However, I'm also open to the idea that you never really know what might happen, and if we decide differently whilst out here, then whatever happens, happens :)

14:18 Zone: Basically I'm looking at staying single until I find where I want to set myself down more permanently - and I expect that to be somewhere in Asia.

14:19 Zone: However - never say never :)

14:24 Zone: hope it all makes sense

14:26 Zone: I guess the other reason I wanted to bring it up - I wanted to find out your thoughts, because if it was now or never for a chance to see if 'us' works, then I honestly don't know what I'd do. I wouldn't want to lose the opportunity to find out.

14:53 Zone: You know, I've never felt able to be so relaxed and open about myself with anyone else. I DO have very strong feelings for you, and I've asked myself a few times out of every person I know, who I could see spending the rest of my life with, and you're always the obvious and 'sensible' choice. I add that last bit because occasionally my mind is distracted by a leggy blonde [none in particular, this is just for 'story' purposes] or some such.

14:57 TeamAiredale: ah wow...well, let's be sensible here....if you have those kinds of feelings for me as I do for you then we need to tread carefully and just see where life takes us. I would hate to push it or close the door out of impatience or timing as we could cock it all up.

14:57 Zone: and please don't feel like that's a slight on you being short and brunette. If I hadn't thought you were hot, we wouldn't have done what we did in Tenerife ;)

14:58 TeamAiredale: ahahaha that's fine! seriously...you're a man....you will always be distracted by leggy blondes....I expect nothing less and could cope with that....so long as you looked and didn't touch ;)

14:59 Zone: that goes without saying.

15:02 TeamAiredale: but alas I am not leggy or blonde. You'd be stuck with a brunette, freckly short arse for your life ;P

15:04 TeamAiredale: though I am disappointed I'd be the 'sensible' choice....dear lord that makes me sound dreadful lol. I want to be the best choice, the No.1 'I can't keep my eyes off her, she lights up my world' choice if it ever happens.

15:05 Zone: sensible in that I know... well... I hesitate to use the phrase, 'perfect for each other'.

Oh. At that point I lost my resolve of finding balance between moving to Egypt for the diving and to be with Nicholas. I hadn't known he felt that strongly about me. As I arrived home on New Year's Eve I recalled that moment and tried to push it away and focus on my plans and not my heart. When I checked my emails one last time for the year, I opened a message from my dear friends overseas. Out of nowhere they were offering me a season of working with great white sharks in South Africa. It was a dream come true and I desperately wanted to reply yes. When I spoke to Nicholas about it he told me I absolutely had to take the job. He didn't want me to lose that opportunity. To me it was a sure sign that we would not be getting together, that he didn't mind if I moved elsewhere, and he was right that I had to go for it. I replied to my friends with a huge heartfelt yes and I saw in New Year's Day with Dad knowing I would be moving to South Africa in four months' time and that it was going to be the best year of my life. It had to be, I couldn't take any more failures and loss.

49

I really did not mean to tell Nicholas I loved him. I had no intention of sharing that information and I did not mean to tell him as we were walking past a smelly, dribbling camel in Egypt that February. I certainly did not mean to tell him when I was tipsy on cheap beer and I definitely did not mean to tell him as I stood there in an oversized woolly hat and had wild post-diving hair. It was not classy and I mostly cannot recall Nicholas's words, thanks to the cheap beer and my disbelief that I had professed my love.

It was Valentine's Day and we were enjoying our week together in Egypt up until that point. I had paid no attention whatsoever to the suitability of the local diving centres for my scuba training, beyond talking to one friendly dive master, and had instead spent the week in bed, on the beach and underwater – all with Nicholas by my side. Evidently my career planning and attempts at being a strong-minded single woman faltered that week.

Because of the day it was, we had vowed not to do something couple-related and had continued to draw our emotional boundaries in the sand all day. Nicholas had talked about women and been less affectionate than usual whilst I kept highlighting the excitement of my move to South Africa and the possibility of meeting new people. In the evening we walked past local restaurants covered in giant plastic hearts and fluffy fairy lights and laughed dismissively at the ridiculousness of it all. We scoffed at love, avoided kissing couples like the plague and yet couldn't resist the offer of a five course buffet that smelled divine. Plus it came with a free glass of fake champagne and a dry old rose that smelt of heavy, sickly perfume; classic Valentine's Day accompaniments. Had we known that the evening would have involved me belly dancing and a random man stuffing a live snake down his trousers I suspect we may have gone elsewhere. As it was we made the most of the delicious, abundant Egyptian cuisine, enjoyed the local beer and, whilst I attempted to belly dance, Nick stole my soup and couldn't stop smiling. We agreed it was the best non-Valentine's evening either of us had ever had and walked home hand in hand whilst dodging the Egyptians haggling and selling their wares.

As we walked along I looked up at Nicholas and, for no sane reason, told him that I loved him. Out of nowhere, I admitted my feelings and watched his big brown eyes widen and his mouth fall open just a touch. Right at that moment an Egyptian approached us yet again to sell their fake designer sunglasses (at night time) and Nicholas, for once, gave him short shrift and pulled me to the side of the walkway. He said a lot of important things, he spoke earnestly and no matter how much I have wracked my brain since then I cannot remember precisely what he said. Oh I laid awake all night trying to commit Nicholas's words to memory but my hangover the next day erased them all and permanently. I do know however that he took hold of my hands and told me that he also thought he loved me but that he wasn't ready to admit it to himself fully yet. I was moving to South Africa, he had plans to follow his dreams to South East Asia and he was fearful of getting hurt. But, he knew deep down that I was the one for him. It just wasn't our time yet.

As we stood at the entrance to my apartment I looked up, still in my woolly hat with wild diving hair, and spoke.

'Nicholas, just promise me one thing. As your friend and nothing more I want the best for you and I want all of your dreams to come true. I know, I really *know,* how it feels to lose someone you love and I know that a true love walking into your life doesn't happen every day. Okay, well maybe it happened a few times for me but that's not the same and they were definitely not true loves. Anyway, just promise me this. If you find the woman for you, whether it is me or not, and if you truly love her don't ever let her go. Reach out, take hold of her hand and don't *ever* let her leave,' I implored.

I held Nicholas's arm firmly as I spoke, as if to emphasise the importance of it all.

'I promise. I promise I will never let *you* go.' Nicholas lifted my chin and kissed me tenderly as my over-sized woolly hat fell across my eyes.

I remembered that moment all the way home more than anything else from our weeks together. It had been said knowing we would not see each other for seven months because I was moving to South Africa. I thought about it often during my remaining months in Cornwall, still trying to convince myself not to love Nicholas, and wondered what he had meant. I then began the task of preparing to move overseas to turn my life into something entirely new. I was flipping terrified and asked myself often what on earth I thought I was doing.

50

I started swimming. Nothing exceptional, I know, but I am not a natural swimmer and in just over six months' time I had to pass swimming tests to become a Dive Master. Real tests, in the sea, where I would be required to not only swim considerable distances but to also survive, tow along someone else with me and look like I knew what I was doing. I was about as good at swimming as a moth that has fallen into a swimming pool and believes it can flap its way out and I had only two months until my flight departed to South Africa. I knew my slow breaststroke would not match up to the course requirements. After my return from Egypt, I decided to start swimming regularly and learn how to do front crawl. It was the perfect distraction from the ongoing heartache of missing my Bears, who were already living an idyllic life with their new family. I missed them so much.

With that in mind, I took to the local pool with my new multicoloured swim hat, pink goggles in hand and, oh, I forgot to shave my legs. Excellent start.

I also discovered that my hat made me look like a Chupa Chup lolly; a Chupa Chup lolly with hairy legs. Nice.

I hadn't been taught front crawl before and I needed to learn how to do it and do it well. I didn't want to be the person who completed their Divemaster swimming tests in the slowest time known to PADI; all red-faced wheezing and half drowned. Just call me No Points? That was so not going to be me. I was going to be the graceful one, first to finish in lightning speed with a smile on my face. All long legs, swaying hair and looking super cool as I nonchalantly rose out of the water like a bond girl. I had something to aim for.

So, front crawl. Exactly how do people do it? I had never been as nervous as during my first trip to the pool, despite my dear family spending time showing me beforehand what to do. My initial attempts involved head butting the end of the pool a number of times, which really confused me. No one else seemed to head butt the end when I watched them swimming. How did they know the end was near? Ah, the dashed line on the pool floor apparently. I learnt that it is the indicator of the end of swimming pools. I thought it was just a pretty decoration. I decided to watch the pool floor at all times and swam into someone's backside. I was so busy watching for the dashed line that I forgot to look up and I headbutted some poor old lady square in the bottom. I thought I should get out and quit.

There was also the issue of how to actually do front crawl. There seemed to be a lot of wind-milling of arms going on, kicking of legs and breathing. With so much wind-milling and kicking and watching the pool floor I found breathing quite tricky. I had been advised by my brother-in-law to pretend I was licking my shoulder to get the right position for breathing whilst continuing to swim.

First attempt at that and what did I do from concentrating so much on the concept? I actually tried to lick my shoulder, choked on a lot of water and promptly burst out laughing in the middle of the deep end and half-drowned in the process. That didn't go down well in a pool full of serious lane swimmers at 7.30am on a Monday morning. I needed to work on my breathing or buy a snorkel.

The part that really filled me with dread was the lanes. The lanes of doom scared me senseless. I was like a sheep without a herd and I just didn't know which lane I belonged in. I decided that, if in doubt, I ought to choose the slow lane. Slow lane was a lovely place to be. It was a very wide lane, it took up most of the pool and it was full of old people that I came to adore. There was the cheery middle-aged lady that was even worse at front crawl than me. She was a learner too. I liked her for the simple fact that we encouraged each other and I could also remind myself quietly that I was not the worst, I was second worst. Then there were the two elderly ladies that didn't appear to do any swimming. They seemed to just hang out at the end like two birds on a wire, wittering away and putting the world to rights. God love those ladies and their hot air. There was the wiry old chap that didn't swim but conducted some form of underwater physiotherapy whilst holding on to the side of the pool. He nearly kicked me in the face a number of times as he rotated his leg and thrust it wildly out into the blue. I rather admired his lack of care and his crazy underwater moves. But my personal favourite was the very old man. Let's call him Burt. He looked like a Burt and he was awesome. He was there week in, week out with a big smile on his face and he is the oldest person I have seen alive. He also appeared to be wearing actual underwear in the pool; both where underwear should be worn and also on his head. I tried to get close enough on a number of occasions to establish if he was in fact wearing pants on his head but then I started to look like a stalker. From what I could tell, they matched his bottom attire and so I came to the conclusion that they were in fact pants. I didn't feel it would be appropriate to ask him outright if he had pants on his head. I mean, I had a Chupa Chup lolly on my head so really I couldn't speak. In addition to his pants, Burt had his own unique style of swimming and I rather liked it. He swam like a very wonky, overenthusiastic frog wearing pants on its head. I felt very at home in the slow lane amongst those people. It was where I came to belong, my comfort zone, my nest. People said hello to me in there but I didn't think that was going to help me pass my Dive Master.

Ugh, the middle lane. It was not quite the fast lane but definitely a different zone to my beloved slow lane. The people in the middle lane were mean and quick and really good swimmers. They were probably all on 'swim faster' drugs, high on their achievements as they flew through the water and whooped when they beat their best times. Oh I hated that lane, hated it. It took me a month to get up the courage to even go and look at that lane. I told myself I had to do it and asked myself really how bad it could be. Very bad, so bad I burst into tears on my first attempt. I tried to keep up with my wind-milling kicking crawl and my awesome hat of many colours but they were so fast! I got halfway through a length, panicked at the demon swimmer approaching me from behind with a look of murder on his face, promptly headbutted the lane barrier and licked my shoulder. Excellent. I retreated into the slow lane and wept into my goggles.

Thankfully things improved since those early days. I became a better swimmer and I can still do a version of front crawl for a number of lengths. I even managed to find myself at home in the middle lane – though I think that was because I bumped everyone up into the fast lane. It seemed crowded in there whenever I went swimming. My problem was then that I became overenthusiastic and of the opinion I could maybe go faster. I decided it would be a great idea to swim a length as fast as I could one Friday, to get an idea of how fast I could swim if I was being chased by a shark. I felt it was important to know that in the event of either a shark chasing me or my wanting to keep up with a shark swimming away from me. I love sharks and would be likely to chase one in the water so I could see it more closely. Anyway, my mini swimming test went well, I was quick(ish) and I didn't head butt anyone. But I was on anti-inflammatory painkillers with a bad back for the next week. I think I was a little too keen. I reverted to the slow lane again upon my return, satisfied with my achievements, and checked out Burt with his pants on his head.

51

Despite my swimming success I still found myself panicking and couldn't begin to imagine being able to take my mask off underwater during my diving courses. Yet I knew I had to do it over and over again and that I had to be confident at doing so as an Instructor. My poor future students would not take too kindly to me, as an Instructor, bursting into tears when I took my mask off underwater and then bolting to the surface without them. I was moving to South Africa in forty-three sleeps and decided to try a course of hypnotherapy to rid me of my fears. I had already spent a day in a swimming pool with my old Instructor Dawn, practising taking my mask off, and that went well. I had sat in the bath and filled my mask with water from my pink elephant watering can again whilst I relaxed with the bubbles and that went well. I survived; I definitely didn't die suddenly on either occasion. My brain by now believed that being underwater in a swimming pool or bath and removing my mask was not a problem. But the ocean…..that was entirely different according to my mind.

When Nicholas and I last went diving in Egypt, the scenery was stunning and we had great visibility. We went deep and I became 'narked' almost immediately – which is a diving term used to describe a condition that leaves you feeling inebriated underwater. It isn't particularly conducive to diving well and safely. I was narked and quite frankly couldn't have cared less if I sank to the bottom of the ocean. I was giggling away to myself, heard music in my ears and really had very little idea of what I was doing. We went shallow to ease the symptoms and pottered about looking at the beautiful reef and did our safety stop at the end of the dive. I was feeling tired by this point and Nicholas kept making me laugh with various underwater impressions from films we had watched together. Some things just make me giggle and I couldn't stop laughing and flooded my mask with water. In the end I had to face away from Nicholas so I could regain some form of control and sort my mask out. I must have been confused from laughing so much, as I turned towards him and thought he gestured for me to try taking my mask off. Nicholas knew all about my fears and would never, ever, ask me to remove my mask.

I was feeling brave and decided I could do it. I could so do it with bells on. I whipped my mask off and looked straight at Nicholas. For a fraction of a second it was okay. I had done it; I had actually not died from taking my mask off in the ocean and then it all went wrong. I panicked; oh I panicked and looked like such an incompetent. Nicholas held me by my waist as I hyperventilated. I kicked like an angry child who'd had her sweets taken away, looked at him pleadingly (at least I think it was pleading, maybe it just looked like insanity?) and I wheeled my arms around trying to explain to him in sign language that I was going to die. I had no mask on and sudden death would occur if I was not removed from the water at that very moment. Being the lovely calm chap that Nicholas is he didn't let go of me as I bolted for the surface. Not that I noticed or cared. I was so far beyond reason it was ridiculous. We made it to the surface and I cried. We made it back to the boat and I cried again. Nicholas tried to reassure me it was no big deal. I cried some more and, in a high-pitched unintelligible voice that sounded somewhat like a seal, I stated I was going to be the worst diving Instructor ever. Another friend of ours then wandered over and asked if it was a good dive, to which I responded by crying some more and resuming the high-pitched seal impression. I am an adult….seriously, not cool. It turned out, unsurprisingly, that Nicholas hadn't been gesturing for me to take my mask off underwater at all.

I reminded myself that I didn't particularly want to go through that kind of embarrassment again as I booked myself onto the course of hypnotherapy. I genuinely believed that my mask fear and my willingness to understand and overcome it would give me compassion and make me a great scuba diving Instructor in due course. Come the day I had a nervous student who couldn't get their head underwater and who had a panic and a wobble of confidence at times, I hoped to be able to help them through it to achieve their dream of becoming a diver. I was hopeful that hypnotherapy would be an incredible experience I could share with people in the future. Thankfully it met up to those expectations.

I was apprehensive when I went for my first introductory chat and I sat there meekly on the chair hoping the therapist could not read my mind and that I would not blurt out too much information. To be honest, I was expecting the therapist to look like Mystic Meg and have the voice of Alice In Wonderland's Caterpillar 'Whooo…are….you?' I expected to be made to look into her eyes, cluck like a chicken when commanded to do so and then be back in the room in five, four, three, two, ONE! The therapist was actually a normal person, there was no looking into eyes and I did not cluck like a chicken. Instead I spent that day and future sessions learning all about fear management, how to reduce anxiety (I knew I needed to master that one) and had a number of kips on a comfy couch whilst retraining my brain in the process. I discovered that I was totally aware of everything my therapist said when I was lying on the couch and the sessions appeared to work. I felt relaxed, calm and able to visualise removing my mask underwater without my pulse going through the roof. That was a good start.

The part that baffled me though was the appropriate etiquette for when being hypnotised. I didn't know how I was supposed to behave when being stared at whilst lying on a couch. How should I look? What should I do? Being stared at is generally un-nerving for most people and I am not a fan of letting anyone ever see me sleep (in case I dribble a lot). As such, I found that part of the situation quite difficult and way outside of my comfort zone. I just couldn't figure out what I should be doing. I gave it a lot of thought and spent a large portion of my time on the couch trying desperately to keep still and to 'look' hypnotised. Yes, that is correct; I tried to look hypnotised as I didn't want my therapist to think I was doing it wrong. It was ridiculous. I found my right leg had a mind of its own every time I was on the couch and I fought a weekly battle to try and stop it from lashing out at my therapist as she told me to relax. Apparently involuntary twitching is normal when under hypnosis. Still, kicking her in the face would seem excessive. I also worried that if my breathing increased she would think I was coming 'out' of being hypnotised. To combat that problem, I started holding my breath for as long as possible so that I looked like I was breathing slowly due to being so relaxed. The only trouble was that I felt a bit short on air at times, my heart started racing and I needed to suck great lungs of air in surreptitiously. That was not easy to get away with in a silent room when I was also trying to look appropriate. I also didn't dare swallow either in case that wasn't supposed to happen – which didn't help with trying to prevent dribbling. An hour is a long time not to swallow. After going through that malarkey for what seemed like ages every session I usually give in and relaxed from sheer exhaustion. I can't help wondering that if I relaxed sooner it may be even more beneficial.

But on the other hand, what if I relaxed too much and let out an almighty fart? Then I really would need therapy.

52

I didn't realise that growing my new water wings would be exciting and yet so exhausting. As I swam into April I was on the verge of leaving behind all that was familiar and safe to me in order to chase my dreams, to live my authentic, creative life surrounded by my true passions and loves. I was going to live in the sunshine as a shark diving guide and Instructor, write, create, sing and hope my life path would inspire others to take a chance on their dreams. It sounded amazing, it was amazing. I just hadn't realised I would feel so tired in between the crazy excitement of those imminent changes.

I lovingly titled my move overseas and the challenges and dreams it would contain as Book Two. I was going to broaden my horizons, my life and spread new wings. Smile at the sun and fly free to be me. No one had stopped me from doing this before but, like many people, I had bowed under the pressure of expectations from myself to conform and be what others expected of me. I had put aside my dreams in order to please others and stay firmly in my conventional, somewhat musty cardboard box. Well stuff that, I was climbing out of my box one step at a time that spring. The path had been ten years in the making. My box was made of quite thick cardboard and I had found myself comfortable in there at times with Graham and then Oscar.

In order to leave feeling truly free I decided to clear out all of my belongings, which also meant I was clearing out my mental clutter and hopefully healing old wounds. It was not an easy task, as I had clung onto every childhood toy and had the remnants of my old life, furniture and things to let go of. But I did it. I spent weeks clearing through every box, relived every moment and cried and laughed my way through it all. I was confronted with happy memories of my beautiful mum, sad memories of the loss of my wonderful woolly Bears and the pain that came with my fiancés walking away and leaving me behind. The best part was the childhood toys. They were hilarious and it had me in stitches when I realised the crap I had kept. My favourite had to be my Take That tour programmes from the 1990s with my handwritten comments from each tour of when a member of Take That waved/winked/pointed at ME. Of course they were waving at me. Evidently I believed I would be marrying Howard from Take That (according to my comments) and yes I also spent a day camped outside Robbie Williams' house once. I was that cool as a teenager. My friend Vicky had tried to steal his pants from his washing line but sadly she couldn't climb over the high garden wall despite our best efforts. Robbie I am very sorry we tried to steal your underwear.

I recycled, sold and gave away everything other than some basic furniture and the clothes I would need to take with me for life overseas. I would like to say it left me feeling free but it left me feeling a wee bit tired and without an identity. I felt like I had pulled a huge sticky plaster off my face and it unexpectedly whipped off my features in the process; eyebrows, lady moustache and all. I didn't expect that to happen.

Having cleared out the old, I became busy growing my new wings and they were fine wings indeed. I was on the most incredible journey and those wings were going to support me through thick and thin. They needed to be both beautiful to the eye and sturdy. Somewhere between angel wings, swan wings and 'built to fly all day' albatross wings. I definitely did not need Dodo stump wings. I was perched on the edge of my cliff, looking at the abyss and testing out my prototype wings before I leapt. It was one month and counting until I would fly.

53

'You don't have to be great to start, but you have to start to be great' – Joe Sabah

That was my inspiration in my final weeks in England as I took deep breaths and put myself out there whilst cutting and pasting my dreams together. I repeated that quote in my head often with emphasis on the 'great'. But then I realised the quote reminded me of Kellogg's Frosties cereal hero Tony the Tiger every time I said 'great'. I had an idea and so my new mantra, said every morning as I looked in the mirror with crazy bed hair and blurry eyes, went like this:

Hey Kathryn!

Bring out the tiger in you!

Earn your stripes!

You're Grrreat!

I said it with a Tony the Tiger voice and a deep throaty grrrrr when I reached the word great. It was essential that I pointed at my reflection in the mirror as I said each line. After all, I was telling myself I was great! It was impossible not to laugh and it was a brilliant start to the day. I also spent a large amount of my time doing visualisation exercises, as I had decided that if my mind believed I could achieve something and it could visualise me doing it repeatedly then success would be certain. I genuinely believed this was the case and I knew it wasn't a new idea. It is something that professional athletes (and others) use all of the time and I put it into practice in my own way and for my own life. The visualisation worked well, so I used it for all of the things I wished to achieve. I was creating the life I dreamed of in my mind and then making it all happen.

In my last two weeks in Cornwall I pondered with my colleagues how I would exit the office on my last day. We came up with the following:

a) Take over the office tannoy system and sings songs to the entire office.

b) Turn up to my customers' sites in a hi-viz bikini instead of wearing my usual hi-viz jacket and hard hat. That would certainly liven up the day but may also be the death of me in the winter weather

c) Make everyone a big cake. No surprises this was the most popular option along with going to the pub after work

I also decided I was going to finish with a flourish at my last lane swimming session by swimming in the fast lane of doom. I was nowhere near fast enough to do that but felt it was important to be able to say I swam in the fast lane. I was just a little bit scared and unsure how it would turn out but I was going to do it and would keep up with the people that inhabited that lane even if it killed me. I hoped that I wouldn't panic like the first time I went in the middle lane, couldn't keep up and swam into the lane barriers.

During my last day at work I rode the adrenaline train with many cups of tea and chocolate caterpillar cake to keep me firing on at least one cylinder that day. In the past twenty-four hours I had lurched from sadness to fear to downright 'so excited I might be sick' emotions. I was like a child at Christmas faced with a mountain of presents and realising they were all for me. How did I get that lucky? Or….how did I find the strength within me to believe in and create such an opportunity?

As promised to myself, I started the day with my final lane swimming session. Never mind actual swimming, my friend and I made up games instead including:

1) Backwards swimming as fast as you can in the slow lane

2) Hanging out chatting with the old people, especially Burt with is pants on his head. It turned out he wasn't called Burt after all, his name was Eric. What a gentleman.

3) Treading water for as long as possible with my swimming partner whilst holding a conversation, holding arms out of the water and avoiding the death stares from the serious swimmers and from the lifeguard.

And in a final flourish of giggles I braved the fast lane. There was a man in the fast lane who was entirely triangular in stature and his shoulders were each bigger than my head. I sidled up to him in order to check that and yes I realised his shoulders were akin to my head size. He was flying up and down the lane like a man possessed. A man with a bee in his swimming trunks that was stinging him for all he was worth. We observed from the middle lane and decided we would have to duck in to the fast lane and swim like crazy to keep up with him. On the word 'Go' we leapt into action and swam as if our lives depended on it. Unfortunately I got confused, hit the lane barrier and stood up laughing…..only to see my friend ploughing straight towards the triangle man's head. Thankfully she realised at the last minute and bailed out into the middle lane with a very high-pitched squeal. It turned out we had navigated the lane in the wrong direction and I clearly just didn't know which way was forwards. We pottered about in the middle lane for a while in a fit of hysterics and discussed tactics. We decided we would try again but this time we would go the right way around the lane and follow the pool markings so we didn't veer. Triangle man must have been getting tired, as we actually kept up and I achieved my dream. I swam in the fast lane.

It seemed to me that the progression from the slow lane was much like a reflection of life in general. We all need to spend periods of time in our comfort zone; the slow lane where life is predictable, comfortable like a well-worn slipper and easy-going on the joints and soul. The beauty of the slow lane is it allows you time to heal, time to think about your dreams and life to date. It allows you time to establish connections with people that make your days that much brighter whilst you consider your next move. I loved spending time with the older generation in my slow lane and it definitely afforded me the time to learn how to do front crawl –a new skill in a comfortable arena, to grow my new mermaid wings and be surrounded by slow-paced wisdom and support. I knew I would genuinely miss seeing Burt (he will always be Burt to me) and the man that did front crawl with a mask and bright green snorkel. Those wonderful people were each on their own journey in the slow lane and I felt privileged to have been a part of their world and kindness.

Then there is the middle lane. The times in our lives when we decide to stretch our wings, test our blossoming dreams and hopes without the commitment of throwing ourselves in at the deep end. It is a time of discovering if our beliefs about ourselves are true and seeing how much potential each of us holds. Can we make anything happen if we try hard enough? For me, the middle lane gave me the confidence to realise that actually I can do front crawl and, more importantly, anything is possible and achievable. All it had taken was consistent effort, a sense of humour and a multicoloured swimming cap. By stretching my wings I started to realise that my future is in my hands, I am capable of more than I realise. I didn't know where that discovery would lead me to. We are all capable of more than we realise and the only limitation is that which we place upon ourselves with our minds, false beliefs and negativity. The middle lane gave me so much more than just earache from front crawl and laughter from head butting the end of the pool.

What of the fast lane? That is where achieving dreams and putting into practice new-found confidence occurs. But it is also where there is no place for hesitation. It is the time and place to shout charge at the top of your voice and swim as if your life depends on it. Swim like never before, with a smile on your face and a mental attitude that says 'let's do this and see what life throws at me'. The fast lane isn't always a smooth ride and inevitably there would be times when I would bail out into the middle lane again and reassess. But I planned on never giving up, believing in my dreams and getting back in there regardless.

On the day of my final swim I was seventeen sleeps away from turning my life upside down. I had fear as my bedside companion and there were moments when I lay awake in the middle of the night wondering why I was moving to the other side of the world alone. In those moments I remembered that I was doing it for the fast lane, for the belief I had more to offer to this world, because life was precious and because I wanted to hug sharks. I hoped to give the very best of me to the people and world around me and to help others to make their dreams come true. It was finally time to walk tall as I left the office behind and stepped into the unknown.

54

Today, I am sitting here after my first day of work on a shark ecotourism boat in South Africa. I have dreamed of pursuing this passion as my 'work' for 10 years. Thanks to the inspiration and confidence I gained, I packed my bags two weeks ago, left the UK and here I am! I couldn't be happier to finally have the courage to follow my dreams. My work is no longer work… it is fun and I get paid to do this!?!

You can go through the darkest times and survive, or even come out winning in the end. My story wasn't unusual, I was not superhuman, just a regular person in her thirties that had some heartache and tried to get through it and fight for something more. At the time I wrote that paragraph in my journal I was living in South Africa. During my final weeks in England I had packed my bags, said tearful goodbyes to my family and friends and then boarded a big shiny aeroplane. I asked myself what I was doing moving to Cape Town throughout the long flight. I had fought hard for my dreams and against my fears for months and it was too late to back down. I settled surprisingly quickly into my cosy cottage by the ocean. I was doing it alone, I was scared of the unfamiliar surroundings and crime levels but I had a smile on my face – or was that tension and fear? Just days after my arrival, I began working on the boat for my friends and began sharing my passion for the oceans with anyone that would listen. I had finally figured out that if I could survive the past few years and still have a smile on my face (which I had done) then I could find the courage to chase my dreams and set myself free. I worked on the boat most days and learnt how to adjust to balancing on rough seas whilst working, how to size people for wetsuits without offending them and how to identify individual sharks from one another. I was nervous and seasick often but I didn't give up. I worked hard on a daily basis whilst I watched the ocean, the guests around me and whispered to myself...*I did this.*

55

South Africa became somewhere I cherished in my heart as home. My friends and family had often asked me why I would chose to live somewhere that has such a high crime rate and is known for its social and political problems. With that in my mind, I expected to feel unsafe and threatened being there alone but instead I found it liberating and more welcoming than any other country I had lived in or visited. I was based near Cape Town, in a relaxed seaside community called Fish Hoek. It wasn't the prettiest of towns but the people were happy, kind and always had the time to stop and say hello. I noticed that the residents of Fish Hoek mostly walked barefoot wherever they went and I enjoyed watching them do their weekly shopping, driving and walking along the high street without shoes and without caring about it.

Fish Hoek beach was my haven that year, with its golden sands and crashing waves. I lost count of the number of my walks there that lasted hours simply because of idle conversations with people passing by and because there was so much to see. There were the elderly ladies that took their daily early morning swim at the southern end of the beach. I watched as they gingerly dipped their wrinkled toes in the water and waded out beyond the small waves, their hair as white as clouds and fragile arms held out for balance. There was an elderly couple present most days and I could see how the years had moulded them into one. The gentleman didn't so much as let go of his lady once whilst they stumbled through the larger waves. I admired their courage (these waters are cold), their love and sense of togetherness. There was the man with the ball; the ruby red ball and the ever-present smile on his face. I saw him every day on his own with his cherished ball. He spent hours playing with that shiny bouncing ball, kicking it round, tossing it in the air and he always looked so content. He even took his ball for a swim. Evidently it must have been an excellent swimming companion and always handy as a float.

There were also walkers with dogs of all shapes and sizes. I found myself veering towards them and adored the companionship of those dogs, especially as I missed the Bears terribly each day. I never saw any Airedale terriers but was lucky enough to meet a sparky and proud Irish terrier that lived by me. He was a corker; all wiry copper blonde hair, wet gumdrop nose and ears pricked and ready for action. His name…Fluff. I bumped into the owner of the dog on my return home and he proudly presented me with his wife and exclaimed 'I've brought my other Irish terrier along this time'.

Finally, there was Prince and we sat and talked on one of the bright red benches by the beach. He was from Zimbabwe and made wire and bead animals to sell on the high street to tourists. He had very little income or possessions and the animals he made were his livelihood. We sat and talked about life and happiness and how broken the world is due to the cruelty of those in charge and the importance placed on wealth. He couldn't go back to Zimbabwe due to the troubles there and he told me how he missed his home. It made Prince deeply sad that the people of Zimbabwe are intelligent, motivated people yet there was no opportunity for them to grow, to earn a living and find a safe place to be. He moved from place to place and all he asked was to be left alone by others and to have peace. He told me of the bad times he has experienced at the hands of other men yet he still smiled as we shared happy stories. He was content that, on the day we met, the sun was shining and the sea was his company whilst he worked.

It struck me that we all come from such different backgrounds and experiences yet we are all the same. We have the same fears and wishes for one another, we all have a heart that can be hurt or healed and we can do something to make a positive change. As Prince finished his work and packed up to go, he gave me a beautiful bead rhinoceros. I tried to argue that he couldn't give me his work for free but he refused. He had so little, yet in his words 'the joy is in the creation, in seeing others smile'.

Away from the beach, my time was taken up with working on the boat and with the sharks. I met my partner in crime and colleague Jane soon after arriving in South Africa and we spent many happy days at sea together in the sunshine during autumn. Jane was the only other crewmember on the boat, a tough cookie, and one to have on your team in times of need. She was far better than me at pulling anchor, was a grounding influence and became a very close friend of mine. The only down sides with our work were that getting up at 5am never got any easier despite months of practice, guests were sometimes sick on my head and down the front of me and there was a box of food onboard that tempted me daily. It was full of sweets, chocolate and crisps and I battled to avoid it and often failed after a twelve hour day at sea and a desperate need for sustenance. Oh and I also had bright orange waterproof dungarees to wear each day, which made me look like a Satsuma.

Jane and I spent hours talking about life, shared our stories and enjoyed the wildlife in the ocean around us whilst the season progressed into winter. We got to know many different sharks that came to our boat, all with distinct and different personalities, and we saw different species of whales and dolphins regularly. It was incredible. When my life took a dramatic turn of events at the end of my time in South Africa Jane was the one who rescued me in the nick of time. I will forever owe her for her persistence and refusal to give up. We knew nothing of that day to come though during our time on the boat and enjoyed the guests that joined us for their marine safaris. We were lucky to meet many people and I found their stories inspiring and uplifting.

One such person was an unassuming, quiet woman who wasn't feeling very well throughout her trip at sea and she lay at the bow of our boat under layers of clothing and towels. She was mostly fast asleep all morning, curled up small and unresponsive to my trying to assist her. I didn't spend a great deal of time with her, knowing she wouldn't want to talk when she felt so seasick. She appeared to be a regular young woman on holiday with her boyfriend, perhaps straight out of university, and I left her in peace to rest.

I met a confident, gentle and well-spoken Asian lady during that working day. She was on her honeymoon and she joined our boat for the day with her husband. Whilst the other guests on board couldn't decide whether to go shark diving she was the first to volunteer. She calmly got ready with her husband by her side, slid into the cage and enjoyed their first dive with a beautiful white shark. I admired her confidence and her ease at being the first to volunteer without hesitation on what was a cold and foggy day. She was tranquil in a situation that most people find challenging at first if they have not dived with sharks before. I assumed she must have been a regular diver with plenty of experience for she had the grace of a mermaid.

When we returned to the harbour I escorted our group to the shop for mugs of tea, hot chocolate and coffee. Hands were warmed around colourful mugs; steam rising to soothe cold cheeks after a brisk morning in the elements. I was afforded more time to get to know the guests as they shared their excitement at seeing the sharks and other wildlife. I asked the quiet young girl if she was feeling better now that we were ashore. What followed was a conversation in which she explained to me that she was visiting Cape Town to investigate moving there in the next couple of years and because she was celebrating opening her first school in Tanzania.

She was from Italy and had spent the three years working in Tanzania with local underprivileged children and had one day decided to build a school for them. She had funded it herself, built the school, obtained the teaching materials and books from overseas, would be teaching the children and training the future teachers. She had achieved that all on her own, overseas, away from family support and the school was opening the following week after we met. She was only twenty-four years old.

She had the good grace and honesty to laugh and admit that most people were surprised when she explained what she had achieved. She knew she looked like every other girl her age, dressed in the latest cool clothing, and hanging out with her peers. Yet one day she woke up and decided she wanted to create a school and so she did it; without any prior experience or qualifications to do so. I was speechless at how she had a dream, a BIG dream, decided that it would happen and made it so. She didn't tell herself she couldn't do it, she didn't give up and she didn't expect others to make it happen for her. She just took one step at a time and tackled each hurdle with confidence. Her walk turned into a run and she was already considering where to open her next school.

But what of the confident gentle honeymooner that was first into the cage? As we talked about how much she enjoyed her cage diving experience her husband gently took her in his arms. With an incredibly proud and loving smile upon his face, he told me this:

His wife had only learnt to swim four weeks ago. She was terrified of water, absolutely terrified, and throughout her life she had only been able to go calf-deep in water before having a panic attack. She literally fell apart mentally at the thought of going into water but she wanted to overcome her fear so she could cage dive with her husband. She wanted to give him that gift with all her heart and so she spent time with a coach in the final weeks before her wedding, learning to swim and overcome her fear. As if pre-wedding preparations and stress were not enough, she took on that challenge as well. It turned out that on our boat she was terrified, she didn't want to get in the water at all and she felt her old familiar panic rising at the prospect of not only being in deep water but also with a shark nearby. Yet she did it without a word of complaint or hint of nervousness to the guests and crew around her. She did it, she loved it and the look in her husband's eyes told me everything I needed to know about overcoming your fears and about true love. I never would have known from the demeanour of those two guests that each would have such a story to tell. I was wrong about them and those two people left a lasting impression upon me.

I realised then that strangers in the street, colleagues, loved ones and the people that pass us by are where the real magic lies. They are where I could find everything I needed to encourage and inspire me if only I truly saw them without judgement. If only I let them in just the way they are and listened with my heart rather than my subjective mind. Then I saw the real person, heard the real story and went home to share it. Went home and curled up with a mug of steaming tea, a smile in my eyes and typed to Nicholas almost daily…

You'll never guess what happened to me today.

56

By the time we were in the depths of winter in South Africa, which was still mild on land compared to England, Jane and I had spent plenty of long, bitterly cold and exhausting days on rough seas and had supported each other throughout it all. We gave words of encouragement when we became progressively more tired from the non-stop pace of work and passed each other strong coffees to keep us going. I continued to enjoy my adventures at sea despite the hectic schedule of work and my time at home was taken up with dive theory studies for my Divemaster course whilst missing Nicholas. We had continued to talk online for months whenever time allowed and there were many evenings when I fell asleep with my laptop open as we tried to talk and the exhaustion of being at sea caught up with me. By the last week of the season I was counting down the days until I returned to England for my diving course and to see family before flying onwards to Egypt and to be reunited with Nicholas.

I didn't want to leave South Africa in many ways and I had adored my work there but knew it was time to move on and face the next set of challenges. I had completed my studies, Nicholas and I had grown ever-closer and, in the final weeks before leaving, it had finally become clear to me that we would most likely be getting together. His dreams of South East Asia were rarely mentioned and instead we talked of returning to South Africa together the following year.

I thought about all of that during my last day at sea and was looking forward to an evening with Jane at my favourite pizzeria to celebrate a successful season of work. I had three days after finishing work during which to pack and move out of my cottage. It was plenty of time and my mind was occupied by the promise of good food as we moored the boat at the jetty. I said my goodbyes to the crew I had worked with for five months, looked at the beautiful blue ocean around us and then caught a lift home with some local acquaintances I often shared a ride with. I didn't know them well but they were two local Rastas, Leon and Mondre, who had kindly offered to drive me home most days.

On the drive home I was admiring the ocean yet again when I noticed a road block ahead of us. I had seen these road blocks often and thought nothing of it as we turned down a side road to get around it. Our vehicle was promptly stopped from doing so by a police van and I noticed Leon and Mondre fidgeting and quickly stubbing out their smokes as a policeman approached. I cottoned on as to why very quickly; Leon and Mondre always smoked marijuana on the way home and I always spent the journey with my head hanging out of the window trying to breathe fresh air. I realised that the police had stopped the vehicle to search it and assumed Leon and Mondre were trying to get rid of any evidence that they had been taking drugs. In my naivety, as a non-smoker and someone that doesn't do drugs, it didn't occur to me I could in any way become implicated in this problem.

We were ushered out of the car and a heated exchange followed between Leon and a police officer. I had no idea what was going on because they spoke in Afrikaans and I just stood there calmly enjoying the afternoon sunshine and thinking I would soon be heading home for pizza with Jane. Then I looked back at the car and saw another police officer holding up what appeared to be an enormous bag of marijuana he had found in the back of Leon's vehicle. I watched as Leon and Mondre were cuffed and shoved into the back of a second police van. At this point a third police officer approached me and, in English, asked me if I understood what was going on. I politely said I thought so and asked for a lift home because it was nothing to do with me and I was merely catching a lift after work. The police officer kindly informed that actually it was everything to do with me. Leon and Mondre had denied all involvement and pointed the proverbial finger at me. I was being arrested for the possession of illegal drugs with intent to supply.

I *still* didn't cotton on to the fact I had been arrested as I was driven to the local police station. I sat in the front seat all the way there chatting happily about life, my work and how I used to assist the police in England during my old career. The police officer had to pull the car over to the side of the road and tell me again I was under arrest and that I would most likely be spending the weekend in jail. At that point it began to sink in and I went numb with shock. This was really happening to little old me. I had never even smoked a cigarette let alone smoked drugs. My idea of a good night out was a glass of wine at home and going to bed with a book and yet there I was being arrested in South Africa for the possession of drugs. I was literally being banged up overseas.

When we arrived at the police station I was taken hold of and ushered unceremoniously onto the *wrong* side of the front desk. By wrong I mean the side where the criminals are processed before being put behind bars. I was surrounded by officials, Leon,

Mondre and a cell to one side that was full of the most terrifying people I have ever encountered. They looked half-wild, as if they might eat me, as they eyed me up and down from behind bars. I began to realise that could be where I was heading and I feared for my safety and panicked. I looked at Leon and Mondre and they both looked away from me and at the floor. My belongings had been taken from me as soon as we arrived, nobody knew I was here, I couldn't contact anyone and no one was speaking up to shout my innocence. Everyone spoke in Afrikaans, I didn't understand a word, but I knew Leon and Mondre said nothing about me. They didn't so much as acknowledge or mention me for the next hour as we stood there being processed. I was more frightened than I have ever been and felt utterly powerless to do anything about it. I didn't know the law in South Africa, I didn't know what to do and I was made to sign a statement that said I understood I was being arrested for the possession of drugs. I felt sick to my stomach and began to shake. I barely held it together and then in walked Jane.

As fate would have it Jane had driven past Leon just as he was being cuffed at the roadside. She had seen me enter a police car and, knowing me as a friend, assumed it was nothing to do with me and that I was being given a lift home. Jane drove home quickly and then back to the police station to see how she could help. Our eyes locked across the desk and she realised I was on the wrong side of it and so must have been arrested.

It is a well-known fact amongst her friends that Jane has an 'Attack Chicken' mode. When Jane's friends are under threat, she goes into attack mode to protect them and becomes a persistent pecking chicken. I had never seen it before but I knew how loyal Jane was and that she would do anything for her loved ones. I was desperately relieved to see her as she leant over the counter to hug me. We were promptly told not to touch by a nearby officer but Jane gave him a look of pure fury and carried on regardless.

As Jane tried to calm me down she explained that, as I had been arrested on a Saturday, I could not get out on bail and would be spending the weekend in a cell until my court case was heard on Monday. I was due to be leaving South Africa on Tuesday and that information threw me over the edge of reason. Just as Jane was explaining that she would do everything in her power to speak to the detective and fight that decision, I was taken away by another officer I didn't know or understand. He obtained a translator and I was asked to undress to show my tattoo on my back so they could record it as a distinguishing mark on my paperwork. I felt humiliated and frightened as I did so and then, after dressing, they took each of my fingerprints. I had so far not cried up until that point but when I saw the ink on my hands and it wouldn't come off I broke down. It was all too much, I had no idea what was happening and I sobbed. Attack Chicken Jane suddenly appeared and calmed me down as she gave the detective she was waiting for a look of pure evil and exclaimed I couldn't possibly be guilty because I was English and crying a LOT. I adored her logic. She told him to look at the state I was in and begged him to realise I was innocent in all of this. He sat there in his purple knitted jumper, portly and friendly-looking in his power, and yet refused to move from his seat. I eyed the half-wild criminals in the cell next to me again and felt sick at the prospect of joining them. Jane assured me I would be put in a cell behind the main station building if she couldn't get me out and she returned to fighting for my release. Meanwhile, I begged any officer that passed me by to please let me go home. I just wanted to go home and have my pizza.

It took four hours to process me and I continued to look bewildered and frightened as I stood by the front desk. Jane did her best to reassure me I would be released today but the officers assured her I would not be released until the following week. Leon and Mondre had been escorted to their cells for the weekend and it was my turn. I couldn't believe it when two straight-faced officers walked me out of the back door and turned me towards a dank and miserable looking cell. I began to shake as I realised the extent of what was happening and I heard Jane's voice fading on the breeze as I walked away from my chance of freedom.

The cell had a thick outer door with huge bolts and an inner barred door. The officers pushed me into the dark cell and bolted both doors noisily behind me. As my eyes adjusted to the lack of light and my nose adjusted to the stench of the area that was supposedly a toilet in the corner of the cell I realised I was not alone. There was a young teenage girl curled up asleep on the one mattress in the cell and she was clutching an orange tightly. She spoke in Afrikaans and I didn't understand most of what she said but she managed to explain she wanted to go home and was innocent. Typically I also told her I was innocent (does everybody do that?). I didn't know what she had done or why she had an orange but she was polite enough and offered me a horrible, scratchy prison blanket. At the realisation that I would need a blanket because I was going to be in a cold cell all weekend without a toilet, food or additional clothing I lost the plot with anger. I was absolutely furious at being treated that way, I had done nothing to deserve it, and I angrily checked my statement of rights – which conveniently confirmed I effectively had no rights at all in my current situation.

I banged my fists on the prison door repeatedly as I shouted in a polite and high-pitched English accent.

'Excuse me. Hello? I am English! Please come and help me! Excuse me, can you hear me? Hello?'

I heard the officers laughing in response at my attempts to be released and nobody came to me despite banging on the door for what felt like hours. I eventually gave up and the girl with the orange merely rolled away from me and blocked her ears.

I was not going to give up and my next plan of attack was to try escaping the cell. I paced furiously in my rotten cell and noticed there was a tiny sink embedded in one wall. There was a tiny window above the sink on the adjacent wall and I decided I could fit through that window if it would open. I began climbing onto the sink to reach the window and an inner voice stopped me.

Kathryn, what are you doing? You can't escape. You are locked up in South Africa, not England. They have arrested you on drugs charges and they will probably shoot you if you make it outside. Shoot you. Seriously, sit down and calm down. You cannot attempt to escape. Don't be that person Kathryn.

That voice was right and I knew it was both unrealistic and unwise to attempt an escape. Nothing good would come of it. I was locked up overseas, I was innocent and yet there was nothing I could do and nobody to help me now. I had no freedom, no rights and nobody cared about my welfare. I was that cliché of banged up abroad. My shoulders began to drop, tears formed in my eyes again and I realised I was trapped. There was nothing I could do other than make myself a nest and sleep the weekend away. In one last attempt to deny my situation I folded the prison blankets in the cell to make it more homely, asked if I could help the girl in any way as she woke up, and then I found a corner and made a nest of blankets and hid within it. It was absolutely freezing cold lying on the floor and I tried to calm my mind. I decided that if there was no escape I would do something positive with my time rather than cry. I closed my eyes and sent good wishes and prayers to everybody I had ever met and spent time with.

My time went on like that for who knows how long and then suddenly I heard footsteps approaching. The officers that had brought me to the cell opened the door wide and took the other prisoner and her orange away. She was beaming a huge smile as she left and hugged me tightly in goodbye. One of the officers smiled at me and promised he would soon be returning for me. I begged him not to lie to me and to please, please come back for me. As he locked the doors again I hid under my blankets and hoped he would return. I had no belief that he would but then he did. As I heard footsteps again I raced to the door and waited. The officer beamed a big smile at me and took my arm to escort me back to the front desk. As I entered the reception area, still on the wrong side of the desk, the detective in purple asked me if I felt better.

'Not really, no. Not until I am on the right side of the desk,' I responded in a shaky voice.

I saw Jane waiting for me and the detective laughed kindly as he allowed me to finally be on the right side of the desk. I signed some paperwork and the detective explained that I had to appear at court on Monday for my hearing and I was extremely lucky to be let out on a warning for the weekend. He advised me that if I explained my innocence at court I should be free to go that very same day, assuming Leon and Mondre pleaded guilty.

Relief washed over me as Jane escorted me outside and I realised it was dark. She had been fighting for me to be released for over seven hours and had finally won. Jane took me straight to the pub and plied me with red wine until my hands stopped shaking, I stopped rambling about tetanus and HIV and I began to calm down. It took a long time, I was extremely stressed and shocked, but eventually I calmed enough for them to take me home. I sent a short message to Nicholas from the pub to explain I was okay and not to worry but then the internet connection failed and I was not able to explain my absence fully. He had been expecting me to be in touch hours ago.

When I was finally left at home alone I messaged Nicholas to explain something had happened and, having realised we could use my mobile to Skype, I called him. It had been months since he had seen my face as we hadn't thought to Skype before, I was an absolute state both physically and emotionally and I didn't care. All I wanted to do was hear Nicholas's voice. I laughed hysterically as I explained the events of the day and that I had to go to court to plead my innocence. I made no sense at all and keep rambling about the scratchy prison blankets and my concerns about having contracted tetanus and HIV. We didn't stop talking for hours and I fell into a fitful sleep.

The following two days were horrendous as I attempted to pack up my life in my cottage, freaked out about court and was too frightened to pack a bottle of wine to take through customs – if I even made it out of the country. I thought the officials might arrest me again. I was supposed to be leaving on Tuesday. I was not rational, Jane kept me company often, and eventually Monday arrived. I was exhausted but arrived on time at court and sat numbly in the waiting area that smelt of urine and fear. Jane tried to distract me with crossword puzzles, the corridors were packed with anxious locals awaiting their trials and the hours dragged by as people in handcuffs passed us and our case was delayed by a murder case being heard. A passing barrister recognised my friend and explained to me that the hearing would only be to confirm my details and would not clear me of charges. I would have to remain either within prison or on bail for up to *six weeks* until my case was heard. My head swam as I considered that latest development, I nearly threw up on the barrister's shiny shoes and, seeing my fear and circumstances, he offered to represent me free of charge. I was beside myself with fear and the barrister spent the rest of his day arranging for our case to be fully heard on Tuesday. I *had* to leave the next day; I could not stay any longer because my visa ran out and I had plans to be elsewhere. I was innocent for crying out loud! The barrister sent me home hours later with an assurance that my case would be fully heard on Tuesday and I would either be free to go or declared guilty and sentenced. All of that was going to occur an hour before my flight was due to leave Cape Town. I couldn't believe it was all happening to me.

It was one of the most surreal moments of my life turning up at court again the following day with my bags packed in the back of a car. I had no idea if I would be able to leave the country or not as my case was heard and I watched the clock constantly. Would I go to prison or would I be free to go home? My family had no idea of what was going on, I had only told Nicholas, and I shook as I stood in the dock next to prisoners in their handcuffs. I watched as they attempted to pass cigarettes to one another when the court staff were not watching. I didn't understand when people spoke, the case was heard in Afrikaans, and I wasn't allowed to speak to declare my innocence. I had no idea why we were all lined up and who the people next to me were other than Leon and Mondre. I was terrified of the outcome as I stood to attention but eventually I was escorted away from the dock. Was I free to go? Was I innocent? It was all very unceremonious, I wasn't sure if it was the end or not, but Jane grabbed hold of me and told me I had been declared innocent. We raced to the car as I tore up my court documents stating my arrest and charges and threw them to the wind. I was free and I had a flight to catch. I didn't dare stop in case somebody changed their mind.

Thankfully the traffic was minimal and I made it to the airport on time to leave South Africa. As I sat down in my aeroplane seat, I took a deep breath and attempted to calm down; an hour ago I was on the verge of being found guilty of possession of drugs overseas and yet now I was free. It was utterly surreal and my head swam as a smart gentleman sat down next to me, introduced himself and enquired if I was on holiday. In my shock I blurted out that actually no, I had just been released from prison. He practically leapt away from me, I shrivelled up in embarrassment and I vowed not to tell anyone what had happened to me other than my family. It hadn't occurred to me that people would think I could be guilty! As the air hostess advised us to fasten our seatbelts, I also vowed never to return to South Africa again. As much as I had loved it there, prison had left a very bitter taste in my mouth called fear.

57

How do you tell your family that you were arrested overseas for the possession of, with intent to distribute, illegal drugs?

I pondered that question throughout the long flight back to England and didn't come up with a good answer other than you just don't tell your family. I knew I was innocent, I knew they would think I was innocent but I was still a little bit mortified at having found myself in such a situation. I am the most unlikely person to be arrested and for the possession of drugs no less. As a teenager I vowed never to smoke a cigarette and never to drink alcohol. I became vegetarian for fifteen years, convinced my family to also go vegetarian for a number of years and was mostly opinionated and self-righteous. My peers were a mystery to me and I didn't suffer so much from peer pressure as from peer exclusion. I would never have taken drugs as a teenager and after fifteen years at the same private school for girls I didn't so much as get one detention. I was that well behaved, naive and innocent as I grew up. As an adult the closest I ever came to drugs was eating a hash cake at university, after which I laughed my face off, fell asleep and then woke up to consume my entire week's worth of groceries. That was my one and only experience with drugs, I have never smoked and after about two glasses of wine I have had my fill. Even my friends would attest that I am more likely to be at home having a cup of English tea that partying the night away. I am that dull and I love it. As I said, I am the most unlikely person to be arrested and I had no idea what to expect from my family when I informed them of my arrest and court case.

I was greeted by my Dad, my sister and her family when I arrived in England and decided that the best place to tell them would be at home. At least then they could react as they chose without any public humiliation on my part as I tried to whisper what had happened to me. I absolutely did not want anyone else to find out and, as I write this, there are only a handful of people in my life that actually know about my prison episode. This is in effect my admission of having been banged up abroad.

As we sat down for dinner that first evening at my sister's I chose my moment and explained I had something to tell my family. They all looked so eager, assuming it was something exciting about my travels I suspected, and beamed at me. I fiddled with my cutlery and tried to explain that I hadn't had my leaving do of pizza and red wine (it still pained me I missed a night at my favourite pizzeria) because instead I had been arrested and spent an afternoon behind bars. The looks on my dad's and sister's faces were absolutely priceless as they tried to comprehend what I was saying and struggled to find words to respond. After a silence mostly filled with them trying to contain their disbelief and laughter, Dad finally spoke up and told me he was so proud of me. I am the first in my family to have ever been arrested and overseas for drugs no less. Well done me! When I told my brother on Skype what had happened he couldn't speak. He laughed so hard that tears ran down his cheeks and he had to leave the room to compose himself. He absolutely could not believe that his younger sister, the bookish geek, had been arrested. Every time he came back to the Skype camera to talk he just burst out laughing again and had to clutch his knees to stop from falling off his chair.

It was such a relief to have told my family but admittedly I was on a knife edge for the next week. It took me a long time to get over that finale in South Africa and I was also due to start my much-feared Divemaster course the following week. I battled with letting go of one nightmare whilst willingly taking on another one. I knew I would be in the company of two fantastic scuba diving Instructors, people who would understand and assist me in overcoming my fears, but I was still nervous as I boarded the train to Cambridgeshire and then settled into my B&B the night before the course began. I scribbled in my journal late into the night and reminded myself that I could and *would* succeed. I had worked hard to get this far and I would not fail myself now.

I really enjoyed being back in the water and I practised my dive skills quite happily with my Instructors each day. I kept thinking about mask removal and knew it was time to conquer my fear of taking my mask off underwater during that course. It terrified me and was my worst fear in life. The idea of swimming without a mask on whilst breathing underwater was quite frankly madness but I found my courage and changed my beliefs. I kicked fear up the backside and did it. It took a while and at first I couldn't get my face underwater at all. Okay, I did well up and nearly quit the course but somehow I regained control of my breathing and my mind and I managed to put my head underwater and eventually removed my mask. It was awful at first but slowly, with practice, my panic subsided. By the end of the course I had swum many lengths without my mask on, with my eyes open and whilst breathing.

With the support of my wonderful Instructors and friends James and Lucie, I had joined the ranks of PADI Professionals as a Dive Master. I couldn't believe I had actually done it and I was lost without my team by my side afterwards but I knew it was just the beginning of the next chapter of our lives. It had started right then. It was time to move to Egypt for my Divemaster internship and Instructor training. In a week's time I would be living by the Red Sea, seeing Nicholas at long last after seven months apart and putting my new-found confidence and skills into practice.

58

I talked during the entire flight to Egypt; I was that excited and nervous about seeing Nicholas and of staying permanently this time. I practically chewed the ear off the couple sitting next to me as I told them all about my move overseas, my diving plans and about the man. I fidgeted in my seat, my heart raced as I spoke and I recalled how Nicholas and I had grown even closer during my time in England. His tone of speech had changed since my last weeks in South Africa and he had spoken about *when* we would get together as a couple rather than *ifs* and *maybes*. He had informed me that, as soon as I arrived in Egypt, he would take me on our first date. My sister and I had spent hours wondering what our date would be after Nicholas's cryptic message about the date itself:

The date will go well but it won't go well for the date.

When I waited at the baggage carousel after my arrival at the airport my hands were shaking with excitement and I hauled my luggage onto a trolley. As I walked through the packed arrivals area my eyes scanned the horizon constantly whilst an airport official checked my documents and I feared I was about to be arrested again. He hadn't checked anyone else's document but then it didn't matter; I saw Nicholas on the other side of the grumpy official. There he was, standing tall as usual above the surrounding heads and shoulders of people. Moments later I was in his arms and neither of us wanted to let go. After months apart, a time filled with self-discovery and adventure for us both, we held each other's hands tightly and haven't stopped doing so since that day. We walked away from the airport and drove past desert landscapes and tourist hotels that lay amidst the crazy traffic and constantly beeping horns. The locals screeched from lane to lane without warning, they hit the accelerator hard whenever possible and seemingly all had an addiction to using their horn for absolutely everything. The noise was constant, the atmosphere was hot and dusty and this was to become my home.

We arrived at Nicholas's apartment and no sooner had we entered the door and placed my baggage down than Nicholas asked me if I would accompany him on a date. Of course I said yes, excitement fizzing inside of me wondering where we would go. I had in mind a romantic dinner by candlelight whilst I watched, bemused, as Nicholas placed a dried date on the floor and stood upon one half of the date. I wondered what he was doing whilst he gestured for me to place my foot on the other said of the date. As I stood there with my foot squashing half of a dried piece of fruit I realised this was our first date...he had asked me if would accompany him on an actual date. Nicholas took my hands as we perched atop the date and asked me if I would be his girlfriend before producing a chilled bottle of champagne with which we could celebrate. It was certainly unique, not exactly what I had in mind, and the rest of the night was one to remember given we had spent such a long time apart.

Nicholas's apartment was absolutely tiny and those first nights we stayed there were incredibly awkward on my part, as I had decided before arriving that I would not trump in the presence of Nicholas *ever*. I wanted to be graceful and polite, the essence of a perfect lady, and ladies do not trump in front of their men folk as far as I am aware. I had never managed to hold it in for long in previous relationships but I had been determined to turn over a new leaf and keep my bottom musicals to myself. It all went well at first, I was trump free, but then we were constantly in one another's company and the bathroom was immediately adjacent to the bedroom, which was also the living room. In fact it was the only room other than the tiny kitchen and we lived there day and night as we folded ourselves into one another in the bliss of a new relationship. There was nowhere I could trump (or do anything else for that matter) without Nicholas hearing and noticing the aroma of the consequences. It was murder holding everything in and at night I clutched my cramping and swollen stomach as I waited and lay awake exhausted until Nicholas was fast asleep. Only then did I let out an absolute symphony of trumps, trills and burps. I am amazed to this day that he did not wake up as I stared nervously at him in the dark watching for any signs of wakefulness before letting out another cloud of gas. Holding off from using the bathroom was even worse and by day three I had the worst stomach cramps of my life. I had tried to eat as little as possible to stave off the inevitable as I could not, would not, do *that* when Nicholas was at home. He would hear everything and I would die of embarrassment. Unfortunately though Nicolas had no diving work and had no need to leave the house. For the love of life why, *why*, couldn't I just explain the need to vacate my bowels and go to my apartment to do so? Because I couldn't even admit to such a thing and also could find no reasonable other excuse to leave, that's why. I was stuck in an impossible situation and spent my days in constant pain until diarrhoea finally saved me and destroyed my plans to be a lady. Within the first weeks of arriving I had contracted the inevitable local stomach bug and spent the next *month* on the toilet in one form or other. I wept to myself and hid my face in embarrassment as I made the most ungodly noises I have ever heard, every single day and night, whilst Nicholas laughed his socks off at me from the bedroom. It should have been a humiliating passion-killer but instead it was one of the funniest times we had in Egypt.

As it turned out, Egypt was not one of the healthiest places to live and I spent the majority of my time living there unwell. Within the first two months I experienced numerous bouts of diarrhoea, grew some kidney stones, visited the local hospital and mostly failed to attend my Divemaster internship at the local dive centre. I barely made it out of bed most days and every time I became well again the next round of illness found me. It was not an ideal start for our relationship and life in Egypt but we did what we could and I only pooped myself once during a day of diving. I would call that a success given the circumstances.

The local culture of Egypt was a huge shock to me. Having always lived in countries where my rights of expression and freedom as a woman were limitless I found it very difficult adjusting to the local culture. I felt undervalued and invisible when I was out and about amongst local people. I noticed that Egyptian women are rarely seen in the area where I lived and the majority of my time in public was spent amongst Egyptian men. What was it about my interactions with the people around me there that left me feeling that way? I must point out that I am not blaming Egyptian men for my feelings of inadequacy whilst living there but I was curious as to what brought this on for me. I wondered how my experiences there had brought about one simple fact for me; I felt like a second-rate citizen, the property of men, purely because I am female. It saddened me deeply and affected my opinion of that little piece of Egypt greatly.

I have been brought up within a loving family and as part of a society where being female had not held me back and had not been of any significance in my life choices. I can honestly say it didn't occur to me until living in Egypt that being female could affect how others believed my life ought to be lived. I thought everyone just saw me as, well, me. How fortunate I was to have been valued for being who I am and for having been allowed every freedom and choice that came my way, irrespective of my gender. My voice has been heard, my opinions respected by others (well, sometimes), I have a career of my choosing and I have experienced great joy being a woman. I have my own unique gifts and strengths and I have expressed them freely.

Lucky me, though surely it should not come down to luck. It should be every person's birthright to be heard and to be free to make their own choices in life. For many people that simply is not the case in our complex world and we limit and divide people for reasons of race, gender, age, religion, money, sexual orientation and so forth. It is not my place to comment on the huge subject of discrimination right now, I am no expert, but I can say that it appals me to think of women being thought of as the lesser sex. It appals me to think of anyone being segregated and labelled at all to be honest. In my opinion there is no place for such attitudes in our world if we ever hope to achieve harmony and see people in their true greatness, regardless of their gender, beliefs and so forth. We are all equal.

So what is it about my interactions with some people in Egypt that left me feeling, quite frankly, like crap? I pondered that over many cups of tea and decided to quietly observe myself and those around me every time I went out in order to understand what on earth was going on. And here is what I observed with as little judgement as possible. It is quite difficult not to judge though as those incidents involved me and I was pretty unimpressed at being treated that way.

Firstly, when I went out alone and got the tiny blue bus into town, nobody would sit next to me. The buses are no larger than a sardine tin and were crammed with people trying to get into town. No matter how busy the bus was, the men that hopped on and off to go about their daily business would not sit anywhere near me unless absolutely necessary. If possible they rearranged themselves when a woman boarded the bus (a very rare occurrence) so the woman and I were sat together away from the men. Furthermore, when we all handed our money forwards to the driver, many of the men would not let me pass their money forwards when I offered to help.

Furthermore, I had the misfortune of being groped by a local man on the blue buses. I was under the impression that because I was a lone white female in a foreign country, where women are rarely seen, I appeared to be a novelty. That or some of the men had no understanding of personal space. I asked other women that lived there and heard many awful reports of being treated that way and worse. It was apparently just the way it was and I felt too intimated on the bus to speak up. Plus the only words I could say in Arabic were yes, no, here, please, thank you, goodbye, crazy, one, two, three, four, five. I suspected that wouldn't get my point across sufficiently.

Secondly, when Nicholas and I went to our local supermarket and I paid with my money, the cashier handed the change back to

Nicholas. He would not pass the money to me, despite the fact I paid. Now that really took the biscuit. That was my money with which to buy large amounts of amazingly sweet Egyptian bread and also tonic to go with my gin. If the other cashiers cottoned on to that and started giving my money to Nicholas all of the time there would be a problem. What if Nicholas didn't share the bread? That prospect needed to be nipped in the bud straightaway but again I don't know how to get my point across in Arabic.

Thirdly, whenever I walked anywhere on my own I was approached by young Egyptian men. They stood in front of me so I could not get away without a big sidestep, which is tricky being so short. I couldn't for the life of me see around those random men and for all I knew I was likely to step on another one. The conversation always went like this:

Man: What is your name?

Me: No thank you (in Arabic and hoping to deter Man)

Man: Where are you from?

Me: Here (We're back to English already. Man is not deterred)

Man: Here?

Me: Yes. Here

Man: You like me?

Me: I don't know you

Man: You have a boyfriend?

Me: Yes

Man: You married?

Me: Not yet   (Note to self. That does not sound cool. Just desperate)

Man: Why not?

Me: My boyfriend has not asked yet   (Wow that sounds even worse)

Man: How old are you?

Me: Thirty-four (Oh here we go. I wince at what is coming next)

Man: You are thirty four and not married yet! Girls here marry at twenty!

Man looks horrified at me, is clearly appalled and then sees an opportunity. I am dying of embarrassment.

Man: You marry me if it doesn't work out?

Me: No

Man: Why not?

Me: Thank you. Have a nice day. Goodbye now

And onwards it went. All whilst I was sidestepping like a lunatic and getting nowhere. To add to the excitement of this I was also being kerb-crawled by taxi drivers in much the same manner. They were quite irate at times when I dared to ignore them and walk on. One tried to run me down but failed miserably. I was impressed at their ability to drive, honk the horn, not hit the kerb and chat me up all at the same time.

It had to be said the taxi drivers were hilarious though. I once counted how many seconds it took to be offered a taxi after leaving my apartment. Ten seconds. And then approximately every ten seconds afterwards all the way along the main road. Once we were offered twenty different taxis within the time it took to walk across the road. Taxis were everywhere. Every single day. The taxi drivers beeped, followed us, slowed down, asked 'taxi?', beeped, kerb-crawled, asked again 'taxi?' and then beeped some more. Their persistence was incredible.

Finally, I loved to go running in the evenings when I was well enough (which was not that often). On my running route I passed a dusty little area where the taxi drivers gathered and chatted whilst waiting for business. It seemed a nice area to congregate and drink tea and I passed them during each run. One day I was running along towards them and fell spectacularly right at their feet. It was a tremendous effort on my part to fall as embarrassingly as possible; I stumbled, flailed, hit the deck with a whooomph sound and skidded along the dirt on my stomach whilst holding my iPod aloft. Clearly my priority of what needed to be saved from the impact was slightly askew. I was a little shaken, grazed and dusty and, as I lay there regaining my senses, none of the taxi drivers so much as blinked or tried to help me. There was no visible reaction. I felt like standing up, waving and shouting 'Hello?! Woman down! Help me!' whilst pointing to my grazed knee and pouting like a child. How they failed to notice me at their feet I do not know but the best part was the response that followed. Once I had dusted myself down and organised my haphazard clothing, I began to limp past them. One of them stepped out in front of me enquiringly.

'Taxi?'

Now I know we are from different cultures, different societies and we all prejudge. I have expectations of how I would have liked the Egyptian men to treat me and they probably had expectations of how they would have liked me to behave. I can only assume that the ones I encountered treated me in a manner that is appropriate for their culture and I cannot speculate as to what they think and feel towards me or women in general. However, I make an exception for the groping. That is entirely not my fault and is inappropriate at any time, any place. I recognise that I am a sensitive soul at heart and have enough self-awareness to realise it is likely my reaction to the above interactions that was the problem. My feelings are my own choice and it is up to me how I respond to others each day. I have a choice. I allowed myself to develop expectations of being treated poorly and of being hassled every time I went out. By expecting to be treated as second-rate and as some kind of ex-pat available for purchase, I was tense all the time. I was in a mindset that would make every interaction seem offensive no matter how innocuous. The power of the mind.

It is with that power of the mind that I tried to turn it around for me. Perhaps the local men did not sit next to me and did not pass me my money because they felt uncomfortable and did not know how to treat me. Not because they thought I was second-rate but because they were trying to be polite and respectful by deferring to what is appropriate for them. Perhaps the young Egyptians that approached me were just being friendly and looking for love. Perhaps they were lonely, being cheeky and hoping to brighten their day with some female company. Perhaps the taxi drivers simply didn't know what to do when I fell over at their feet. Perhaps it would be inappropriate amongst their peers for them to offer assistance to a foreign lady sprawled at their feet in lycra and covered in dust.

Put simply, perhaps I got it wrong. Perhaps I just need to get a grip and stop being offended. I spoke at length with a lovely Egyptian friend of mine (who is also a taxi driver and a very nice one at that) and he confirmed kindly that what I had experienced was fairly common and perhaps they had thought I was marriage material.

Call me naive. Call me an optimist but I chose to ignore those facts and focussed on seeing the good in the people around me. As I approached my third month of living in Egypt I smiled at everyone and assumed they meant well. I did my best to be gracious and kind and it worked. It turned the experience around for me and it was bliss.

59

Without a doubt the best part of living in Egypt was the easy access to the world-class diving within the Red Sea. The dive sites were incredibly beautiful and in the approach to my Instructor Development Course (IDC), the final part of my training to become a scuba diving instructor, I had managed the occasional day aboard the dive boats to explore the local, colourful reefs. I hadn't been well enough to do a great deal of diving but the sites I did visit were beautiful. My mask removal fears remained in the distant past and I dropped happily to depths of 30m off the back of the boats and admired the shoals of fish that surrounded me. I saw fish of all shapes and sizes, turtles and even eagle rays on one occasion. As long as the current wasn't strong, I was a content and confident diver and capable of looking after myself throughout the dives. The variety of marine life was staggering and the clear warm water soothed me, improving my confidence further. By the time I began my IDC I was healthy and ready for the final diving challenge I had worked so hard towards. I was nervous, the entire group was when we first met at the dive centre, but I felt confident that I could complete the course and hoped I would be able to cope with the two day Instructor Exam at the end. That was to be the real test of my skills.

During the first day of our course the group got to know each other and Lucie and James put us all at ease about what was expected of us throughout the IDC. As with my Divemaster course, the focus was on having fun and they reassured us that our learning would be more effective if we relaxed and enjoyed every day. The entire course followed on that way and we were in fits of laughter as we learnt about teaching techniques and practised demonstrating our diving skills to one another. The group were wonderful; there were nerves and moments of doubt amongst us all, depending on what we felt were our weak spots, but we had such a positive time together. The members of the group supported each other, we cheered each other on and helped one another with the confusion of dive table calculations when it all became too much at the end of the day. I came to realise that we each had our own fears related to diving and teaching and my mask removal fear was no worse than others' different fears. I was not alone. I found myself asking to demonstrate mask removal as my skill during the IDC and, each time I did it, I felt an inner sense of pride and success. Removing a mask underwater may have been a small gesture for other divers who didn't understand why mask removal had elicited such panic in me but I felt like I had conquered the world. Thankfully I was comfortable speaking in front of others and the teaching aspects of the course that followed passed by smoothly for me.

By the time we reached the end of ten days of training, the group had all become confident speakers, divers and teachers and we had completed the skills required of us. We had spent hours in the classroom and swimming pool practising our teaching techniques and we had visited a beautiful local dive site to practice further. I had learnt that the Red Sea is extremely salty when I took my mask off underwater at the dive site and opened my eyes, but I soon adjusted. It was no worse than the freezing cold water of Gildenburgh quarry from months previous.

By the eve of our Instructor Exam we had achieved everything we set out to as a group and had learnt a great deal about each other along the way. When we walked into the dive centre to begin our two day exam we were confident of success (mostly), a united front and our nerves didn't get the better of us; apart from when I assembled my dive gear back to front during my first attempt at doing so. It wasn't the best start but nobody noticed outside of our group. The exam consisted of a number of teaching and dive skill assessments within the bay and, as it was almost Christmas, we decided to wear Santa hats throughout the exam. Our examiner was less than impressed with our jolly attitude and quickly put us in place with his short sharp comments about taking the tests seriously. Not to be deterred, we wore our hats anyway, muttered a little behind his back and stuck mental fingers up at his attitude. We were taking it seriously but we were also being positive and ensuring we enjoyed ourselves. Sadly the examiner's attitude didn't improve throughout the exam and he spent his time criticising our skills heavily whilst limiting his praise to none whatsoever. We were skilled divers, we knew what we were doing and our tests were executed seamlessly as a group, but the critical attitude of our examiner dampened our spirits to the point of neglecting to wear our Santa hats by the second day. Some of us had a sleepless night, others were angry and the entire morale of our group was exceptionally low throughout our final day. We tried our best to support one another but our morale only lifted when we excitedly finished the last assessment, the examiner confirmed we had passed and each of us realised we had become PADI Open Water Scuba Instructors. We had made it and success was ours. Well, everyone except me had become an Instructor. I was delighted at my achievement of passing the exam but I still had to complete more dives in order to reach one hundred and officially qualify. I was almost there but reined myself in until the one hundredth dive was completed.

We celebrated our success that night mostly by sleeping, it had been a long and tiring exam, and then Nicholas and I set ourselves the task of reaching one hundred dives in the New Year. We had decided to move to South Africa together and I needed to qualify as an Instructor before we departed for a season with the white sharks again- evidently prison had been long forgotten.

60

We had six weeks left in Egypt after Christmas and we were in and out of the water most days at the local bay, enjoying dive sites to ourselves as we pottered about admiring fish and ancient coral structures. We met an inquisitive local turtle, admired groups of eagle rays passing overhead and followed blue spotted stingrays as they settled upon hummocks of sand each day. We came to know the reefs intimately and there was not a soul to be seen when we swam along hand in hand and explored.

It was a quiet time of reflection as the number of dives in my log book steadily increased and my one hundredth dive was soon upon us. It is a tradition amongst scuba divers that dive No.100 is completed naked and I had no idea how we would manage that. As a compromise I decided to only wear my bikini during that dive, which was going to be freezing given the relatively chilly winter water of the Red Sea. I looked quite spectacularly stupid walking along the beach in my bikini with heavy boots and a neoprene hood on whilst other divers exiting the water were in dry suits or thick wetsuits. I beamed knowing I may be cold but I would exit the water later that day as a qualified Instructor. As Nicholas and I shivered, swore at the temperature and descended we finned to one of our favourite reefs to warm up. We were soon alone, surrounded by colourful fish and dappled sunshine from above. The water was clear blue as usual and the sandy bottom sloped away from us gently. It wasn't as cold as I had expected if I kept moving and didn't focus on the temperature. The dive itself was less spectacular than previous ones but it was tranquil, there were plenty of small fish to admire and, as I swam along, I looked back to the past few years of my life and everything I had fought against to survive.

There had been so many times when I felt like giving up, so many times when the worst happened to me over and over again and I had been filled with shame, humiliation and defeat. Yet somehow I had gotten up off the floor, dusted myself down and survived repeatedly. I don't doubt that people go through worse, mine is just a small story about one small person, but it is *my* story and I had not only survived my own version of hell but I had painted a bright new canvas for myself. As I admired the fish dipping in and out of their coral hideaways I realised I had achieved more than I ever thought possible simply by dreaming big and refusing to give up.

I am a very ordinary person, with very ordinary skills and I am full of those human neuroses and fears we all have, yet there I was swimming along as an almost-qualified scuba diving Instructor. That achievement had been beyond my wildest dreams (and nightmares) and, as I looked back upon the old version of me that had been terrified to even consider diving or living overseas, I realised how much I had grown. As I banked around the reef I thought about the highs and lows of each year and of how I continued to miss Mum and the Bears each day. I had made my dreams a reality in honour of them but it hadn't been easy. I had done it to create something positive out of heartache and loss and I was so thankful I hadn't given up on myself.

The changes in my life since those difficult times had been brought about by determination and effort, not by being incredibly talented or exceptional, and it made me realise that anything is possible in life if you just commit to it and *do it*. With that in mind, I remembered that my one hundredth dive should be naked and I could do it, so I did. As I struggled and wriggled out of my bikini, Nicholas held on tightly to the top of my head (where else could he hold me whilst I was half-naked during a dive?) in a bid to stop me from floating off to the surface without my dive weights on whilst I undressed. As I laughed, my bikini released in a flourish, I put my dive gear back on and then I finned away from my inhibitions; naked and free.

I was without a care in the world as I swam around the reef with my white bottom wiggling and jiggling like a big fat jelly and I spread my arms wide like wings in celebration of the person I had come to be. Nicholas had tied my bikini to the top of his head and was merrily filming my moment of abandon. I jiggled my bottom past him and around the corals, with my white belly hanging free like a soft, squidgy (and hairy) anemone. I glided over the sandy hummocks and grazed them with my nipples as I smiled. I realised that, in spite of it all, in spite of wanting to give up on life, I had finally and happily just become me.

Epilogue

Since writing this book Kathryn has continued to follow her dreams and she lives happily with Nicholas. They returned to South Africa for a second season of working with great white sharks in 2014. After the season ended, they returned to England and visited Hester and Paddington for a bouncy, lively and emotional reunion. The Bears are happy and well. Kathryn and Nicholas have gone on to create a marine conservation cause to highlight the plight of sharks and the oceans and this is called Friends for Sharks. They are travelling the world in 2015 to educate others about the importance of marine conservation.

Did you enjoy No Damage?

Please help the author by leaving a review on Amazon & Goodreads

Follow Kathryn Hodgson

@bourbontea

https://www.facebook.com/NoDamageKAH

www.KathrynHodgsonAuthor.com

About the Author

Kathryn Hodgson (1979) was born in England and spent her childhood exploring the rugged beauty of Cornwall. She pursued her love of nature as an adult and created a successful career within environmental enforcement in England and then as a scuba diving instructor in Egypt and Great White Shark wildlife guide in South Africa. She is co-founder of the marine conservation cause Friends for Sharks and author of No Damage.

Made in the USA
Charleston, SC
02 September 2015